FOUR WHITE HORSES AND A BRASS BAND:
True Confessions from the World of Medicine Shows,
Pitchmen, Chumps, Suckers, Fixers, and Shills
by Violet McNeal

Four White Horses and a Brass Band was originally published in 1947
by Doubleday and Co, Inc.

©2019 Feral House
ISBN: 9781627310833
Printed in the United States of America
10 9 8 7 6 5 4 3 2 1

Feral House
1240 W. Sims Way, Suite 124
Port Townsend, WA 98368
www.FeralHouse.com

Design by Sean Tejaratchi
Cover illustration by Mahendra Singh

FOUR WHITE HORSES
AND A BRASS BAND

TRUE CONFESSIONS
≫ FROM THE WORLD OF ≪

MEDICINE SHOWS,
PITCHMEN
CHUMPS
SUCKERS
FIXERS
AND SHILLS

BY VIOLET McNEAL

FERAL HOUSE

⇉ TABLE OF CONTENTS ⇇

APPENDICES

→ CHAPTER ONE ←
MAKING MEDICINE

BEDBUGS DECIDED MY FATE and changed the pattern of my life.

Quite a few things influenced it, of course, before the bedbugs took over. There were the farm, which I hated, and the dark handsome lady from Minneapolis, and the books by Bertha M. Clay[1]. But it was rebellion against the biting of the bedbugs in a St. Paul tenement that led me finally to Will, whose brain had been tainted by the devil. The bedbugs and a two-line newspaper want ad opened the door to the fabulous world of medicine shows.

It was a swashbuckling world, peopled by a few geniuses and a great many rascals. It was a world in which the romance of the four corners of the world could be found in the flame of the pitchman's gasoline torch. The torches are gone, but the names they led to fame are not. Silk Hat Harry, Prince Nanzetta, Brother John, and Hal the Healer are only a few.

I had never encountered a bedbug when in 1904 I took the train from our little town, bound for St. Paul. I was sixteen years old. My parents be-

---

1 Bertha M. Clay is a literary pseudonym first used by Charlotte Mary Brame. After her death in 1884, Brame's daughter began to write under the name.

At the same time the pseudonym became a house name of Street & Smith Publishing, where dozens of male writers used the name. Between 1876 and 1928, 27 different publishers issued titles under the name Bertha M. Clay. Eighty-eight titles have been attributed to Clay, some remaining in print for nearly 50 years.

lieved I intended merely to visit a friend during a Fourth of July celebration. I knew when I mounted the high iron steps of the day coach I was never going back.

Taking the trip had meant scrimping for months. We had always been poor, and everyone in our family had to work at home or work out. I refused to do housework. I loathed washing dishes and cleaning rooms, so I had got a job copying documents at the courthouse.

Most of my work, for which I received fifty cents a day on Saturdays and school holidays, was done in the vaults. My boss was a middle-aged man with baggy pants and a scraggly gray mustache. I thought he was loathsome-looking. He had a habit of patting my shoulder or accidentally touching my hands. I could stand that, thinking of the greasy dishes I would have to wash if I quit. But one day in the vault he put his hand against the bosom of my dress. I slapped his face and left.

Hurrying home, I told my father. He called me a liar and said the man was married and wouldn't do such a thing. It was clear I would have to get another job, so I undertook to mislead my folks and plan my own life. The first move was to write a letter to my friend in St. Paul, asking her to invite me up for the celebration.

At that time I was half child, half woman, and what I longed for most was love and approval. I had not received much attention at home, as my younger sister had diabetes. When company came they always brought presents and exclaimed consolingly over her. I was healthy as a pig and used to stand in the background, longing for someone to notice me.

I used to end my prayers every night with the words, "Please, God, make me sick like Sister." To me she was the luckiest person in the world. She always caught every disease that came along. I didn't altogether depend on God to make me sick. When my sister came down with the whooping cough I sneaked into her room at night and got her to blow her breath in my face. I tried to catch the chickenpox from her, but I couldn't even catch a cold.

The only time people noticed me as a child was when I made them cry at prayer meetings. I was honestly religious. I went to church, Sunday school, and Epworth League[2] meetings. I had a good contralto voice and was always asked to sing "Come Unto Me" at revival meetings. I sang it with such feeling that the congregation would begin to weep and come to the altar. I got a kick out of that, as much because it was I, Vi, making them cry as because they were saved. I was quite an exhibitionist. I took music lessons, and my teacher always had me play the duet with her on recital days. No sniveling or forgetting for me. I always performed best before the largest audiences. I believed in heaven and hell, and my life was patterned accordingly.

In those days girls married early. Nearly all of my relatives and friends had married at sixteen; a girl of nineteen was an old maid, and a woman of thirty was an ancient crone. If we were good girls our beaux could go just so far in their petting. Hugging and kissing by the hour were allowed, but just let them go too far and we would remind them we were good girls, and if they didn't behave we would tell Papa. I firmly believed I must go to heaven a virgin if I died, and to my husband a virgin if I lived. I got on that day coach to St. Paul with fewer fears for my future than I have crossing a highway today.

At home we had three or four books written by Bertha M. Clay, and I read them many times. Invariably the beautiful farm girl was seen by some rich man who fell in love with her virtue and beauty and married her, despite opposition. If she didn't know her knives and forks, so to speak, he provided the proper instruction. All went well, and they lived happily ever after. The fade-out revealed the grandparents and three or four grandchildren playing happily on the lawn.

I was sure I was beautiful, and I knew I was virtuous. I was going to a town where there must be many rich men, so if I could just eat long enough, one of them was sure to lay his hand and fortune at my feet. In the meantime, I would get a job.

My girlfriend had a job cooking free lunch in the back of a saloon—a fact I hadn't mentioned to my parents. Also, I had a card in my pocket. It was from

---

2   Founded in 1889, the Epworth League is a Methodist young adult association for people aged 18 to 35. It had its beginning at Cleveland's Central Methodist Church on May 15, 1889. The League takes its name from the village of Epworth in Lincolnshire, England, the birthplace of John Wesley and Charles Wesley. Its members are known as Epworthians.

a lady, dark and very striking, who had come to our town the previous summer. She stayed at the hotel and talked to the young girls. Before she left she gave me and two other girls a card and told us we could make lots of money in Minneapolis. If we got tired of the old home town, she told us, we were to look her up and we would have a job at once.

The train ride seemed endless. I must have gone to the ice-water tank and into the toilet dozens of times. I combed my hair and tried to make myself look more dreamy-eyed—someone had called me his dreamy-eyed sweetheart once, and I had tried to live up to it from then on. I had some cornstarch in an envelope, and I put a little on my face.

What scared me most on my first glimpse of St. Paul was the number of people, but my friend found me without any trouble. We took my little grip to her home on St. Peter Street. It was the tenement district, but I didn't know it. She and her parents lived in three tiny rooms, with the bath in the outside hall, but the constricted establishment looked as grand as a mansion.

First of all I had to see the town. We walked miles and miles and looked in all the store windows. It seemed like a fairy world. I saw the different things, but still it didn't seem possible they could be there. We went home for supper, and my feet hurt. I took off my shoes, and my feet were blistered. Walking on cement wasn't as easy as walking on board sidewalks. Ada told me her fellow and a friend he was bringing were going to take us to a dance at the amusement park that night. The blisters ceased to matter. I soaked my feet, we primped up, and the men came. To my delight they were dressed in the blue uniforms of the Spanish-American War. I had never seen soldiers in uniform before. I thought they were wonderful, and at the very least must run the whole Army.

We rode out on the streetcar, with the soldiers' arms resting on the back of the seat and lightly on our shoulders. Even the park entrance was a wonderland to me, with all the electric lights and such sweet music sounding in the air. We had pop and lemonade and played some games, but the merry-go-round was my meat. The only time I had seen one was when a carnival had come to our home town. We got on and rode to celestial music. After two or three rides the others wanted to go, but I didn't. I could have stayed on that merry-go-round until I died. When we finally got to the dance hall my sore feet were forgotten. We danced until the last car left, and I was certain I had never lived before.

Ada and I went to bed. About two o'clock in the morning I woke up with things crawling and biting all over me. I turned back the covers and saw a multitude of little bugs crawling through the bed. I woke Ada and asked her what they were.

"Bedbugs. Don't pay any attention to them." She rolled over and went back to sleep.

I tried sleeping on the floor. They followed me. I woke Ada again and asked her if they had them every night. She said yes, it was impossible to get rid of them. Right then and there the bedbugs made my great decision for me. I had to find a job and get out of there.

We got up early the next morning and went down to the saloon where Ada cooked the free lunch in a back room. She explained, but I couldn't understand how anyone could make money when so much food was given away. The saloonkeeper was a fat and jolly man who teased us about our beaux. "Eat all you want, girls," he invited. My conception of saloonkeepers as villains vanished. To me they were all jolly and gave you lots to eat.

We took the streetcar to Minneapolis to look up the dark lady who had promised me a job. Ada had something else to do, so I inquired and found the address. I was a little surprised to discover it was a theater, but, so far as I was concerned, a theater was a theater, and I supposed it was like the opera house in my home town. I bought a ticket for fifteen cents and went in, expecting to see the lady inside. I sat down in one of the back seats.

A funnily dressed man was talking on the stage, and when he finished a lot of young pretty girls came out. To my horrified eyes they appeared to be naked, except for a little skirt and some little things over their breasts. And of all things, they had hats on, as if they were going someplace. I blushed harder than I ever had in my life, ashamed and humiliated at being in such a terrible place. My mother had told me she had never undressed in front of my father, and my sister and I turned our backs to each other when we undressed for bed. I was ashamed of my naked body, although when I was dressed up in long skirts I was proud if someone told me I had a swell shape.

Frightened and beginning to cry, I hurried to the door of the theater. I was afraid I would be stopped and forced to live a life of shame. No one stopped me or even seemed to notice me. I was scared to death, but I wasn't ready to quit. I was still determined not to go home but to get a job and become grand and noble and rich.

Ada was mildly scornful. Probably all they had wanted, she said, was to have me dance like the other girls. She said she wished she weren't so fat and had my chance. We discussed my whole problem, and it was she who decided I must investigate the want ads. I pored over them the next morning. There was only one that seemed to fit me. It read: "Wanted, an office girl. One with some knowledge of stenography preferred. Apply at 10 A.M." The address was an office building on a prominent corner in St. Paul.

The next morning at ten o'clock I was there. I opened the door lettered "Remedy Co." and walked in. A big homely Swedish girl told me to sit down. My heart sank as I looked around. About ten other girls were waiting. It seemed to me they were dressed in the height of fashion. I couldn't see where I stood a chance. I was dressed in a white lawn shirt-waist and a gray linen skirt with a ruffle around the bottom that came to my feet. My stockings had been knit by my mother, and I had on country shoes. My petticoat was made of flour sacks, and my most intimate piece of underwear had XXX's across the seat. We could boil out the "Pillsbury's Best," but the XXX's were there to stay.

Thinking of my sleepless nights with the bedbugs made me decide to wait. A little later a small dark man came in. He didn't look like any man I had ever seen before. He had black hair and hazel eyes and was smooth-shaven. He had beautiful white delicate hands. He wasn't built strong like the country men and boys I had known, but still he looked to me as if he could do more things than anyone I had ever known. He wore a blue-and-white-checkered velvet vest and gray-striped trousers and a long-tailed coat and a diamond as big as a hazelnut in a blue tie. He was the most gorgeous man I had ever met. He gave a quick look around at us all. He pointed to me and said:

"Young lady, come in here."

I followed him into a small office.

6

"Are you looking for a job?"

"Yes, sir."

"Where do you live?"

I told him I had just come from Iowa and was stopping with a friend.

"The wages are five dollars a week to start," he said.

I told him I was satisfied. He went to the door and told the other girls to go, that he had hired me. He talked to me a few minutes longer, and then told me to come back at ten o'clock the next morning. I didn't walk out; I rolled out on a pink cloud. I had a job with a handsome boss who wore beautiful clothes. The diamond in his tie might as well have been a piece of glass; it didn't indicate a thing. But that checkered vest meant riches and grandeur.

Before ten o'clock the next morning I was hanging around the hall outside the office. When I went in, the Swedish girl knocked on a door and my boss came in. He took me into another room furnished like a parlor, except that at one side was a broad couch. There were two pillows on the couch, and in the middle of it was a lovely black wooden tray. On the tray was a copper lamp with a round globe, not very tall, that shone dimly. Beside the lamp was a black sponge on a dish, a needle which resembled a knitting needle, and some unfamiliar tools and little boxes.

I noticed, in an offhand way, that my boss's face was peculiarly pale. In my eyes he was an old man, about forty; but, oddly enough, that made no difference whatever. Something about him completely absorbed me. He was short, no more than five feet five inches tall, and weighed about a hundred and thirty-five pounds. Not only his jaw, which was the most solid and determined imaginable, but also some indefinable quality about him expressed exceptional power. His voice was low and compelling. It was a melodious, pipe-organ sort of voice. When you heard it you wanted to believe it and do what it told you to do.

"Young lady, can you be trusted?" he asked.

I assured him I could be.

"I am a famous doctor," he said, and listening to him was like being in church. "I have made a wonderful discovery which will cure consumption. Others are trying to steal this discovery, so you must never let anyone in this room or speak to them of it. I am going to let you help me manufacture the medicine."

I had never been so proud in my life. My heart swelled as if it would burst. I could hardly breathe. It seemed almost like a fairy tale that a great doctor would trust me with his secret. At that moment my blind, unreasoning adoration for Will began. I would have died to defend him or his secret. I promised him I would never disclose it.

"Thank you, my child," he said, and the touch of his voice was like the delicate stroke of fingers on my forehead.

He lay down beside the tray on the couch and told me to lie down across from him. He took up the long needle and dipped it into one of the little boxes which contained what looked like black molasses. He cooked the needle's tip over the lamp for a time, shaping the black substance into a small pill. Then he picked up a slender ivory tube about two feet long. Screwed into the tube about a third of the way from one end was what resembled a dirty dark doorknob. He stuck the pill over a little hole in the doorknob and started to inhale and blow out smoke. Then he showed me how to do it.

After the first three or four puffs I began to get dizzy. The smoke got down into my lungs. I choked and coughed. He watched me with fatherly concern. I was afraid that, asked to do the simplest thing in the world, I was failing and that he would discharge me.

"Are you all right?" he asked.

"Yes," I said. "I like it." I went into another fit of coughing. My stomach began to reel. The smoke didn't smell like the smoke from my father's pipe or the smoke from our kitchen stove or the smoke from fires we had built to clean up debris in the yard. There was a sweetish taste to it.

"Perhaps you had better stop for this time," he said.

"I don't want to stop," I said. I took one more puff. The walls of the room began spinning. I laid the pipe down. His face looked like two faces mixed up together.

"Never mind," he said. "That's the way it is at first. You'll get used to it."

I put my head on the pillow and fought to keep my stomach from turning inside out. He smoked again for a time and then unscrewed the doorknob, picked up another tool, and scraped some dry stuff out of the bowl. He put this in a box, saying: "This is the medicine. It's worth five hundred dollars a pound, so be very careful of it."

My duties seemed to consist entirely of making this medicine with him and answering a few personal letters. Gradually I got over being sick when I smoked. I began to look forward to it. No matter how tired I was, I always felt rested after we had smoked a little while. Things I had been worrying about didn't seem important. I felt there was nothing in the world I couldn't do if I chose to get up off the couch and do it. I felt completely satisfied and flooded with quiet happiness.

Two or three days after I went to work the doctor told me I must have some new clothes. He would select them, he told me, and I could pay him back out of my wages. When we walked into a department store my new life began. It became a combination of Alice in Wonderland, Cinderella, and a huge Christmas tree with all the presents marked "Vi." And the man I was working for represented Santa Claus, God, and the Count of Monte Cristo rolled into one.

He took me first to the corset department and asked for a Lily of France corset. Never before or since has anything given me the feeling of grandeur that corset did. At the time I was wearing a funny makeshift thing which had been washed so many times the horn buttons had turned a deep yellow. The doctor told the saleslady to fit me with corset, underwear, and silk stockings. When it came to undressing in front of her I balked, but she said I would have to be fitted. After she had got the garments on my squirming body she produced a silk underskirt that made a noise like kicking tissue paper when I walked. I was torn between admiring myself in the mirror and walking so as to get the most noise out of my underskirt.

When the bill came and the doctor started to pay it I was dreadfully upset.

"It's more than I can ever pay you back," I said miserably.

"My child," he said, "you're such a help to me I'm going to raise your wages."

I was easily persuaded to keep the clothes. It seemed to me I had never met anyone so good and kind. He never tried to put his hands on me, and he called me his "child" or his "dear child." He never asked me to stay in the office evenings, but the night of the clothes-buying expedition he invited me to go to a circus with him. It was my first circus and represented all the glories of the world combined. I shivered with terror when the animals growled at their trainers; the people on the flying trapeze were angels floating in the air.

A day or so later the doctor took Anna, the Swedish office girl, and me to dinner at one of the best restaurants in St. Paul. Never having been in such a place before, I was confused and bashful. He ordered, and the waiter brought me half a broiled chicken, French-fried potatoes, salad, and peas. I sat there, not touching a thing, but looking longingly at it.

"Aren't you hungry?" he asked at last.

"Yes," I said. "But what piece of chicken can I have?"

In the most kindly way imaginable he explained it was all for me. Reassured, I devoured everything in sight. Quantity was what I wanted in those days, where food was concerned. I was always hungry.

That first week I always felt important, too. All I did was lie on the couch and smoke the funny pipe with the doctor. We took turns smoking, and I was supremely proud to be helping him. He talked to me and asked what I thought about marriage, love, the Bible, and other subjects. He was the first person who had ever been interested in my opinions; it was a delight to present my views and be listened to with such respect. I loved him for so many things. He was as glamorous to me as a movie star would be to a country boy. He was always clean-shaven, and his hair had a nice smell. His fingers were slender and deft. The country boys I had kept company with had hard callused hands, and they always smelled of sweat or the stables. Even to a girl who took her weekly bath in a wooden washtub they were offensive.

That week the doctor paid me ten dollars and gravely took back two dollars as the first installment on my clothes. He also asked me to go out to Lake Como with him on Sunday. I would have crawled miles on my hands and knees if it had meant being with him. We rented a boat and rowed slowly around the lake. I trailed my hand in the water, and he sang to me. The water made his soft rich voice even more thrilling. I silently thanked God for being so good to me.

The next day as we were lying on the couch making medicine he very quietly said:

"My dear child, how would you like to marry me?"

Did I want to go to heaven when I died? I was actually panting for breath when I told him how much I loved him. Words just flew out of my mouth as I started to make plans to go home and be married. I wanted to show the folks back home what a prize I had won.

He held up his hand. "My dear, I am older than you and know what is best for us. Our wedding must be held very quietly here in the office. I'll have the minister and a couple of friends come up this afternoon."

I was disappointed, but I would have consented to anything rather than lose him. I had been to only one wedding in my life. As I was five years old at the time and had mumps, my ideas of weddings were vague. Will, as he told me to call him, left the office. I went on idly making medicine and dreaming of a future of silk clothes, circuses, and moonlight excursions on lakes. I was sure now I was beautiful, and Bertha M. Clay was right.

Will had measured my finger with a string before he left. When he came back he put a diamond ring on my finger and showed me a wide gold band which was to be my wedding ring. Late that afternoon three men came up to the office. Will introduced one of them to me as the Reverend Stevens, who was to marry us, and the other two as friends of his who, he said, were to be witnesses. We were married, and I was handed what to me was the key to heaven on earth. It was such a lovely marriage certificate. At the top were two clasped hands, around which a wreath of roses was entwined.

We went to a hotel, and for the first time I saw a room with an adjoining bath.

"Can I go in there any time I want to," I asked, "and no one else is allowed to come in?"

Will smiled. "No one at all, my dear. It's yours."

At our wedding supper that night Will patted my hand tenderly. "Let's have a drink to celebrate our marriage."

"Oh no," I said. "I couldn't. I signed a pledge in Sunday school."

"Just one won't hurt you. You're a married woman now."

"I just can't," I said miserably.

Will's hazel eyes were so understanding I almost burst into tears.

"Very well. We'll have a nice cold drink instead."

He ordered dinner and said, "Waiter, bring us two absinthe frappes at once." When the milky-looking drinks came Will held up his glass. "We are drinking this to my precious little girl-wife. May she always love me as much as she does today."

I swore I would.

"Now, my dear, just sip the drink slowly," he said.

I wrote a glowing letter to my mother, telling her how I had married a rich doctor who was good to me. My mother wrote back, blessing our marriage and sending us a pair of feather pillows for a wedding present.

Marriage didn't change our routine much. Now, however, we made medicine in the office in the evening. Will would turn out the electric lights, and only the dim light he used for smoking would be burning. He talked to me by the hour. He told me about Confucius, Buddha, and Mohammed, about Ulysses and Penelope. He knew endless strange folk stories and myths. I lay beside him, entranced, soaking up all he said like a sponge. He took me out and pointed to the different stars and told me their names and how and why they were named. I had dreamed of romance, and here it was personified. At home on the farm the men came in exhausted, and of course my mother was always tired. About the only conversation I had heard concerned the spreading of manure or the price of hogs.

I now had money in my pocketbook, so I could indulge myself whenever Will let me go out alone. One day I asked Will if I could go down the street and get an ice-cream soda, as I had had only three or four in my life. I started at the top of the menu and began to eat my way down. I was getting pretty well filled up when I ordered a banana split. The counterman came over to my table, looking disturbed.

"Say," he said, "you can't have any more. What are you trying to do, commit suicide?"

I didn't argue. I was feeling pretty dizzy. The bill was more than three dollars. I went back to the office and was sick. I thought I was going to die.

We had been married several weeks when a friend from my home town, having learned our address from my mother, came to call on us. Will was away from the office, but I was overjoyed. Here was a chance to strut my stuff in front of the home folks. I conducted the man on a tour of the office, and then a happy thought struck me. I was Will's wife and could do as I pleased. I proudly took Elmer into the room where we made medicine. I lit the little lamp, threw myself down, and rolled and started to smoke the little pill. I looked up. I wanted to see the look of astonishment on his face before I told him what I was doing.

His look certainly showed astonishment. It also showed horror.

"My God, Vi!" he burst out. "What are you doing smoking opium?"

I sprang up and started to cry and rushed at him, hitting him on the chest with my fists.

"I'm making medicine!" I screamed. "Get out of here or my husband will kill you when he gets back!"

I was still crying when Will returned. "Will! Elmer said I was smoking opium!"

He didn't say a word. He drew back his fist and hit me on the jaw, knocking me completely out.

→ CHAPTER TWO ←

ONLY SUCKERS WORK

WHEN I CAME TO, Will was kneeling beside me on the floor and holding me in his arms.

"I'm sorry I had to hit you," he said, "but you must learn to obey me."

"I want to go home," I blubbered.

He put his hand over my mouth and continued to talk to me. "I am your husband and I know what is best for you. Do you think I would let you do anything that would hurt you? Now, if you'll talk quietly, I'll let you talk."

I nodded my head, and he took his hand away.

"But I don't want to smoke opium," I said. "I'll get to look like the pictures in the foreign mission books."

"Don't be childish," he said. "They only print those pictures so people will give money to foreign missions. You feel all right, don't you?"

"Yes," I faltered.

"And you don't look horrible. Neither do I. You can see how silly you are. Where is Elmer stopping?"

I told him the name of the rooming house.

"Now dry your eyes, my dear, and give me a nice kiss. You don't want me to take all your pretty clothes away and send you home, do you?"

I began to cry again and begged him not to send me home.

"Then do as I say. Go to Elmer's room and tell him I am a doctor and have had opium in the office only two or three days. Tell him that as a medical experiment I was using it briefly to judge its reaction on people. Tell him you had never smoked it before, that you were just trying to show off, and that if he will not tell your parents you will never smoke again."

I went to Elmer and told him what Will had told me to say. It must have been convincing, for he didn't tell my parents.

When I went back to the office Will took me in his arms. "Dear child," he said, "I am older than you are and know the world, and you must let me decide what is best for us. Now shut your eyes. I have a surprise for you."

I felt him fumbling with my shirtwaist, and when I opened my eyes I found he had pinned a gold watch near my shoulder. The blow was forgotten. My mind was a funny jumble. I knew you were supposed to stay with your husband until "death do us part." I had known women whose husbands hit them, and they didn't get gold watches afterward, either. As for smoking opium, it was impossible for me to think it was dangerous. I had been smoking it, and it hadn't hurt me. So I believed Will. I not only believed him, I loved him. And I didn't want to give up my lovely rings and watch and silk clothes.

A few days later Will asked me if I would like to go to the St. Louis Fair. We bought more clothes and some luggage. My brain was in a whirl. I seemed to be going from one grand experience to another. Will praised my looks to the skies, and I thought he was the grandest man in the world.

Sometime before we were to leave, as we sat down to dinner, Will ordered drinks and said: "Vi, you're going to be with a great many people who drink. There's no harm in it. Every drink you've had with me has had liquor in it. Don't you think it's time for you to stop acting like an ignorant child? After all, you're a woman of the world now."

A few weeks before I would have been horrified. Now I was secretly thrilled to be considered a woman of the world and didn't mind drinking if that was how one proved it.

We went to St. Louis by way of Chicago, and there I met the man who had contributed more to Will's personality than any other individual. He was Dr. Lop Chung, a tall, dignified Chinese who spoke English perfectly.

We went into a room decorated lavishly with embroidered hangings and lay down to smoke opium. When we got up to go Dr. Lop brought out twelve pieces of embroidery about a foot square. They were worked so beautifully they seemed to be painted. He also gave me a funny-shaped kimono of ivory satin, embroidered on one side with pink cherry blossoms, and on the other with white cherry blossoms against a pale pink background.

"These are an unworthy gift to the wife of my friend," he said.

I thought he was crazy to call them unworthy. They were the loveliest things I had ever seen.

Contrast, however, came swiftly. We were having dinner that night at the Palmer House, and Will asked if the steaks were good.

"Sir," replied the waiter, "we never serve a piece of beef here unless it has hung for at least six weeks."

That finished me so far as dinner was concerned. I was certain the meat was rotten. On the farm my father would kill a beef in the morning, and we would probably have a steak for supper.

The World's Fair was even grander than the amusement park in St. Paul, and the best part of it was the Ferris wheel. I rode on it as long as Will would let me. The thrill of it was still in my head when we went into the Chinese Building, where my husband examined two gorgeous mandarin coats. Inquiring the price, he was told by the attendant he could have the pair for a hundred and fifty dollars.

Will pulled a railroad ticket from his pocket and showed it to the Chinese.

"I'm going to Oklahoma City tomorrow," he said, "and all I have left is ninety dollars. I can't give you any more."

"Why, Will," I said, "you had over four hundred this morning."

"I have only the ninety dollars left," he said.

"Why, Will, I've been with you all the time. Look through your pockets."

"Just a minute," said Will. "I have a friend somewhere in the building. We'll see if we can find him."

He took me out of the room, behind some big pillars. Holding me with one hand, he slapped me with the other. Then he started shaking me.

"You fool! Do you think I've suddenly gone insane and don't know how much money I have? You may as well learn now. Never contradict anything I say in front of a third person. If I say a wall is black, agree with me, even though you can see it is red. No matter what I say, I know what I'm doing. Now stay here until I come back."

In a few minutes he was back with the mandarin coats. He had paid ninety dollars for them. "One of them is for you," he said. "Wipe your eyes. We're going downtown and eat."

He never argued with me. He told me a thing once. If I didn't remember and it was important, he slapped or hit me. Then he bought me a dress or fur.

The next day we went to Oklahoma City and got a hotel room. Will went out for a while, and when he came back he told me he was going to pitch that night. I asked what he meant. Men who lectured on the street from a hack and sold medicine, he said, were called pitchmen, and the lecture was called the pitch.

Perhaps an hour later a lean, curly-haired man with a derby hat sloped back on his head came up to the room. "Going to work tonight?" he asked.

Will said he was, and introduced me.

The curly-haired man looked me over. "What does she do?"

"Nothing," Will said.

The man looked at me again. "She's excess baggage. I can teach her something in an hour or so, and she can ballyhoo your crowd for you."

"How?"

"A mind-reading act. Just a little one—twenty-six articles on the alphabet code. She'll know just what you're going to touch next and can answer you."

The monster, as I thought of him, got a paper and pencil and wrote down twenty-six items. They were articles easily found in any ordinary crowd—hat, necktie, handkerchief, stickpin, watch charm, and so on. Will and I had to learn them in alphabetical order. In no case did the opening letter of the word correspond with the letter used to designate it in the alphabetical sequence.

The three of us worked in the room most of the afternoon. Finally the man with the derby hat left. I still thought I could get out of doing it. I begged and pleaded. I cried. I dreaded the prospect so much I even vomited. At last the hack arrived at the hotel. I had cried so much I was a sight, and Will put the bandage over my eyes before we left the room. He led me through the lobby and put me into the vehicle. I could hear him announcing a free show right down on the next corner, starting immediately.

The hack was open. I was sitting on one seat and Will was standing on the other.

The clop of the horses' hoofs on the cobbles sounded like the rattle of doom. I began to shake; I was so frightened and ashamed. The hack stopped. I could hear the stir of other traffic and the scraping of boots as the crowd gathered. Behind the bandage over my eyes I visualized the most terrible assortment of faces staring at me curiously. I cringed lower and lower in my seat.

"Sit here until I get the gasoline torch lit," Will directed. I heard the scrape of a match and then, as the flame caught the torch, the little puff of sound that later was to become so familiar. Will touched my shoulder and I stood up.

Will's magnificent voice rolled out with that persuasive, compelling quality which never failed to capture attention.

"Step this way, gentlemen, and I will have the little lady read your minds." There was an obedient shuffling. "To an infinitesimal number of persons in a generation," Will continued, "is granted the rare power of probing the thoughts of others. The dark mystery of this skill—this dread and supernatural skill, if you please—has never been traced or explained by science. Some of the world's foremost medical men have come to scoff at the demonstration you are about to witness—and have remained, baffled and bewildered, to praise the inexplicable talents of the little lady you see before you. These profound and unfathomable secrets of the human mind are beyond the ability of man to explore. We can, however, observe and marvel.

"I will show you how this little lady, blinded and immobile, can strip away the bone and flesh which separate her mind from yours. To her, the innermost thought processes of each and every one of you are as clear as the pages of a book.

"I am now going to pass among you. Silently and at random I shall indicate some article of apparel or adornment visible to all of you but unseen by the little lady. I shall ask the owner of the article to concentrate on its name. Powerful and precise, his thoughts will flow across space and be read by her.

"Now, gentlemen, we are ready to proceed."

Will stepped down into the audience. Article A on my memorized list was "hat." Will selected the nearest man wearing one, pointed to it so the crowd could see, and asked, "What is this article?" I replied, of course, that it was a hat.

Article B on the list was "spectacles." Will found a pair, and I answered his standard question, "What is this article?" correctly.

Article C was "handkerchief." I got that and went on down the alphabet without a hitch. There never had been anything wrong with my memory, and by the time I was halfway through I began to be proud of the murmurs of surprise and puzzlement which were running through the crowd. I felt a little like I had when my singing of "Come Unto Me" had made people cry at revival meetings.

The alphabet code was, of course, the simplest thing of its kind in existence. Will and I later worked out a more complicated code. This involved men's descriptions. We divided men into two general classifications, dark and light. A dark man could be tall and slender or heavy-set. He could have a mustache or be clean-shaven. His hair could be straight or curly, and it might have some gray in it. The same divisions were applied to blonds.

Among Will's friends were men who became models for each one of these divisions. A friend named Harry, for instance, was tall, dark, slender, smooth-shaven, with curly hair. As I stood blindfolded Will would say, "Have you any idea what this man looks like?" The code word was "have," the two opening letters, h-a, indicating Harry, whom I would describe. If the man fitted the same general description but wore a mustache, Will would say, "Madame, have you any idea of the description of this man?" The "madame" meant mustache. When the man's hair was straight, Will didn't mention it, and I knew it was straight. When he said, "Describe his hair," I knew it was curly. When he said, "Go on and tell me if you can as to his hair," I would reply that there seemed to be gray in it. With a key model to work from in each division, it was easy. Will, of course, always picked out the men in the audience I was to describe. For big blonds we used a friend named Hubert for the model. Will would code me by saying, "Hurry up and answer this question." The h-u in "hurry" told me whom he meant. We worked fast. We had to or the yokels would have caught on. Will kept up a flow of talk which buried the code words in a flood of language.

When we had descriptions down pat we started in on numbers. This was considerably more difficult. We translated the numbers one to ten into words which could be used easily in any sentence. One was yes; two, go; three, slow; four, see; five, numbers; six, look; seven, tell; eight, please; nine, ready; ten, now.

Will never addressed me personally except to ask me the bare question. He coded me while he was talking to the chump. For example, he would say to the chump, "I want you to whisper in my ear, so no one can hear you, a certain sum of money." Assume the chump mentioned $645. Will would say to him, "So you want the little lady to look and see the numbers of the money you are thinking of?" The three key words gave me the sum at once. Will would turn impressively to me as I stood blindfolded and say, "Tell us the amount of money this man is thinking of," and I would rattle off the figure. If the sum mentioned happened to be $6.45 instead of $645, Will would cue me by saying, "Tell us the dollars and cents this man is thinking of."

Sometimes Will would vary this after he had coded me by telling the chump to walk up and ask me himself. He would come up and I would ask him to give me his hand. I would press his fingers against my forehead while he asked me the question. This always went over big because men never failed to be impressed by games which permitted them to touch even the forehead of a strange woman. I would say, "Think! Think! No, you are not thinking hard enough," and I would allow my hand holding his to tremble so that his hand quivered on my forehead. Then I would give him the answer.

Perhaps the chump would want to know the date of his birthday. After learning it in a whispered conversation, Will would say to him a trifle impatiently, "Yes, yes, of course she can tell months and numbers and dates of birthdays." He went on talking, but I paid attention only to the number code. The first "yes" meant "one," or January. The second "yes" and the word "numbers" meant "fifteen." So his birthday was January fifteenth. If he wanted the year of his birth he could also have that after a little more conversation with Will.

We went on to build up a code for states and towns, and I got so I could tell the chump the town and state from which a letter in his pocket had been mailed. The codes worked because of Will's tremendous vocabulary and his quick-wittedness. His first sentence usually gave me the general idea of what was wanted. Then I would know what to look for in his casual conversation.

We got into serious trouble with the mind-reading act only once, and that was in Yakima, Washington, months after my first jittery experience. Will had quit hitting me and blacking my eyes by that time, as I had become valuable and it cost him money when I was laid up. He had devised instead an even more painful method of correction. Whenever I failed to do as well at something as he thought I should, he would find an excuse to return to the hack or platform, reach in, and pinch the calf of my leg.

When I went out to do my mind-reading ballyhoo in Yakima, Will was a little drunker than usual. He started to code me an article but was so drunk he coded me wrong. I stalled and said, "I can't see what the article is." Will coded me wrong again. I guessed and missed. I was standing up in the hack, the door of which was open. Will reached in, as if looking for something, and grabbed a hunk of the flesh of my leg and twisted it.

Some yokel saw him do it and began to shout, "Don't abuse that woman! You're killing her, trying to make her see things! What you need, mister, is a poke in the jaw!"

The crowd began to talk rough and surge in around the hack. Will climbed up in back and explained the code to them. They wouldn't believe him. They were convinced I really read minds and that he had to torture me to make me do it. Will's explanation was drowned, finally, in the uproar. Someone yelled, "Get a rope and lynch him to that telephone pole!" It was nip and tuck for a moment, but the police chief heard the row and came on the run. He got Will away from the crowd, with me following. He escorted us to our hotel room for our luggage and then down to the depot. He stayed right with us until the first train pulled in, and it didn't matter to Will which direction that train was going.

But this was long after my initial experience in ballyhooing a crowd. For the first time in front of an audience I had gone through the alphabetical code without a hitch. I stood there in the back of the hack, still shaking a little. But now that it was over I was only ten per cent scared and ninety per cent proud.

I thought, "I didn't make a mistake. Not one. I can do it again." I could hear Will's voice and feel him beside me in the hack. I knew the gasoline torch was flaming at my elbow; all at once I liked to have it there. The mental picture of faces staring up no longer terrified me.

Will's voice was unruffled. "Slip off the bandage," he whispered, "and go back to the hotel."

I climbed down out of the hack and, lifting up my skirts, scampered up the street. Waiting in the hotel room, I was in a fever of uncertainty, wondering how the pitch had gone. I nearly wore out the window curtain pulling it aside to see if Will was coming up the walk.

It was a couple of hours before Will arrived. He was all smiles. "I did pretty well," he told me. "I sold forty dollars' worth of medicine." He counted it all out and handed me five dollars. "Buy something tomorrow. You helped make it."

I couldn't believe my eyes. "Why, you didn't do anything but talk," I said, "and just an hour or so. Our hired man on the farm worked all month for twenty dollars."

"Always remember, my child," Will said, "no one but a sucker ever works."

→ CHAPTER THREE ←
PERFUME
BEANS
AND
PICKPOCKETS

THE VIRUS had started to work on me. Something for nothing. Nights, after the lecture, Will and I would lie on the bed and smoke opium. A fascinating storyteller, he would relate the histories of different lands, the habits of their people, their punishments and methods of revenge. He selected books for me to read, starting me off on Gibbon's *The History of the Decline and Fall of the Roman Empire*. I read Plato on Socrates—whom I called the Hemlock Kid—Darwin, Schopenhauer, and others.

Also, while we smoked, Will spoke more freely of his background than at any other time. Bit by bit I picked up the story of his early life and his start in the medicine-show business. His mother was a gentle, sensitive woman, slightly hunchbacked, whom Will adored. The adoration amounted to a mother complex which colored Will's actions throughout his life. His father was a robust man, much larger than Will, with a roving eye for a trim-looking leg. Reading was Will's passion; they called him the crazy student. His only excitement was running around with a bunch of young thugs whose game at the time was robbing pushcarts. Many of them graduated later to assault, robbery, and passing counterfeit money.

His parents were divorced, and both remarried. As Will detested his stepfather, he left his mother and went to board with a family in Wisconsin when he was about fourteen. The husband was a traveling man, the wife a beautiful blonde of about twenty-eight years. One night during the absence of her husband on a prolonged trip, the wife seduced Will, and they continued to live together until he was seventeen. The husband at length became suspicious and trapped the pair. He must have been allergic to this double-take home life, because he jumped Will. The upshot was that Will and his ladylove departed for Chicago with her two children. There she got a job doing housework while he went to work as a delivery boy for a drugstore.

The woman, whose name was Mary, never returned to her husband. Although Will never married her, he supported her and they remained emotionally bound to each other for the rest of their lives.

The drugstore was on the edge of Chicago's red-light district. His deliveries were restricted to this area and some office buildings nearby. Will was a rosy-cheeked, black-haired young fellow with a way about him. He became a favorite with the prostitutes and even their pimps and associates.

While delivering medicine he came in contact with Dr. Lop Chung, who was immediately attracted by Will's inquiring mind. The liking increased, and the cultured Chinese had long talks with the alert boy, eventually hiring tutors to provide him with a classical education. Will continued his studies throughout his life.

When I met him he had become the brilliant, dominant personality who was a legend in the medicine-show business. Despite his short stature and his opium-induced pallor—Will made a habit of touching up his cheeks with rouge—he was an overawing figure. I never heard him raise his voice under any circumstances, yet it was a voice no one could resist. He had very odd eyes. They were an off hazel, and at times, when he was angry, they seemed to be flecked with burnt umber and jade green. He dominated everyone, man or woman, with whom he came in contact. It was simply a question of will power. And it seemed to be understood that he knew everything. When he addressed any one of us medicine-show people as "my child" or "my boy" and said, "I am older than you are and know best," I believe we would have committed murder for him if he had insisted on it.

One of his chief delights was to gather a bunch of medicine people together and answer the stiffest questions they could ask. We would demand, for example, the population of Peru. How much wheat did Russia raise during the current year? What were the exports and imports of Greece? He never failed. Those who doubted him now and then checked his replies in the World Almanac and invariably found he was right. The control of others was a source of particular satisfaction to him. When other holds failed, he found that by starting a young person off on opium he could continue to exert his influence.

Will himself had begun smoking opium when he was about eighteen. Whether he was started by the Chinese doctor, who was an addict, or by someone in the red-light district, he never said. His start in the medicine business, however, was easily traceable.

While strolling home one day he observed a man lecturing on a street corner with such energy that a crowd had collected. The youthful Will, his imagination caught, remained long enough to watch the speaker offer for sale tins of salve at fifty cents and quickly collect six or eight dollars.

Will rushed back to Dr. Lop's office and breathlessly described the incident. "I can do it just as easily as he did," he exclaimed. "I know it."

Dr. Lop, though pleased, was not overwhelmed. "I believe you could," he said. "But why not do it a little differently? I will lend you a Chinese costume, and you can sell vials of Chinese headache oil."

To this Will agreed enthusiastically. The oil was put up in tiny green vials containing about twenty drops and cost about five cents a vial. He hurried to Chinatown, financed by the doctor, and laid in a supply.

The following day he put on the costume, equipped himself with a box of the vials, and took up a station in front of the Board of Trade Building.

Even on that first occasion his knack with crowds was apparent. He stood in the street beside the curb and began to extol the merits of his preparation. Something about the diminutive, pink-cheeked youth with the black hair and convincing voice persuaded passers-by to listen. Will was completely oblivious of the hustling traffic about him. He explained that one drop of his precious imported fluid rubbed on each temple would cure the most painful headache. So beneficial was it, he declared, that in most cases the same result would be achieved by simply inhaling the odor. Warming to his spiel and savoring the attentiveness of his hearers, he invented fresh benefits on the spur of the moment. Rubbed briskly over the back, he asserted, the preparation would relieve lumbago or kidney trouble.

He was disposing of the vials as rapidly as he could make change when a hand fell on his shoulder.

"Where, me lad," said the Law, "is your license to sell medicine?"

"License? Do you have to have a license?"

"Sure, and they'll explain it all to you at headquarters. Come along."

Will got his license, a new supply of vials, and the first Oriental Medicine Man was born. From then on Will was identified with things Chinese, and his warmest personal interest centered on the subject.

During those early nights as we smoked in Oklahoma City, he recalled tale after tale of the Chinese heroes of history.

We had been in Oklahoma City only a short while when Will got a letter from another medicine man, Arizona Bill, asking Will to join him in Ponca City. Arizona Bill had a medicine show playing theaters and needed a partner. An itchier-footed lot than medicine men has never been born. The letter had scarcely stopped crackling in Will's fingers before we were on our way.

We found Ponca City plastered with bills advertising the show. As a matter of course Will asked for theatrical rates at the hotel. The troupe of actors was a rather dilapidated bunch. They made a somewhat distressing effort to be jaunty as we sat together at lunch, but were agreeable enough. There was a girl, young and good-looking, a couple of young men, one of whom had a habit of scowling and tugging at his mustache, and a husband and wife. The wife bobbed her head at her husband, like a bird pecking at food, whenever she spoke to him.

We went to the opera house that night to see the show. Medicine shows were divided into two parts, with the pitches sandwiched in between, the actors doubled.

In this show the leading lady of the afterpiece played the piano while the audience filed into the theater. The entertainment itself began with one of the actors giving imitations on the violin. He played "Listen to the Mocking Bird" with variations and imitated different birds. Next came the leading lady, singing "I'll Be with You When the Roses Bloom Again" and "Break the News to Mother." Even Arizona Bill had to double. Dressed in a frock coat and silk hat, he contributed to the festivities by rendering a tune or two on the accordion, and replied to an encore with a song which involved the challenging line, "Oh, I'm going home to Arkansas tomorrow; why the hell won't you go back today?" The husband and wife concluded the first part of the program by parodying a bullfight.

The curtain went down and then rose again to a drumfire burst from the piano to reveal Arizona Bill, the Great Benefactor of Mankind, attired now in buckskins. He wore a long mustache, and his hair hung below his shoulders, after the manner of dime-novel Indian scouts.

His story was a mixture of heartbreaking tragedy and spine-chilling peril. He had, he told the audience, been stolen by Indians when he was an infant. The chief of the tribe had adopted him, and thus he had had access to their most intimate tribal secrets. He had studied the mysteries of their miraculous herbal cures and at length had determined to escape in order to bring these marvels to the white race. He had indeed managed to free himself, pursued by hideous danger at every step, and now was able to share his discoveries with friends of his own race at the modest price of one dollar a bottle. He had been able to salvage, also, the formula for a liniment of peculiar and powerful properties known as Rattlesnake Oil. The Indians rubbed themselves with this to prevent rheumatism, he explained, and used it to keep limber on marches, and for cuts, and so on. Arizona Bill was actually a Welshman and spoke with a cockney accent, but that didn't make any difference to the yokels. They still bought. All the other actors hustled through the audience, selling the herbs and oil and shouting, "Sold out again, Doctor!" whenever their immediate supply was exhausted. When the last loose dollar had been extracted from snap purses, Arizona Bill bowed off the stage, and the curtain lifted once more on the short afterpiece.

The show spurred Will to a new scheme. Back at the hotel, he sat up writing after I had gone to bed. The next morning he handed me nine sheets of paper covered with tight script.

"Learn this," he said. "I'll make up the stock as soon as you have it memorized."

What he had produced was a new pitch which I was to deliver. I read it through and stammered, "But, Will, I can't—get up and talk—I—"

"Certainly you can. Why can't you?"

"But with a lot of people looking at me—"

"They looked at you when you sang at revival meetings, didn't they? Was your voice impaired? Of course it wasn't. You sang better because they were looking at you."

The memory of those tear-drenched triumphs was persuasive. I was frightened, but I was intrigued too. I began to memorize the pitch. I even let myself believe, just a tiny bit, that I had done what it said I had.

The story had a flavor, all right. It dealt with what was described as the Mexican perfume bean and a soap known as Ou Yah Nut Soap. These perfume beans, the story explained, grew only in a remote section of the interior of Mexico. They possessed a haunting, individual odor of great loveliness which lasted as long as the bean itself. When placed in clothing the beans imparted this wonderful odor to the garment and also killed all moths and bugs. The region in which this bean grew was inhabited by an extremely ferocious tribe of natives, but, indifferent to peril, we entered it. A peculiarity of this tribe was the fact that all its members had long, luxuriant hair and beautiful complexions. It was apparent that their use of a soap, made from a closely guarded formula, accounted for this phenomenon. At the risk of our lives we remained with this native tribe until we discovered the priceless secret of this soap's manufacture. We were now offering both the beans and the soap to the public for the very low price of twenty-five cents.

The next morning Will had the labels printed. He bought a sack of speckled beans, a bottle of perfume, some long white bars of soap, and some tin foil. We cut the soap into small pieces and wrapped them in the foil. After sprinkling the beans with perfume, we put them in a glass fruit jar.

I went to the show every night, feeling very gay again because I didn't have to do any mind reading.

Then abruptly the company's leading lady fell ill. Arizona Bill asked Will if I could play a secondary role in a scene from East Lynn. I cried, I begged, I groveled. It was no use. The actors were called, and I was forced to rehearse with them. Whenever I thought I might have to do a thing I disliked, I turned to and learned to the best of my ability, but always with a secret conviction that Providence would intervene before the event. In this case nothing happened. When the time came to go on I was on the verge of collapse. Will got some whisky and gave me a couple of drinks. The curtain went up and I tottered out onto the stage. Somehow or other I got through the scene.

The next night I had to play Mrs. Bibbs in *Bibbs and Bibbs*. The whole show went wrong this time, probably because of my inexperience. The man with the violin got drunk and kept on playing in spite of commands from the wings. They had to lasso him and drag him off the stage, trying to pretend it was part of the act. After the show the husband-and-wife act got into a fight. Everyone was jittery. Even Will had had enough. He gave me up as an actress and promised we would leave the show as soon as we could get our things together.

The next day we labeled the beans and the soap and bought a sponge. Will took the sponge to the room and dampened it. He then got out some shaving soap and carefully rubbed the sponge full of it. The following morning we left for Blackwell, Oklahoma. Probably there never was a more desolate town—empty streets ankle-deep in mud, wooden sidewalks lined with a few broken-down hitching racks. It made my spine crawl to look at it.

We got a hotel room with decayed wallpaper and went down to the livery stable to rent a rig and driver for the day and evening. We got a hack—a four-wheeled vehicle which broke in the center and folded back, something like a sport coupe. The pitchman stood on the back seat while he was talking. At night the light for the lecture was supplied by our gasoline torch, which was tied on a pole and secured to a rear wheel. We always taught some kid to light the torch and bring it down and fix it to the wheel. In those days "carrying the torch" for a pitchman involved a good deal of emotion for a boy, but not the kind referred to by the term today.

Before we left the livery stable Will took one of the wheels off the hack and carefully removed the dirty axle grease. He then packed the wheel with tar soap, which is very black but an effective cleansing agent. We drove to the town's main intersection. It was about eleven o'clock in the morning, Saturday, and people were beginning to come into town on horseback, in wagons, and in buggies. We went to the hotel, picked up our stock, a pan, and a pail of water. Will handed me into the hack, stepped up on the back seat, and in his rich voice announced the opening of a free show.

I began to shake, but not as much as I had before. The noises of the gathering crowd still sent chills racing through me. Blindfolded, I could imagine their faces gathered in a tight ring just beyond Will's back. Every muttered remark seemed to be directed at me. To get the rising panic out of my mind I hastily rehearsed the codes we had worked out.

Once we got under way I couldn't concentrate on anything but the mind reading. It was over far too soon, and Will had whipped off the bandage, and there I was, feeling absolutely alone and terrified. I couldn't get a word out of my throat. The faces seemed a hundred times larger than they were. I still remember one man who used a grimy forefinger to curl down his mustache so he could chew on the end of it. It seemed to me they were all about to break into shouts of laughter.

"Start on the beans," Will hissed.

I started—scared, sweating, and stuttering. I grabbed for that story of perfume beans found in the remote and dangerous interior of Mexico. It was something to hang onto. I gradually straightened out and then started on the soap. Somehow I felt comfortable talking about that tribe of natives in Mexico; compared with the crowd jammed around the hack, they were friends of mine.

"See," I concluded, "how little soap it takes," and picked up the loaded sponge. I rubbed it once or twice across the soap and dipped it into the pail of water. In less than a minute I had great gobs of lather piled around me.

"The wheel," Will whispered.

I rattled along, instructing the driver to remove a wheel—the one we had fixed. When he had it off I took a clean handkerchief and wiped what appeared to be black axle grease off onto it. I held it up so the audience could see how filthy it was with grease and dirt. Men don't get very excited about things like that, but they were mighty quiet while I gave the handkerchief a swipe with our soap and swiftly rubbed out the black.

"Gentlemen," I said, "you have seen how this wonderful soap removes all grit, grease, and dirt. The price of this soap, together with the perfume bean, is only twenty-five cents. Who wants a package?"

No one moved, and that dull, stubborn quiet was more appalling than any words. My heart began to pound, and I could feel the tears crowding into the corners of my eyes.

One man pressed in against the hack, and an instant later there were a dozen more jamming around him. What looked like a thousand hands clutching silver and gold were being flourished in my face. The tears never fell. They were lost in a rush of happy excitement.

When the last sale had been made Will smiled at me. "Well, how did you do?"

I looked into the grip. All the stock was gone, and I had only about a dollar in change.

"Someone stole it!" I cried. "Someone stole the money!"

"Keep your voice down," Will said.

"But someone stole all the money!"

"Not in the way you think. Do you remember when you were so busy selling and you had so much trouble changing a ten-dollar gold piece for a man? He had to come back the second time to get it right. Well, he short-changed you. Never forget the way he did it. Don't get rattled. Make change for each person before you sell to anyone else."

I never made a mistake in changing money again, and I never found out whether I was really short-changed or if Will framed me with one of the gang to teach me a lesson through experience. Will praised me to the sky and I took it as my just due. I was proud as a peacock. I had lied my head off and the yokels had believed me and handed me their money. Will had proved his point—no one but a sucker ever worked. All working and telling the truth had ever got me was fifty cents a day. I felt as great a sense of power as if I were a queen. I was so eager to pitch that whenever I saw four or five people on the street I wanted to go out and tell them my story again. I felt I could convince the whole world. We stayed in Blackwell several days, and I pitched every day. It seemed to me we were growing unbelievably rich, although judged by later standards I was making only chicken feed.

Customers began to thin out in Blackwell, and we jumped to Hot Springs, Arkansas. While looking for an apartment we stayed at the Arlington, a lovely rambling hotel, and I had a gorgeous time. In the morning I rode a blooded horse through the hills. I had been used to riding astride on the farm, but Will got me a long skirt and taught me to ride sidesaddle. When a groom handed me up into the saddle I immediately became the bored Southern belle with a hundred retainers.

The main street of Hot Springs was lined with bathhouses and gambling houses. Will seemed to know everybody of importance. In the bathhouses or at the races he introduced me to race-track followers, gamblers, prize fighters, actors, and medicine men and their wives, or women. No one could have been more smug or virtuous than I when Will told me some were not married.

We spent the afternoon taking mineral baths and loafing on the sun porches. I was rapidly becoming a favorite with Will's friends. So long as he picked out my clothes and ordered my meals and I kept quiet unless he told me what to say, I did very well. The other women acted bored, but I listened to everyone with openmouthed and wide-eyed amazement. Some gambler was always showing me how he could deal crooked and betting I couldn't catch him. Then he would try to teach me how. Short-change artists, prize fighters, and pickpockets all gave me exhibitions of their pet punches or tricks. I was so awe-struck I must have been good for their morale.

I gradually discovered there was a very strict line of caste among these people. A "high-pitch" medicine man belonged to the aristocracy of the pitch world. The term "high pitch" sprang from the fact that he was always elevated above his audience in a hack, on a stage, or on a platform. He also paid the highest license fees. A "low-pitch" man put his wares on a tripod and stood either on the pavement or on a low box. If a "high" elected to pitch on a certain street, the "low" had to stop until he was through. Whereas a "high" usually made his pitch and quit, a "low" might stand and sell, or grind, as we called it, all day. A "high-pitch" man never associated with carnival followers or even circus performers, although they had an aristocracy as rigid as our own. It was permissible, however, to associate with circus owners. I could mingle with saloon owners, managers of gambling houses, race-horse owners, bookmakers, politicians, and high-class thieves, both men and women. In the last-named category were penny-weighters (diamond thieves), madames of houses of prostitution, and confidence men.

Strictly taboo were prostitutes, pimps, bartenders, hack drivers, waiters, moll buzzers (men who snatched women's purses), clock men (who stole only watches), and sneak thieves. We never tried to associate with our prospects. Contact with them was only in the line of business.

Two-timing men or women were given the cold shoulder. If you fell in love with someone other than your husband or wife or lover, you were supposed to pack your trunk, split your bank roll, and leave with the one of your choice and live decent. There was no haphazard kissing at parties. If you tried that you were liable to hit the morgue. More often than not a couple worked together, each in a way being the meal ticket of the other.

Among the people I met that winter were Kid Herman, the fighter, and May Abbott. May was classed with Kittie Fitzgibbon and Annie Piggott as one of the three greatest women thieves of their time. She was a pickpocket and could take out and put back either hard or soft. This meant she could not only remove currency or gold coins from a pocket, but also could replace them with a temporarily satisfactory substitute. To a sucker giving himself a quick frisk in a crowd, scissored newspapers resembled currency, and the jingle of silver coins approximated that of gold. Before the exchange was discovered, May had made her getaway. May, like everyone else, wore an overload of diamonds. In those days members of the sporting world carried most of their bank roll in diamonds, and men and women wore them.

We had had two or three weeks of this careless living when Will came in one afternoon and announced we would have to go to work. A license fee was prohibitive, he said, but he believed a special permit might be obtained. I was to pay a visit to the mayor in the city hall.

"Tell him I'm a consumptive," Will instructed me, "and we have to make a living. I'll walk up and down the opposite side of the street, and you can point me out if they want to see me. Put on your plainest dress." He handed me one hundred and fifty dollars. "Get a month's license. Whatever you save out of this you can have."

I was still riding on the confidence my pitching success had inspired. The city hall didn't look big, and it didn't look hard to beat. The mayor was courteous, but he shunted me off to another official. This second man listened to my story. He was stout, with the shiniest half-bald head I'd ever seen, and his eyes were very quiet. They seemed like dead eyes.

"How old are you?"

"Nineteen," I said, giving myself three extra years.

"And where is your husband?"

I pointed out the window. He got up, his hands clasped behind him, and stood for nearly a minute staring across at Will with a kind of cold lifelessness.

"Broke?"

"Just about."

He sat down abruptly at his desk and wrote out a permit to lecture and sell medicine on a good corner in town. He dug down in a pocket and handed me a twenty-dollar gold piece along with the permit.

"Use this to get on your feet," he said. "Come back here every Monday and Friday and let me know how you are getting along."

Back in the hotel room, I jubilantly spread the unneeded hundred and fifty on the bureau and made the gold piece ring as I slapped it down. I told Will what had happened.

Will carefully folded the greenbacks together and placed the twenty-dollar gold piece on top of them. "My dear," he said, "you're a smart girl. I'll keep this for you."

At dinner that night Will showed the permit to some friends and told how I had gotten it. They congratulated me on being such a skillful fixer, but one man who knew the official said, "Don't cross that guy, Will. He's a killer."

Will laughed. "My boy, the hick politician who can trim me hasn't been born."

We started to work, and I reported according to instructions. The first time the official contented himself with remarking on what a pretty girl I was and wasn't it a little hard on me, having a sick husband? I always had to repeat to Will the things other people said, and he told me what to do.

"His next move," Will predicted, "will be to ask you to go out to dinner. Tell him you never go out."

Sure enough, that was what happened. The official did not press the issue, but by the time of the next visit he had been down to watch us work and knew we were doing well. The dinner question came up again. I tried to stall. He leaned back in his chair, his thumbs hooked in the belt over his big belly. His dead eyes kept looking at me.

"My dear, aren't you forgetting that I've done a great many things for you just because you asked me to?"

"Oh, I couldn't ever forget that," I said. "And my poor husband couldn't either. He appreciates it just as much as I do."

He picked up a paper and began to tap it on the desk. "This is a permit I had to take away from a man. He neglected to be obliging after he got it."

"I don't know how we could live if you took our permit away," I said, pretending I was about to cry.

"Now, my dear, I'm not going to take your permit away unless you make me. Surely you can't believe I mean you any harm. I'm just a lonely man who wants a little youthful company."

"There must be dozens of girls who'd be as happy as I would to go out with you if I weren't married," I said.

"Don't you like me?"

"Oh yes, I like you very much, but I never go out with anyone but my husband."

He didn't insist, but he said, "You think about it."

Two nights later Will and I were eating dinner when the friend who had warned us earlier came rushing into the dining room. He sat down at the table and began to swipe jerkily at a lock of yellow hair that kept tumbling into his eyes.

"Will," he said, "you've got to get out of here. Through the kitchen if you can. That guy has put the finger on you, and there's a man waiting in the lobby to kill you."

"Nonsense," Will said. "What are you talking about?"

"I tell you it's true. That guy is crazy about your wife, and he's had you tailed. He knows about your smoking. He figures he can get Vi."

"He can't."

"He figures different. You aren't going to walk ten steps past the hotel door."

"Don't be ridiculous. I'll walk as far as I like."

"Not this time. It's all rigged, Will. As soon as you get outside this man is going to jostle you. There'll be an argument and a fight, and then he's to kill you."

"He'll do nothing of the kind. For God's sake, stop fiddling with your hair. Cut it off or plaster it down. Will you have some dessert with us? Waiter! Bring me a piece of watermelon."

Will finished the meal very calmly. I was terrified, but I didn't dare speak. Will stood up. "Just walk beside me as if nothing were the matter," he said.

We went out into the lobby. A heavy-set man in a brown overcoat was standing beside the door. He went through it just as we did, shouldering into Will and brushing him off balance. He whirled around, grabbed one of the lapels of Will's coat, and said: "Why, damn you, you did that on purpose!"

Will began to cough and choke. "Be careful!" he gasped. "I have ulcers of the stomach. I'll have a hemorrhage."

The man gawked at him a little, but he kept trying to act mad. "I'll learn you a thing or two," he said.

Will kept on coughing. He spat a red substance out onto the sidewalk, and all at once understanding hit me—that watermelon!

"Now see what you've done," Will whispered. "It's a hemorrhage. Get me to a doctor. I'll die if I don't get to a doctor!"

The man in the brown overcoat was stupefied. He kept looking from Will to the sidewalk and back again. He let go of Will's lapel.

"Don't just stand there," Will choked. "Do something. I'm dying, I tell you!"

Brown Overcoat took two backward steps before he spun around and started legging it as fast as he could go.

"Jump up to the room and get our bags," Will said to me. "I'll meet you at the livery stable."

We hired a rig to take us to a small town nearby and from there caught the train for Little Rock. Will talked to me sadly and sweetly on the train.

"He would have killed me, your husband and protector, on your account," he mused.

I threw my arms around his neck.

"I am much older than you, my child," he added, "and my life must be devoted to building up a fortune for you. When I am dead you will still be a young woman, and I want you protected."

I was crying before he had finished. My feeling was tigerishly maternal. I was desperately in love, but my passion was tender, not physical. Will had explained to me that his lack of ardor was not lack of love for me but simply his way of protecting my youth. I thought the reason I accepted his occasional husbandly advances with tranquility was because I was a good girl. We were, of course, simply explaining away one of the effects of opium.

After we had been in Little Rock a few days Will told me to take the train to a town a few miles away and find out how much a license to sell medicine would cost. On the way the engine and tender ran off the track.

When I got back to Little Rock that night I was full of the story. "Will, the engine ran off the track and the cars were lopsided. The conductor said the train might tip over, but it didn't."

He was interested at once. "Anyone hurt?"

"I don't think so."

"There was a considerable jar, though, when the accident happened?"

"Oh yes."

"And you were thrown against something?"

"Yes, I bumped into the seat ahead of me, but—"

"Good God, Vi!" Will exclaimed. "You've lost your child!"

"What?" I screamed. "Oh," I said.

"Get into bed. I'm going to telephone the railroad doctor." When he got back I was in bed.

"All you have to do is keep your mouth shut," he said. "Just tell them you have terrible pains in your abdomen. I will do all the talking. Don't get scared and don't deny anything I say."

It wasn't long before two doctors arrived. I was already so alarmed I could scarcely speak. Their sober, slightly frowning looks added to my fright. Will told them everything that was supposed to have happened.

One of the doctors frowned still more. "We will have to make an examination, of course."

I was so frightened my head throbbed and I was sweating all over. They examined me and the doctor who had done most of the frowning said, "Your wife has a temperature. I think it would be best for her to be in a hospital. We can watch her tonight and, if necessary, operate in the morning."

I began to cry. I said I would rather die than go to the hospital. Will was very firm, too, and it was finally agreed that he would take my temperature during the night, and if it got worse he would telephone the doctors. The doctors returned the next morning, and of course my temperature was down. I put in seven days of hell. Will never knew when the doctors were coming, and I had to stay in bed all the time. Will had lovely trays of food sent up from a restaurant but would let me touch only a mouthful or two. What was left he would mess up and send back by a waiter. All I really got to eat were hamburgers he brought me in his pockets. One day, unable to stand it any longer, I got up and went dancing and kicking around the room. Will took me by the shoulders and shook me hard. "Haven't you got any sense?" he said. "Someone might be looking through the keyhole." He dragged me over to the bed and threw me down on it.

I began to cry. I had just got well started when there was a knock at the door. It was the claim agent for the railroad. He made a clucking sound when he saw I had been crying.

"What's the matter, my child?"

"I want to go home to my mother," I whimpered.

"Yes," Will said. "Her mother is in Los Angeles. I want to take her there as soon as I can."

I nearly told him my mother was in Iowa, but I didn't dare, and deep in my heart I didn't really want to go home.

The claim agent patted my head. "Don't worry. We'll see that you get home to your mother."

The upshot was that we were provided with two tickets and a drawing room to Los Angeles. Driving down to the depot in a hack, Will was pleased and cheerful.

"You must be ready," he said, "to take opportunity wherever you find it. If you happen to be passing a streetcar which has just had a wreck, for example, lie down on the pavement beside it and begin to scream. One way or another, there will be money in it."

→ CHAPTER FOUR ←
TAPEWORMS
AND
TIGER FAT

EVERY MEDICINE MAN whose bank roll or ingenuity permitted it headed for Los Angeles to spend the winter. Medicine men were divided roughly into three categories—the Indian doctors, the "Quaker" doctors, and the oriental doctors, of whom Will was the founder.

Even in the early 1900s the Indian medicine shows had become almost legendary. So far as I know, they were the first of the lot. Wherever medicine men met they talked of the glories of the old-timers, Healy and Bigelow, the Kickapoo Medicine Men, who sold Kickapoo Indian Sagwa. The initial formula for Sagwa, it was reported, was stale beer and aloes. This concoction used to be stirred up on the lot where the show was playing. While rented Indians from the reservation were dancing and yelling, the country people lined up with their quart jars or other containers and bought hand over fist. These Indian medicine men always dressed as Indian chiefs or Indian scouts. Their shows used a few white performers, together with the hired Indians who served as "flash" or atmosphere. The reservation redskins, of course, were always painted up for war; they carried tomahawks and bows and arrows and did a full-scale war dance with appropriate sound accompaniment. Principal locale of their operations was the Middle West, where authentic Indians had thinned out considerably. Another famous Indian show was the Ketonka Medicine Company, featuring White Star, who lectured in an Indian-scout costume and was reputed to be part Indian. The Indian shows usually rented a large lot in whatever town they happened to be playing and put up tepees for the Indians and tents for the white performers. They also had a cook tent. They generally sold herbs, rattlesnake oil, and soap, besides peddling popcorn and candy between the acts. Medicine men had to be versatile in those days. Sometimes the show would stay for weeks on one lot, and the performance had to be changed every night.

Pitchmen's sagas record one veteran preparation which fell into none of the basic groupings but was one of the earliest and most popular of them all. This was Hamlin's Wizard Oil. According to the story, Hamlin was a magician out of a job. He went to another old-timer, a medicine man, who provided him with a simple and inexpensive formula for a liniment. A man of imagination, Hamlin achieved distinction by naming his product "Wizard Oil." He attracted his crowds by performing the feats of magic which formerly had been his bread and butter and promising solemnly that those who rubbed their hands with his oil would presently be able to duplicate his legerdemain. This promise was accepted at face value by the natives—a term used by pitchmen to describe their customers.

They swarmed up in droves to purchase the magical substance that would enable them to dupe their friends. The only flaw in the scheme was that pitching a second time in the same territory involved troublesome explanations. Hamlin's problem was solved for him when a native, who was not without imagination himself, announced that application of the oil to his back had cured him of rheumatism. As a result, Hamlin's Wizard Oil came to be renowned as a medicine of value for muscular ailments. Hamlin thereafter placed his personal confidence in the virtues of massage, and his oil continued to have a gratifying sale.

For some reason, many yokels had a fundamental faith in Quakers. Perhaps this was because Quakers were understood to be a group activated to a high degree by the motives of gentleness and honesty. At any rate, "Quaker" doctors did a very flourishing business. They called everyone Thee and Thou and Brother. They dressed in fawn-colored clothes and wore wide-brimmed, low-crowned beaver hats. Their trousers were known as "barn-door" pants, being unusual in that they buttoned up the side instead of the front.

Three of the most famous "Quaker" medicine men, Beason, Ferdon (who threw hatfuls of small change to the children in his audiences), and Anderson, came from the same town, Litchfield, Illinois. Brother Benjamin was another "Quaker" doctor of note, but perhaps Brother John's pitch was the most striking. All these men had big shows when they worked, some of them requiring special railroad cars for transportation. Brother John, who was known mysteriously as the Great Kamama, lectured from a chariot drawn by four horses. With a great flourish the chariot, bearing Brother John, would sweep up to the platform used by his performers to attract an audience with ballyhoo.

Brother John, in addition to offering various medicinal bargains, pulled teeth. If business began to slow down during the first days of a week, he had a sure-fire build-up for Saturday night. He would step from his chariot to the platform, beaming with the delight of a man who has received overwhelmingly good news. His delight, he would assure his audience, was so great he could not refrain from sharing it with them. In his hand was a telegram from Brother Josiah Baker, his great-grandfather and a wonderful "Quaker." The distinguished old gentleman was on his way to pay him a visit and would arrive Saturday. An elderly man of great understanding and appreciation, he wished to say a few words to the people who came to hear his grandson's shows. Would the audience tell their friends? He wanted to give the grand old man a fitting reception.

Saturday night the lot would be crowded. The show would start. Presently Brother John would totter out, supported on the arm of an assistant. Clutched in his trembling fingers would be another telegram. The tragedy of the news it contained would be reflected in Brother John's drawn countenance, and in a broken voice he would proceed to read its contents aloud. While crossing the Rocky Mountains, Brother Josiah had contracted a cold. His frail but courageous body had been unable to fling off the affliction, and at the moment of reading he was lying at death's door in a San Francisco hospital. Disclosure of this situation would leave Brother John in a pitiable state, barely able to stand, tears streaming from his eyes. By this time many of the women in his audience would be weeping also.

"My friends, I am overcome," Brother John would whisper. "I can say but a few words. You can show your sympathy for me and for this dear, aged man by buying this medicine without forcing me to tear my heart out with more words."

He would signal to his performers to go through the audience with the remedies. Invariably the response was tremendous. Swabbing at their eyes with bandannas, tenderhearted yokels would crowd up to buy. Women, normally far more suspicious and money-conscious than the men, would prod their husbands into making purchases. Brother John, meanwhile, would stagger to a chair and remain there, wrapped in his grief, permitting the natives to step up and shake his hand while expressing their sympathy. Brother John eventually met with misfortune. A peeved performer grew so rebellious that he exposed the Great Kamama's tale of an expiring great-grandfather on the stand. The show broke up, and Brother John died later in a state hospital. As a matter of fact, I can count on the fingers of two hands the medicine men who died or retired with money. A far greater percentage died broke or in state or county hospitals.

The oriental medicine men were perhaps the most colorful of the entire clan because their pitches were based on happenings in far-off and mysterious lands. Even their costumes had the flavor of distant, dangerous places.

When Will and I reached Los Angeles—on the tickets donated by the railroad—we went to a large two-story house between Fifth and Sixth on Main Street. The establishment, which had the appearance of an old-fashioned residence, had been rented by the first contingent of oriental medicine men to arrive in the pitchmen's winter Mecca. It was set about seventy-five feet back from the street and had a large front porch. On the porch was a piano, and chained to one of the posts was a chimpanzee. The pitchmen lived in the house and lectured from the front porch. The piano was used in their ballyhoo, and the ape was an attention-getter. People will stop to look at an animal in captivity when nothing else can whet their interest.

I was fascinated at the thought of being in Los Angeles, and even more fascinated by the men with the fabulous names who lived in the house or trouped through it during the course of the winter. All of them had a deep respect for Will. He had started many of them in the medicine business. His supply of information, as well as his background, was far deeper than theirs, and he had that indefinable quality of a leader. There was no real reason for it, except perhaps Will's sheer individual strength, but the relationship between them was that of master and servant in the life-and-death oriental sense. They took turns lecturing—Will himself worked once a day—and kept the front porch active through most of the day and well into the night.

The first three men Will introduced me to were Prince Nanzetta, Charley Tryon, and Arthur Hammer.

Prince Nanzetta, a half-breed Mexican, was only eighteen. He wore a long crimson robe lavishly decorated with gold tinsel and tiny round mirrors. He carried a short sword in an ivory case. This he referred to as the Royal Sword of Tibet. Around his neck was a chain, hanging almost to his knees, which supported a round seal inscribed with some Chinese characters. This was the Royal Seal of Tibet.

Prince Nanzetta's story was a variation of the Indian-abducts-child pitch. As a youngster, so the pitch went, he had accompanied his father on an expedition into the remote vastness of the Himalayan Mountains. There the natives had captured the group. With the bloodthirsty callousness historically associated with their race they had put to death, employing intricate tortures, the entire party with the exception of young Nanzetta. Him they had spared for training as a slave. He was taken to the forbidden city of Lhasa, where he was made to wait on the priests. So proficient did he become in the art of medicine as practiced by the priests that they made him a prince. It was their hope that he would come to live and think like a native Tibetan, but he resisted this change and plotted a means of escape. A grown man, he finally eluded his captors and was now bringing their wonderful secrets of healing to his own people.

The prince was the vainest man I have ever met. He was always accompanied by a large Negro who acted as his valet. The Negro's wages depended on how many times he called Prince Nanzetta "Your Royal Highness" in public.

The prince made his act so good that one time when he was staying at a hotel in a town in which Mark Hanna[3] was scheduled to speak, he was asked to occupy a chair on the platform with the other bigwigs. This he did with considerable condescension.

Charley Tryon and Arthur Hammer were both from Napa, California. Tryon had a bothersome habit of drinking the alcohol in which were preserved the tapeworms used for display purposes. He was also something of a ladies' man, and on one occasion he came down with a case of pneumonia because the unexpected arrival of a husband had compelled him to remain, unsuitably clad, on a fire escape for a number of hours.

Arthur Hammer had a wonderful ballyhoo called the "Australian Murder Mystery." He opened it by having a member of the audience blindfold him. He then asked that a pocketknife be given to one of his listeners, picked at random. The recipient of the knife was to pretend to stab someone, then hide the knife in the clothes of a third person. With the hand of one of the spectators on his wrist, Hammer then worked through the audience, still blindfolded, and identified the murderer, the victim, and the knife. Hammer probably was the greatest of all the muscle readers.

Muscle reading was an art which involved both psychology and a sensitive touch. There was no faking about it. With the knife planted and the audience waiting expectantly, Hammer would begin his tour of the crowd. The yokel, clinging to his wrist, would be dragged along with him. Hammer would move rapidly at first, almost at a dogtrot. He would weave in and out and around in the crowd with what appeared to be aimlessness. It wouldn't be long before the audience came to the conclusion that he was hopelessly at fault. They would begin to snicker, and the yokel, wheeling around like the tail of a kite, would become embarrassed. He had become part of the act and felt the snickers were directed at him. No matter how honest the yokel might be in not wanting to give signals, there would be an involuntary twitching of his

---

3   Marcus Alonzo Hanna (September 24, 1837 – February 15, 1904) was an American businessman and Republican politician, who served as a United States Senator from Ohio and chairman of the Republican National Committee. A friend and political ally of President William McKinley, Hanna used his wealth and business skills to successfully manage McKinley's presidential campaigns in 1896 and 1900.

muscles when he came close to the murderer and, subsequently, to the victim and the holder of the knife. The twitching of his muscles, of course, was communicated to Hammer's wrist. Hammer's skill lay in interpreting the slightest change in the yokel's grip.

Hammer had a dramatic version of this ballyhoo. He guaranteed to drive a buggy while blindfolded for a distance of several blocks. The route, involving the turning of two or three corners, would be laid out by a committee appointed for the purpose. Obviously, the route would be a mystery to Hammer. Staging of this event was always preceded by a flood of publicity and was as important to a town as the appearance of Katharine Cornell[4] or the Lunts[5] would be today. Spectators would crowd every foot of the route. The blindfolding of Hammer would be done with a great deal of ceremony by a committee which generally included one or two of the city officials. A yokel, selected for his integrity, would climb to the seat beside Hammer, who held the lines, and grasp Hammer's wrist. While the crowd watched in expectant silence, Hammer would speak to the team, and off it would start. An actor to the soles of his shoes, Hammer would spur the team on vocally until it moved at a fast trot. He never missed, and I asked him once how in the world he dared do it.

"Dangerous?" Hammer said. "Hell, no. That damned fool up on the seat with me doesn't want to get killed any more than I do. The faster we drive, the more muscle signals he gives me. If there was any real danger, he'd grab the lines."

Successful termination of the drive was Hammer's opportunity to go into

4   Katharine Cornell (February 16, 1893 – June 9, 1974) was an American stage actress, writer, theater owner and producer. She was born in Berlin to American parents and raised in Buffalo, New York.

Dubbed "The First Lady of the Theatre" by the New Yorker Magazine, Cornell was the first performer to receive the Drama League Award, for Romeo and Juliet in 1935.

5   Alfred Davis Lunt, Jr. (August 12, 1892 – August 3, 1977) was an American stage director and actor who had a long-time professional partnership with his wife, actress Lynn Fontanne. Lunt was one of 20th-century Broadway's leading male stars, and Lynn Fontanne (December 6, 1887 – July 30, 1983) was a British-born American-based actress for over 40 years. Broadway's Lunt-Fontanne Theatre was named for them.

his pitch. His agreement with the city officials included the provision that if he negotiated the route without error he would be permitted to pitch without a license. Hammer didn't mind making the drive, but he hated to exchange the big cities with their opium joints for rural communities, and consequently only the pressure of necessity made him attempt it.

Both Hammer and Tryon worked in silk hats and frock coats and were impeccable fashion plates when they stepped out to lecture. They were distinguished in their profession, but no more so than others in the long parade of medicine men who turned up at one time or another on the Los Angeles premises. The place was a rallying point. Any medicine man who dropped in was welcome to work a few days and replenish his bank roll. During the course of the winter all the big medicine men who worked in the East, as well as those who worked in the hinterlands of California, would visit Los Angeles to refresh themselves with the climate and renew old acquaintances.

Among the visitors were Will Cooper, of Tanlac[6] fame, who buttoned his coat with twenty-dollar gold pieces and his vest with tens; Phenomenal Kraus, known to thousands for his watch chain made of solid gold nuggets, in each of which a diamond was set; and Wonderful Walton, whose private nickname was the Iron Gall Kid.

Big Foot Bill Wallace was another of the rare ones. He always began his pitch with the words, "I'm Big Foot Bill from over the hill; I never worked and I never will." He then loaded down the natives with what he claimed were electric belts. They looked swell, being covered with purple satin. Their gimmick was an area of zinc, dosed with vinegar, which produced a temporary tingle when placed next to the skin. Wallace had to keep on the move because in some instances the suckers developed sores on their backs and began looking for their benefactor with a scatter-gun.

Professor Herzog was an old-timer who dispensed a hair tonic, offering as proof of its virtues the fact that his own hair had grown down to the level of his waist. This unusual growth was achieved, he explained, by application of the tonic after his original crop of hair had all but disappeared. He also

---

6   Tanlac was a wine-based patent medicine purported to cure "stomach ailments." It was 17% alcohol and contained laxatives.

sold Resurrection Oil, a medicinal substance allegedly capable of making old muscles young if applied with sufficient energy.

Henry Gale was famous across the country for his corn cure, a preparation known to the trade as "corn slum." Its chief ingredient was collodion, which had very little effect on corns. Gale had supplied himself with a couple of pseudo corns whittled from a horse's hoof. They were rather startling as to size but were triangular in shape and fitted the average yokel's conception of what a corn should look like. After making his pitch Gale would summon to his chair on the platform some yokel who had shown particular interest in his remarks. He would cut out the usually small corn of which the yokel complained, carefully palm it, and display one of the frightening items of equine origin. Considerably unsettled by the sight, his audience would then be prepared to listen to any reasonable solution to the corn problem. Surgery, Gale told the natives solemnly, was not necessary. They could avoid the horror of the knife by applying his preparation nightly for three nights. At the end of that time the corn either would be dissolved or could be lifted without difficulty from its socket.

When he planned to be in town more than a week Gale would add, "Repeat applications if necessary in stubborn cases."

Gale was quite a ladies' man. He was small in stature and about twenty-five years old when he reached his peak as a pitchman. Girls would cluster in droves at the edge of his crowd, waiting for him to end his pitch. The more there were, the better he liked it, and he made no distinction between those who were married and those who were not. The period during which he favored any one girl with his attention seldom lasted more than two weeks. Not long after visiting Los Angeles he made the mistake of attempting a semi-permanent arrangement. While pitching in the South he picked up a doctor's wife and took her with him to Florida. This attachment endured for several weeks, although it terminated eventually, as had the others, in a separation more desirable to him than to his partner. Several months later Gale made his second mistake when he returned to the same town from which he and the doctor's wife had fled. He had no more than begun his pitch when the doctor, apparently narrow-minded about the whole affair, stepped up and fairly blew him apart with a sawed-off shotgun.

In a class by himself was Ray Black, who ballyhooed with a skull, a Bible and a rope. First he set up a folding table which held his satchel of medicine, called a "med case" or "med keister." Then he spread out the skull, Bible, and rope on the ground nearby. It was impossible for the curious natives to resist this assortment of articles. Black paid no attention to the yokels as they began to gather. He kept his back to them. Frowning, and pausing at intervals to study different effects, he would arrange and rearrange the items, as absorbed as if he were alone in the world. When a sidelong glance assured him he had enough of a crowd to start, he would wheel around and go into his pitch.

Black's pitch was the lengthiest known to the medicine business. Sometimes he lectured for as long as five hours without a break, escorting his hearers on a tour of the world which neglected none of the major points of interest. I asked him once why he pitched for five hours instead of breaking it up into three or four pitches of one hour each.

"Vi," he said, "if they stay with me to the end, they're sure to buy. When I get through with them their heels are round. After standing for five hours their backs are aching and they're certain they have lumbago or kidney trouble."

Black's pitch bore down heavily on kidney trouble. He was traveling one time in Australia, he told his listeners, when he observed some beautiful birds which were strange to him, although they somewhat resembled parrots. These birds were drinking water from various springs in a remote section of the country. He became so interested in the lovely fowl that he made inquiries of the natives. The birds, he learned, were known to have a life span of at least five hundred years. Nor were the curious powers of the springs associated solely with longevity. The natives collected the crystals from the edge of the springs, finding them a surefire medicine for kidney trouble. Black had, he asserted, gathered huge quantities of the crystals and brought them back to this country.

Black always closed his pitch with a shocker. "Kidney trouble," he would say, "sneaks up on you like a snake in the grass. Like a thief in the night. It spares neither rich nor poor. The Archbishop of Canterbury was descending the steps of that great English cathedral when he fell down like an ox smitten in the shambles, stone dead! They held an autopsy; there was nothing wrong with his stomach, heart, or lungs. But, gentlemen, when they turned him over and looked at his kidneys"—Ray would lower his voice impressively—"gentlemen, they looked just like a rotten tomato."

On with the sale! The price of the "precious little box of crystals" was one dollar. The crystals themselves were manufactured from Epsom salts, with a dash of flavoring to disguise the taste.

Black could neither read nor write. He had to draw his name when he signed a document. Nevertheless, he enjoyed posing as if he were reading.

One day he was sitting in a hotel lobby and a yokel stepped over to him and said, "Mister, don't you know your paper is bottom side up?" Black lifted eyes filled with disgust. "What of it? Any damned fool can read a paper right side up. Reading it this way exercises my eyes and my brain."

Another pitchman category included the Gummy-Ga-Ho men. Standing on a box, they worked from a grip set on a tripod. They sold a glue for mending dishes and furniture. It actually did the work, although the margin of profit was greater than the yokels supposed.

Then there were the razor-strop-dressing pitchmen. They sold a cheap razor strop and a small box of salve which contained a quantity of carborundum[7]. For the purpose of demonstration they sharpened their razors at home until they could split a hair. They also worked from a tripod or a table. After rubbing some salve on the strop, they would give the razor a couple of light swipes. Part of their equipment was an old toupee. They plucked a hair from the toupee, held it up, and dramatically sliced off sections of it. The wonderful "kangaroo-hide" razor strop and dressing sold for one dollar, of which seventy-five cents was profit.

Another group of particular interest was the Look-Back pitchmen. One of them who visited Los Angeles used a rattlesnake for his ballyhoo, draping the reptile—the fangs of which had been removed—around his neck. The Look-Backs were cardboard boxes about one-and-a-half by four inches in size, punctured with a couple of holes. Inside the box was a mirror. A Look-Back

---

7   Silicon carbide, also known as carborundum, is a semiconductor containing silicon and carbon. It occurs in nature as the extremely rare mineral moissanite. Synthetic silicon carbide powder has been mass-produced since 1893 for use as an abrasive.

pitchman always began his pitch with the warning that the lecture was for men only. Anyone using the little box, he pointed out, would be able to see behind him. He called two or three men up from the audience, and of course the mirror enabled them to look to the rear. The pitchman called attention to the fun which could be had at parties, as the owner of a Look-Back could tell his friends what was happening while his back was turned.

The Look-Back had other possibilities, he added. Adjustment of the mirror enlarged the field of vision in peculiar and unusual ways. Here the lecturer usually frowned and shook his head. Certain evil-minded men had discovered that a minor alteration in the mirror's position permitted them to look through keyholes and over transoms. He, the lecturer, would not be a party to any such use of the device. He absolutely refused to make the adjustment required for such an unworthy purpose, and he was sure no one in his audience would consider it. The Look-Backs sold like hot cakes for ten or fifteen cents. There was never a complaint from low-minded characters who failed to get the hang of tilting the mirror for keyhole-peeping purposes.

Hal the Healer was one of the best of the "painless" tooth extractors. His method was simple and infallible. He put his left arm around the chump's neck, with the edge of his hand just above the Adam's apple. He pulled the tooth with his right hand and choked off the chump's wind with his left. At Hal's signal his band would strike up a lively tune, and if the chump did get out a gurgle or two, no one heard him. After it was all over the chump was so pleased to be rid of his aching molar he never said a word.

The first medicine woman I ever heard of was Madame du Bois or, as she was sometimes known, Madame du Plat. She and her husband pulled teeth and sold medicine from a great chariot and had a brass band.

Not all of the old medicine men and performers were narcotic addicts, but most of them were heavy drinkers. One of them, a painless dentist, never could get through his lecture and the extracting without two or three drinks. So he had three colored bottles and glasses put on the platform; when he had gone as long as he could without a bracer, he would look up and pretend he had heard someone say something. "I heard you," he would say sternly. "You say it is harmful—this wonderful painkiller. No. It is as harmless as a mother's milk. I'll show you." He would proceed to pour out a slug of whisky and put it down the hatch, frowning, meanwhile, at the imaginary yokel whose doubts had given him this opportunity. He would pull this off with different variations two or three times during his lecture.

Successful pitchmen all had quick wits. One "doctor" I remember got up to sell hair restorer. He was as bald as an egg. As he was getting warmed up in his lecture someone in the audience shouted, "Why don't you use some of that stuff yourself?" He was too old a hand to let the audience get to laughing. "Young man," he replied, "I heard you. You asked why I didn't use tonic of this wonderful hair restorer myself. Would to God I had been able to! But I didn't know of it until I had lost every hair on my head." His voice grew sad. "It was too late. If I had heard someone like myself speaking before I became totally bald, my hair would have been saved. Let this be a lesson to you." The heckler was one of the first to buy.

Those were the days of the tapeworm. A medicine show would not have been a show without several large glass containers with enormous tapeworms gracefully arranged inside. We got our tapeworms at the stockyards, where for five dollars a butcher would rescue a generous assortment of all sizes. We whittled a wooden or cork stopper for our jars. Bent wires, around which the worms were draped, were suspended from the stopper. Worms and stoppers were eased gently into the one- or two-quart jars, leaving just enough room for the grain alcohol. I never saw a yokel who could resist stopping to look at a bunch of tapeworms, and of course nearly every member of the audience was sure he had a tapeworm by the time he had heard the lecture.

The medicine men sold a preparation which really would remove a worm if the patient happened to have one. When this rare but happy occurrence took place, both "doctor" and yokel were proud. An announcement to that effect would be made by the doctor from the platform the following night, with the proud native standing beside him to offer embarrassed but elated verification. If there was no worm, the "doctor" had an alibi. This was an exceptional case in which the medicine had dissolved the tapeworm entirely. This however, was a rather hit-or-miss proposition, so some wise guy manufactured an artificial tapeworm out of some kind of composition. It was rolled tightly, placed in a large capsule, and swallowed by the patient as the first step in the treatment. Next came a dose of the famous worm remedy. Well, the gelatin capsule melted, the physic acted, and there was never a miss. The "doctor" had his money, the native had a glance at his tapeworm, and everybody was satisfied.

These medicine men were my idols. They made lots of money and spent lots of money. I think I never saw more wealth in one small place than I saw when Will and I went to visit Phenomenal Kraus. As casually as if they had been jelly beans, Kraus poured half a cup of unset diamonds on the table for us to look at. No one ever knew when a hasty departure might become advisable, and diamonds were quick collateral anywhere.

For some reason the wives of the medicine men didn't make much impression on me. They were lovely ladies, bejeweled and beautifully dressed, but they didn't do anything. They weren't spectacular.

As for myself, I wasn't satisfied just to ballyhoo. I had visions of greater things. Whenever I had a chance I talked to old-time "Quaker" and Kickapoo doctors about Madame du Bois, trying to learn everything about her. They assured me she was the only woman who had ever had a medicine show. I decided I would become the second medicine woman in the United States, and perhaps in the world. Without saying a word to Will, I began to haunt the other medicine shows.

As there was none better than Hal the Healer in the dental line, I went day after day to watch him work, listening to his pitch and studying his methods. Eventually, I asked him to get me a set of dental instruments and show me how to pull teeth. He thought I was just hero-worshiping and never dreamed I was planning to beat the men at their own game. He got me the instruments and, very amused by it all, gave me several lessons. I was as busy as a puppy chasing its tail. I had to have someone to practice on, so I got the newsboys to let me pull their loose teeth for ten cents apiece. This was all right for a beginning, but it soon became too easy. By this time Will knew what I was up to. When I began to lose interest he suggested I go after tougher game. This was fine with me, so Will went down to the skid road and picked up some bums and brought them to our room, where I could practice on them. The extraction price had gone up. I had to pay them twenty-five cents a tooth. And the peak of my training period came when one of them consented to let me pull a good tooth for one dollar. Perspiring like a coal heaver, ignoring the curses and groans from my victim, I eventually produced my bloody trophy. Will praised me for my hard-won achievement and told me I had progressed far enough in that field for the present.

We had been in Los Angeles several months when Will asked me casually how I would like to be a medicine woman. His hazel eyes seldom revealed what he was thinking, and they didn't then. I couldn't see anything but polite interest in his dark, heavy-jawed face.

"If you care to," he suggested, "you could be the world's second medicine woman. Madame du Bois, I believe, died worth a million dollars." He put one of his slender white hands on my arm and smiled. "You can be greater than any of them. Madame du Bois was certainly not so beautiful. You will make more money than any man because you'll be a novelty."

If he had told me I could be Queen of England I would have gone over there and demanded the crown. I threw my arms around his neck and kissed him again and again.

"Will, how did you guess? I'd rather be a medicine woman than anything else in the world!"

"I want you to be happy, my child."

"I will be. I'll do anything you tell me. Can I have a big golden chariot and four white horses and a brass band?"

"If you like. You can have anything at all if you will learn your pitch."

I swore that no amount of studying would be too much if he would only tell me what to do.

"Very well," Will said. "I'll write the pitch out for you word for word later, but this is the general idea. We will say you're twenty-six years old. I'll get you a Chinese costume—the best to be had—a headpiece, trousers, jacket, and slippers. You will do your hair with Chinese fan combs. I will be in Chinese dress also, and we will say we are brother and sister. Our parents were a Scotch missionary doctor and a Chinese princess."

"What about my name?" I said. "I'll have to have a name."

"Will Lotus Blossom do?"

I thought it was the loveliest, most delightful name I had ever heard. I could imagine myself in those brilliant and beautiful clothes, with the audience listening to me and perhaps weeping, as they had when I sang at revival meetings.

"Go on," I pleaded. "What will the rest of it be?"

Will smiled at me and then began speaking in his deep, persuasive voice. "The Chinese secrets of medicine descend through the nobility on the female side of the house. That will explain why it is you and not I who does the talking. At one time in China, you will say, the people lost most of their virility. The birth rate was low, and family life was disintegrating. So the Emperor issued a proclamation offering a reward the equivalent of ten thousand dollars to the person who would make a discovery capable of restoring their normal vitality to the people. Scientists, doctors, and others scoured the country looking for a remedy. All their efforts met with failure until a man by the name of He Tuck Chaw, while exploring in the volcanic region, noticed countless thousands of small turtle-like animals. Virtually all of them were similar in appearance. At rare intervals, however, He Tuck Chaw discovered one distinguished by beautiful golden stripes. He was interested but not impressed at first by this phenomenon. Presently, however, he began to wonder what accounted for the scarcity of those with the golden stripes. The animal itself was a familiar one, known as the Kup Ki See. His curiosity aroused, He Tuck Chaw caught and examined a great number of the turtles. He discovered that the brilliantly colored animals were males, and estimated that there was one male for every thousand females. Sure now that he was close to a medical discovery of the greatest importance, He Tuck Chaw pushed forward his scientific studies with the greatest dispatch. The answer to the fate of his country lay in determining the source of this animal's incredible vitality. He found that the male differed from the female in that it possessed a small pouch at the base of the brain. This he called the Quali Quah pouch. He removed the pouches from the male animals, dried and powdered them, and gave tiny portions to the Chinese people. The reaction was both swift and effective. He Tuck Chaw was loaded with honors and money. There is, gentlemen, a sufficient quantity of this same substance in these Vital Sparks I am going to offer tonight to restore you to health, virility, and happiness."

Will paused and watched my face. "Do you think you can do it?"

"I know I can!" I was so happy I wanted to sing. "Will darling, I can't wait to start."

"We'll tie it in with Tiger Fat," Will said. Tiger Fat, which was simply a cheap salve, had been Will's specialty. He had done so well with it that "Tiger Fat" had become his nickname.

"Your pitch," Will continued, "will go on something like this: A visiting prince came to go on a tiger hunt with your family. When he was in the back country he wounded a tiger, which mauled him badly. The tiger was killed by one of the retainers. There was no medicine available, however, and when infection set in the prince's life was despaired of. One of my relatives, you will say, had the tiger skinned and cut up. He took the backbone of the Royal Bengal Tiger, chopped it up, put it in a pot, and rendered the fat and marrow. With this substance he anointed the injured prince, who made a miraculous and rapid recovery. Further investigation of the curative powers of this Tiger Fat was made, and it was discovered to be of great value for cuts, bruises, bums, rheumatism, backache, and other ailments. The price of the Vital Sparks is five dollars. The price of the Tiger Fat is one dollar. To everyone who buys the Tiger Fat for one dollar, we are going to make a present of the five-dollar package of Vital Sparks, so you all can discover for yourselves what they will do."

→ CHAPTER FIVE ←

A FIFTY-CENT FLOP
AND A
ONE-DOLLAR TOY

I SPENT TWO HOURS every day learning to deliver this lecture until it pleased Will. At one point I had to use the word "God." Will coached me on that word alone for hours. "No, you say it coarsely. Say it reverently and singingly." I would try and try until at last he was satisfied.

We also worked an hour a day on the mind-reading act, making it longer and more complicated, until finally I could get everything he coded me perfectly. I was willing and eager to learn. I was convinced I must be much smarter than other women so Will would never cease to love me and so everyone would notice and praise me. Studying was a small price to pay if it meant I would eventually go rolling down the street in my chariot, with a band which would center everyone's attention on me.

I read for two or three hours every day, and while we smoked opium in the mornings Will would talk over what I had read. Among others, I read Darwin and Shakespeare. One of my most delightful and impressive discoveries at the time was the story of Venus and Adonis. The affection I displayed toward my thirty-eight-year-old, opium-smoking husband as a result of its influence must have been very embarrassing. Probably the most enjoyable moments of my life then were the evenings we spent smoking opium. As we lay beside the dimly burning lamp Will would tell me stories of the Spartans and Chinese. My heart would beat faster at the tales of bravery and self-sacrifice and intrigue.

The men we met and worked with seemed to like me, but it bothered me that the women didn't take any pains to conceal the fact that they disliked me thoroughly.

"Just jealousy, Vi," Will told me when I said I was hurt by the things they said. "You're young and beautiful. They hate you for being ambitious. All they do is gossip and go to shows, and they dislike anyone who shows them up."

I contented myself by feeling superior to them, but there was one thing I wanted. We all had wonderful clothes, and actually the men were as vain as the women. They had their full-dress clothes, their tuxedoes, their opera hats, and their English walking suits. We women were dressed like a picture out of fairyland. None of us ever wore a tailored suit that cost less than one hundred dollars, and our evening dresses cost up to three hundred and fifty dollars. Our hats cost close to one hundred dollars. They were covered with great willowy ostrich plumes, and some even sported a bird of paradise. We all had our seal-skin jackets and other furs. I had twenty-seven diamond rings. I had diamond bracelets and lockets and one of the Hope diamonds—a six-carat stone set in a brooch. We called them sunbursts.

But I still needed something. I felt that if I was superior to the other women I was entitled to everything they had, and I had been envying them their diamond earrings. I was the only woman of the medicine bunch who didn't have a pair. One day as Will and I were walking by a jewelry store I saw some lovely diamond eardrops. I stopped.

"Will, I want a pair of diamond earrings. May I have them?"

"Certainly, my dear. One day I will have your ears pierced, and then I will get them for you."

"Does it hurt much to have your ears pierced? How do they do it?"

It was simple, he told me, but there was some pain involved. "A doctor puts a block behind your ear and runs a needle with a linen thread through the lobe. He leaves the thread in the hole and draws it back and forth each day so the hole won't close."

We finished our errands and went back to our rooms. After pondering the matter all day and evening I decided I was going to have my earrings right now. The next morning I bought a spool of linen thread and some darning needles.

Back home again, I went into the bathroom, got a small looking glass, and put a pencil mark where I wanted the holes to be. I threaded the needle, put the spool behind my ear, and plunged the needle through the lobe. It didn't hurt as much as I had expected it to. I left about a foot of thread in my ear and pierced the other one. I walked into the next room, where Will was reading.

"Look, Will. When can I have my earrings?"

He gave one look and jumped from the couch. "You damned little fool! Don't you know you might have infected yourself?"

He put a lot of peroxide on my ears and tied the thread in loops. I thought he was angry with me, but the next day he was telling the other medicine men how much determination I had when I wanted something.

By way of a change Will decided we would go to San Diego for a few days. We took the train, and it was such a warm and lovely day we sat on the rear platform of the observation car. I was sitting on a folding stool in front of Will. We were rounding a curve about halfway to San Diego when my stool suddenly flew out from under me, and I landed on my back on the platform.

As I started to struggle Will put a hand on my shoulder, restraining me. "Don't try to get up," he said in the kindest tone imaginable. "You might be hurt."

The train stopped. Everyone left the platform, wondering what had happened.

"You kicked my stool."

"Of course. As we went into that curve I saw the engine jump the track. I thought there would be a heavy jar. I wanted to be sure we would get damages if there was any chance."

"Is there?"

"Not this time. The wreck didn't amount to enough."

I was still scared and I began to cry. "But, Will, you might have hurt me."

"Shut up and come inside," he said. "People are coming back."

In San Diego we went to a natatorium, and after we had fooled around in the water for a while Will told me he was going to teach me to hold my breath under water. He put his hand on the back of my neck and pushed me down. My breath ran short. I began to struggle. I thought, "My God, he's trying to drown me!" I tried to scream under water. Water clogged my throat. I went half mad and began to fight frantically. I was so fierce I threw Will to one side and got my head above water.

Will was staring at me with an odd expression in his hazel eyes. "What in the world is wrong with you?"

"I—I thought I was drowning," I gasped.

With the warm, steamy air of the pool around me and all the other people nearby, it seemed foolish to believe he had tried to kill me. He was tenderness itself as he told me how sorry he was that I had been frightened. Yet from then on, deep inside me, there was a tincture of fear. I was afraid of Will, and the fear never wholly left me.

Once we were back in Los Angeles, memory of the incident faded out. I was too busy learning my pitch and living the gay life of the medicine men to dwell on it. I loved the theater and had a box reserved one night a week in three theaters. Will rarely accompanied me, but he would take me and call for me.

My theatrical experience had begun in Minneapolis, where I met Al Jolson[8] and his brother, and Joe Palmer, who was a cousin of Will's. The act was billed as Jolson, Palmer, and Jolson. Palmer had rheumatism and couldn't walk, so in the act he was the invalid guest in a hotel, and the Jolson brothers were bellhops. His brother was a good singer, but Al Jolson brought down the house with his whistling.

At the Grand Theater on Main Street they were offering the-villain-still-pursued-her type of drama. There was more life on Main Street than on any street in town. Will and I and others of the bunch used to dine at Al Levy's Café on First and Main. We didn't grab a barbecued sandwich and a bottle of beer in those days. The men liked women with curves. Nothing was too

---

8   Al Jolson (born Asa Yoelson; May 26, 1886 – October 23, 1950) was a Russian-born American singer, comedian, and actor. At the peak of his career, he was dubbed "The World's Greatest Entertainer." His performing style was brash and extroverted, and he popularized many songs that benefited from his "shamelessly sentimental, melodramatic approach." Jolson has been dubbed "the king of blackface" performers, a theatrical convention since the mid-19th century.

good, and for us Al Levy produced the choicest canvasback and mallard ducks, twenty-minute broil, Eastern blue-point oysters, and soft-shelled crabs. Nor did we gallop around a dance floor while our food spoiled. No lady smoked in public. We all dressed in our best, for each night was an event. We medicine show people were among the prized customers of any restaurant. Headwaiters would hurry up, bow deeply, and inquire where we would like to sit. Waiters who knew us would straighten like soldiers and look expectantly at us. I used to strut over to the table with my silk petticoats rustling and my train trailing behind, firmly believing this attention was bestowed on us because of my fascinating qualities or Will's popularity. I hadn't then associated service with large tips, and I regarded as personal conquests even the bus boys who brought my footstool.

Saturday night and Sunday were our times of real celebration. Wherever we went we ordered champagne by the case. Most of the men drank heavily. Will was a "still" drunkard. He drank virtually all the time, but it was rarely possible to detect it. We ladies, glittering in our diamonds, furs, and trains, drank very little. All of us depended on our wits, or were married to or lived with some big shot, but we would have fought as tigerishly for our virtue as a virgin. We might live with a lover, but we were not promiscuous.

It was on these Saturday-night excursions that I met the top prize fighters of the period. Among them were Abe[9] and Monte[10] Attell, Mike and Jack

---

9   Abraham Washington "Abe" Attell (February 22, 1883 – February 7, 1970), often referred to by newspapers as "The Little Hebrew," was a boxer who became known for his record-setting, six-year consecutive reign as World Featherweight Champion from 1906–1912, and his nearly consecutive ten-year reign starting in 1902. Said to be a friend of the gangster Arnold Rothstein, Attell was charged with game fixing in the Black Sox Scandal in 1919, but the charges were dismissed before trial. He also was suspected of other infractions including fixing fights, and using drugs during a fight.

10   Monte Attell (July 28, 1885 – November 11, 1960), born in the Nob Hill neighborhood of San Francisco, California was an American boxer who took the vacant World Bantamweight title on June 19, 1909.

"Twin" Sullivan[11], Ad Wolgast[12]. Everyone, the medicine men, the politicians, the gamblers, and race-horse men, played together. I was only sixteen then, and to me all the women were beautiful. All the men were heroes, even if some of them did have cauliflower ears. The bigger the cauliflower ear, the better fighter I thought the man was.

Sundays I usually would take the streetcar to a riding academy on Washington Street and rent a horse for the morning. When I got back to the house we would rent a hack. With the top down, decked out in our best bib and tucker, holding gaily colored parasols over our heads, we would ride out to Casa Verdugo for a Spanish dinner. At night we would go to the theater or return to the Main Street house, where one of the rooms was fixed up like a hop joint, and smoke until two or three o'clock in the morning.

By this time I was thoroughly familiar with opium smoking and with opium joints. Opium still produced in me that same sense of well-being I had experienced after the first period of nausea had worn off. Now, however, the sense of comfort was greater. Opium doesn't put a smoker to sleep, and it doesn't fill his mind with visions. If he is smart it increases his mental alertness. If he is dull he becomes a little more so. It seems somehow to intensify the characteristics of the smoker, in addition to creating a glow of warm satisfaction. To a smoker, misery is less miserable, happiness more keen. Many persons have smoked opium for forty years and more without physical or mental dam-

---

11   Mike "Twin" Sullivan (September 23, 1878 – October 31, 1937) was an American boxer frequently credited with taking the Welterweight Championship of the World on April 23, 1907 when he soundly defeated William "Honey" Mellody in Los Angeles in a 20-round bout. He vacated the title in the late fall of 1908, when he could not make weight. Many, though not all, sanctioning bodies active today recognize his claim to the title during this period.

He had a twin brother Jack, the origin of his nickname, "twin," and was the youngest in an Irish family of several siblings. His twin Jack was an accomplished middleweight boxer as well, once claiming the Middleweight Championship of the World when he defeated Tommy Burns on March 7, 1905. Jack fought top talent as did Mike, and they shared a few of the same opponents.

12   Adolphus "Ad" Wolgast (February 8, 1888 – April 14, 1955), nicknamed Michigan Wildcat, was a World Lightweight champion.

age. Its most serious effect is apt to be a drying up of the secretions of the body. This is reflected initially in a loss of sexual vigor which is more pronounced in men than in women. Prolonged use, as a rule, causes total impotency.

Will and I had smoked regularly in his office in St. Paul, but the first real opium joint he took me to was in Hot Springs. One evening during the season there, as we were going out to dinner, he told me to wrap up a thin kimono and my bedroom slippers and take them with me. We went to a very nice place called California Jack's, where we had a splendid dinner. As Will was paying the bill he whispered to a waiter. When we stood up, ostensibly to leave, the waiter found occasion to come to the table and said in a low voice, "Follow me." He led us to a side door, down a hallway, and into a room at the rear. It was my first view of a hop joint, or opium den, as the missionary books called them.

The room was a large one. On each side wall were two continuous shelves, about six feet deep, the top one three feet or more above the lower. Down the middle of the room was a wide aisle. The shelves, or bunks, were covered with straw matting, and against the wall was a long bolster-like affair with a clean white cover. Both ends of the room were curtained. A woman came out from one curtained end. Will told me to go behind the curtain and remove my corset and shoes.

There was good reason for that. We wore our corsets tight around our waists to display our hips and busts. We were afraid to take a good long breath. Flat-breasted, boyish figures hadn't been heard of. If nature had failed to endow us, we made up for it. We wore a bustle on our hips and pinned over our busts either a cloth with a ruffle on it or a rubber contraption which, if not too closely inspected, would pass. During the day, or when wearing woolen clothes, we wore high shoes, either buttoned or laced. Our shoes and gloves were always about a size too small. If I doubled my hand hard I always split my glove across the palm. Femininity was so pronounced among us that no one ever dreamed of exchanging shoes with a boyfriend to see who had the smaller feet.

When I went back into the room, wearing kimono and slippers, Will was waiting. He nodded to the attendant, a lean man with sagging mustaches which fell below his chin.

"A fifty-cent flop and a one-dollar toy," Will said.

The attendant went behind the curtain at the opposite end of the room and returned with a tray and a pipe. He led us over to an unoccupied section of the lower shelf. He put down the tray and pipe and handed Will what looked like a bone pillbox with a bone cover.

This is called the "toy" and contains the opium. The damp sponge is called the "souey pow," and the needle on the tip of which the opium is held is called the "yen hok." The pipe is also called the "stem." What I had thought of as a dirty dark doorknob when Will introduced me to opium was, of course, the "bowl." We lay down on the bunk, one on each side of the tray. The person in the adjoining section lay with his back to me, facing his smoking partner. It was an orderly place. No one raised his voice. The people on the lower bunks seemed to know each other and, if they were near, would gossip with each other.

If they were too far away to chat in a low voice they would move from one bunk to another, asking friends how they were, where they had been, and how conditions were in other sections of the country.

One of the men must have known Will very well. He sat down on the edge of the bunk, and presently Will asked him to lie down and smoke a pill, as the little pellet of opium cooked over the lamp and stuck on the bowl was called. Will moved over a few inches, and the visitor curled up and rested his head on Will's hip while they smoked and talked. I lay quietly and listened. The newcomer asked Will how long he had used the junk, and Will said since he was eighteen.

I got my first understanding of the caste that prevailed among opium smokers that night. A man came in and asked for a "two-bit flop." His tray was put on an upper bunk. People on the lower bunks did not talk to people on the upper bunks.

So far as I was concerned, there was no sense of horror or degradation connected with being in an opium joint. What I wanted to avoid most was being made fun of as an ignorant country girl. Smoking and talking with a lot of well-dressed men and women was fun, like the ice-cream socials we had at home once or twice each summer.

In those days every big city had at least one opium joint, and usually more. Only rarely was there trouble from the police. Going from one town to another by train, Will and I on several occasions smoked opium together in a lower berth.

So far as drugs in general were concerned, San Francisco probably was as wide open as any city in the country. The Snake Drug Store was only one of a dozen or so in which it was possible to buy a dram of morphine sulphate for sixty-five cents. It was as simple as buying a box of cough drops today. Addicts who were broke could panhandle five or ten cents and obtain a smaller amount at a little store on Kearny Street called the Bindle Joint.

Another favorite among addicts was Bernay's Catarrh[13] Cure, which was available everywhere. Most addicts carried a little box of it, together with a small glass tube to which was attached a short length of rubber tubing. It was simple to take. You dipped the glass in the powder and inserted it into a nostril. Then you put the end of the rubber tubing in your mouth and blew the powder up your nose. Almost at once your nose went numb. Bernay's must have been at least one-third cocaine. Thousands of people, unaware of the drug in its ingredients, bought it as a sure cure for catarrh. It would relieve catarrh and sinus trouble, all right, but about the third sniff and you could have all your teeth pulled and never know it.

In San Francisco there were half a dozen opium joints within a block of the Hall of Justice. We did most of our smoking at Yen Shee Ben's and Turkey Neck Joe's in St. Mary's Alley. Joe's neck looked all right to me, but his eyes bulged out, and he had a cataract on one eye.

The men and women who frequented the San Francisco opium dens were of a different class from those we had met in Hot Springs. There were more thieves and what were called the "hot-money" boys. By and large they were a tougher lot. Medicine men and gamblers, bookmakers and race-horse people weren't regarded as criminals; they were the "easy-money" or "smart-money" class. Instead of using a club to get their money, they used their brains. Sooner or later most famous thieves turned up at Joe's.

---

13   Catarrh is inflammation of the mucous membranes in one of the airways or cavities of the body, usually with reference to the throat and paranasal sinuses. The word is no longer used in American medical practice.

Among those I met was Big Tobe. Six foot six in height and very genial in manner, he not long ago did a term in a federal penitentiary for harboring Baby Face Nelson and his wife in his Vallejo hospital. In those days Big Tobe worked with a partner of ordinary size. He always wore a long coat when on a job and would bend his knees until he was the same height as his partner. When the rap went in to headquarters the wanted pair would be described as being of normal height, and the police couldn't put the finger on Tobe.

Will bought my first pair of diamond eardrops from New York Sammy, a notorious pennyweighter, or diamond thief. I knew the jewelry was hot, but I was as proud as if they had come from Tiffany's.

There were some rough times in some of the joints, but the police seldom caught up with them. One time Will and I were smoking in place a half block from the Hall of Justice. A gambler friend of ours was smoking at the tray next to ours. His partner, whom we didn't know, was lying with his back within a few inches of mine. Will spoke to the gambler, and as he did I got a glimpse of his partner.

It seemed to me he looked funny, but I supposed he had dozed off. A little later I went to the rest room; as I came back I looked at him again. I told Will I thought the man had had a stroke or something—his color was queer. Will got up and shook him, listened to his heart, and told the gambler the man was dead. The man who ran the joint called in a Chinese doctor, who also pronounced the man dead. We were asked to leave and come back in half an hour. We loitered a block or so away, came back, and all started to smoke again. The next day the papers reported that an unidentified man had been found dead in an alley nearby.

At intervals the police would put on a drive to prove to the gullible they were doing their job. During those periods the joints would be run from pillar to post. We smoked in one on Ellis Street for a couple of weeks; then it closed. We moved out to another on Divisadero Street until it, too, shut down. We even smoked in a shack out on the sand dunes behind the car barns for about a month, until the drive tapered off.

The San Francisco crowd was much rougher in its attitude toward police. To them all cops were rats. As they lay smoking beside the trays, the men would tell stories of experiences they had had with the law, singling out specific officers for abuse and describing all detectives or harness bulls as chiselers, crooks, and killers. This was a little bewildering, because as a girl I had been raised on tales of the integrity and loyalty of the Northwest Mounted Police in Canada. But there wasn't much integrity or loyalty in the San Francisco cops I saw. I watched them come into the joints and haul out this thief or that one who happened to be smoking there. Eventually the thief would come back and tell the others how much he had been shaken down for. More than half of the cases which got as far as the courts could be fixed. And when I paid out money to fix crooked cops so we could sell medicine without going through the regular license I began to think the cops were worse than the thieves. I had been taught by my parents to hate a liar or a thief and to look up to all police and officials. Now I was taught they were all crooked. But even the thieves said the Canadian police couldn't be fixed. Attempts to make moral distinctions threw me into such a state of confusion that I gave up trying.

The world was topsy-turvy. My old copybook sayings, "Honesty is the best policy" and "The early bird catches the worm," seemed wrong. Dishonesty paid off, and there were plenty of worms for the late birds. The sermons and talks I had heard at Chautauquas[14] described in vivid detail the rearing of vice's ugly head and advised immediate flight. Yet in their eagerness to convince, the speakers made their horrible examples too horrible. The Sunday-school tracts portrayed all addicts as emaciated, repulsive individuals with matted hair. But I had seen hundreds of addicts, and they looked well fed and well dressed. They weren't noisy and they didn't go around picking things out of the air. As described in Sunday school, all the fancy ladies, as they were called in my home town, were sad, weeping women whose hair blew in the breeze as they begged to be rescued. Actually they looked happier than the hard-working, childbearing farm women I had known.

Will, to whom I turned for a clear thread of reasoning in my confusion,

---

14   Chautauqua was an adult education movement that was highly popular in the late 19th and early 20th centuries. Chautauqua assemblies expanded and spread throughout rural areas until the mid-1920s. The Chautauqua brought entertainment and culture for the whole community, with speakers, teachers, musicians, showmen, preachers, and specialists of the day.

was no help. He used to lecture on different subjects, such as astronomy, ancient history, or politics, for about an hour before he started his medicine pitch. One night he talked on God's love for all humans. He was a striking and handsome figure as he quoted in his beautiful voice from the Sermon on the Mount. It was so touching and beautiful that my eyes as well as many of those in the audience were filled with tears. My heart thrilled with love for Will and his ideals. When it was over he told the audience to bring their friends on the following night, as he intended to continue his lecture. To my horror, when he resumed he spoke of a jealous, wrathful God of war and the rape of innocents. He quoted the Old Testament. Then he went on to Robert G. Ingersoll[15]. He concluded by thundering, "If there is such a God, He is a monster and I want none of Him!" The second lecture was as great a masterpiece as the one on the preceding night.

I had clenched my hands until the nails bit into my flesh. I could hardly wait to get back to the room to ask him which lecture he had meant.

He gave me a funny smile and stroked my hair tenderly. "My child, they were both just lectures."

---

15   Robert Green "Bob" Ingersoll (August 11, 1833 – July 21, 1899) was an American writer and orator during the Golden Age of Free Thought, who campaigned in defense of agnosticism. He was nicknamed "The Great Agnostic."

⇢ CHAPTER SIX ⇠
PRINCESS LOTUS BLOSSOM

BIT BY BIT I was picking up the lore of the medicine-show business. Liquid medicine was called "slum," and salve was called "grease." Herbs of any sort were called "chopped grass." Powdered herbs were "flea powder."

By spring I had my pitch down pat, and Will decided it was time for me to start in. We left Los Angeles and went back to Will's old stamping grounds, St. Paul, but I objected to making my first pitch there. The town was filled with pitchmen, many of whom were friends, and if I pulled a bloomer I didn't want them to know about it. So we went to Grand Rapids, Michigan.

As I dressed for the evening in my mandarin coat and little Chinese skullcap I was nervous but not really afraid. I couldn't get my hair put up to suit me, and I had to do it three times. I had a feeling that if the tiniest thing went wrong, or if I didn't look just right, the whole venture would be a flop. I tried to pretend I was calm, although inside I was seething with excitement. Still, it wasn't my first experience in front of a crowd. We had been doing the mind-reading act all winter in Los Angeles, and I had learned a good deal about handling people. An audience is easy to dominate, but there is a certain trickiness to it. If you are sure of yourself and talk as if there is no question at all about the things you say, an audience follows along like a lot of sheep. If you show signs of hesitation or uncertainty, the people in the audience figure they know more than you do; then they either laugh at you or call you a fool. What frightened me most was the thought that the audience might not listen to me because I was a woman. They were used to men. If I failed to make a hit they would jeer me out of town.

We drove in an open hack to the corner where I was to lecture. Now and again I stole a look at Will's profile with its noble forehead and jutting jaw. He always rode with a supremely confident air, as if he were a monarch who had descended to the level of his subjects. Some of his confidence seeped into me. I rode with my head up, trying to match his manner.

We came to the location Will had picked. Each corner of the intersection boasted a saloon. Will blindfolded me and, as usual, the sight of us there—a distinguished-looking man in a colorful Chinese costume tying a scarf over the eyes of a brilliantly costumed and beautiful woman—attracted a crowd. We did our mind-reading act, and Will unknotted the scarf. He turned to the audience.

"Gentlemen, it is our privilege now to hear a few words from Princess Lotus Blossom, who brings to the world and to us the unknown healing secrets of the Orient. You have witnessed a demonstration of the profound and mysterious workings of the human mind—an art brought to its peak by the Great Ones of the ageless East. In that distant land obscure and unplumbed rites have been developed; likewise, the science of medicine. For countless centuries the wisdom of the East has been focused on man's misfortunes. The lore of healing, far from being despised or regarded with indifference, is held to be one of the most generous gifts of a beneficent God. Its practice elevates both men and women to a level far above that of lesser mortals. With such reverence is the art regarded, indeed, that oriental rulers have decreed that the most precious secrets of medicine shall be transmitted to posterity only through the nobility on the female side of the house. This is because, since the dawn of time, women have filled the role of gentle and understanding healers. They have dressed the desperate wounds sustained by men in battle. In the dark moments of disastrous illness they have nursed men, heedless of danger to themselves. Wherever there has been pain, prodigious hurt, devastating sickness—women have been found. In Princess Lotus Blossom there is something of all her selfless sisters. Although she has pledged her life to the bringing of relief to sickness-ridden mankind, her sacrifice is no greater than theirs. Although she brings to you blessed remedies which never before have left the rich medical treasuries of the East, she is doing no more than countless women, in their own small way, have done before her.

"Gentlemen, I give you Princess Lotus Blossom!"

As he slipped off his Chinese coat and stepped from the hack Will whispered, "Talk until I get back." It was then about eight o'clock.

Will was gone and I was alone in the hack. My heart suddenly felt frozen. My hands were too big; the collar of the mandarin coat chafed my neck; my hair was awry. The hinge on one of the batwing doors of the nearest saloon needed oiling, and it squalled intermittently. Something seemed to be wrong with the gasoline torch; the flame was ragged.

My voice came out of my throat in a broken croak:

"In the faraway land which is my home there is a story which has come down to the present through the misty corridors of many decades.

"It is the story of peril, of overwhelming danger, of a dread and mysterious ailment which threatened to wipe from the face of the earth the great people of the Chinese nation."

Somehow the flow of the words banished my doubts. I could feel Will beside me, as he had been during those endless hours of training. "No, damn it, you must make your voice appealing. Let it throb!" The croaking stopped. Across the street a man stepped through the saloon's swinging doors, hesitated, and came ambling over to listen.

"This nation," I continued, "which had contributed so much to the world through its teachers, its philosophers, and its physicians, was losing its virility. To the honor of all who were aware of the impending tragedy, it seemed inevitable that this mighty race must perish. Its life force was gone. Its manhood no longer possessed the strength required for perpetuation of the strain which had existed throughout history."

And I went on to tell them of the emperor's proclamation and of the discovery by Dr. He Tuck Chaw of the turtle-like animals with the beautiful golden stripes. I finished the pitch and sold the Vital Sparks and Tiger Fat. Breathlessly I looked around for Will. He wasn't there. I expected him to come striding around the corner at any moment, but he didn't come. I felt empty inside, empty and frightened. A few hangers-on who hadn't bought still lingered by the hack, eying me curiously. The hack driver looked bored.

I was a scared seventeen-year-old girl who had been taught to do one thing, so I did it again. I began at the beginning and ran through the pitch. Still no Will. I sent the hack driver into a saloon for a glass of lemonade, as I was getting a little hoarse. I kept on pitching and sending him in for lemonade. I was afraid Will would hit me if I stopped. I delivered that pitch backward and forward and both ways from the middle, until I couldn't speak above a whisper.

A little after eleven o'clock Will showed up. He was drunk, celebrating because he had at last found a meal ticket who could produce. Although he normally drank a quart of whisky a day, I saw him really drunk only two or three times in my life. He had been making the rounds of the saloons and had accidentally come by the corner and remembered he had a wife. I was so glad to see him I forgot the agony of the experience.

When we got back to the hotel room I counted the money in the pitch case with my own hands. There was more than fifty dollars in it. Proud?

I couldn't have been prouder if I had received an ovation at the Met. Very few men who work singlehanded had ever equaled it.

The next day we went back to St. Paul and I started pitching on the street there. One night when I got home and counted up my grip I found I had made one hundred and one dollars. I danced, I laughed, I cried. It was the greatest moment of my life. I went down to the telegraph office and sent wires to all our friends: "Made a century tonight, one pitch, Vi."

Immediately, of course, I began to demand my chariot and brass band and four white horses. Will talked me out of it. "You don't need anything like that," he said. "You're so good you don't need the flash. Show them you can get as much money as they can without it." I was terribly disappointed. I had pictured myself in that chariot so often. But he had set me another moon to shoot at. I had to outstrip the other medicine men who used elaborate shows as background for a pitch.

About that time Will got a letter from another medicine man asking him to send me to Winnipeg, Canada, to fix the town for them. Fixing a town—that is, making the necessary arrangements with the city officials—could be simple or complicated. In San Francisco it was as simple as walking up to a harness bull on Saturday night, shaking hands with him, and leaving a five-dollar gold piece in his palm. Or it could be as involved as my maneuvers with the murderous Hot Springs politician. At any rate, it was an art in itself. Anything could be fixed. Circuses paid huge salaries to advance men who arranged for the big top to go up in restricted, but favorable, areas. A good location would make thousands of dollars' difference in the take. Crooked gamblers fixed the police and were allowed to open their games. Even pickpockets could fix to pick pockets on certain streets. Pitchmen had to fix with headquarters, or the cop on the beat would go through their audience with a night stick just before the sale. The excuse was always that the pitchman was blocking traffic.

Usually there was a go-between who contacted both the city officials and the person who wanted something fixed. In most cases he was the owner of a saloon, or a lawyer. Bartenders always knew how a town was run and whom to go to. When I went into a town to make a fix I headed for one of the good saloons, went in through the ladies' entrance, and had a chat with the bartender at the first opportunity. He could tell me who the fixer for the town was.

It got so I did more and more fixing, not only for Will but for his friends. Being young and attractive, I could strike better bargains than the men could. Before I contacted the fixer himself Will would coach me on exactly what to say. He told me what I was to wear, how I was to act, and how I was to make the approach. Before making the contact with the fixer I always spent a day or two learning all I could about him. I had to find out whether he was married or single, whether he was a chaser, what he did for amusement, and what his favorite sport was. When I got to talking to him it was simply a case of fixing for as little as I could. There was no use lying about how much money we expected to make, as the go-between would check up and hoist the ante if I lied. It was harder, of course, for a woman to deal with fixers than it would have been for a man. Normally the go-between—someone trusted by the higher-ups—would keep a certain percentage and pass along the rest. Will taught me to go to Mr.

Big and eliminate the go-between, because it saved us money if it could be worked. The higher-ups were downright scared of fixing with a woman. They thought a woman would go out and brag about her influence. I always made it a point to pay cash on the line and let it be understood that I wouldn't tell an outsider so much as the time of day.

Some of those higher-ups were so damn nice when I gave them a sob story about my sick husband that I couldn't stand tricking them. I went back to Will and told him there was no fix. Then there were the women chasers, who wouldn't take money but thought they could cash in on what they believed to be my adversity. With this crew I had to figure the length of our stay in a town very closely. We tried to get out just before it came to the point of my having to hit them over the head with a club.

Once in a while I got a break I wasn't expecting. In one town in Canada, for example, I went to the police chief and asked for a permit to lecture on the street. He refused it. I went over his head to the mayor and got the permit. There was no fix of any kind. The mayor was simply being kind to a woman who was earning her living. Naturally the chief had it in for me. It happened that a strike was brewing at the time. The mayor left town and the strike was called. While I was lecturing two uniformed men came up and read aloud what they said was the Riot Act, afterward dispersing the audience. When I went to see the chief about it he laughed me out of his office. What he didn't know was that the mayor had heard of the strike, had got off the train, and started back. I got to the mayor same night. He called in the chief, raked him over the coals, and told him sternly that he was to leave this harmless, hard-working woman—meaning me—alone.

Although I made scores of fixes over a period of years, that first trip I made to Winnipeg was the most important, for a particular reason.

As Will put me on the train he handed me a box of Yenshee. This is the residue scraped from the bowl of the pipe after the opium is smoked. "Take a quarter of a teaspoon before breakfast and another at bedtime," he said. I put it in my grip and forgot about it. I arrived in Winnipeg the next morning. About the middle of the morning, long after the time for my usual morning smoke, I began to feel sick. That night I couldn't sleep. By next morning I was having stomach pains and vomiting. At first I thought I had caught some sickness. Then I remembered that Will had told me to take the Yenshee. I swallowed a half teaspoonful and took a drink of water. In thirty minutes I was feeling so good I could have done a family washing and was on my way out to make the connection with the go-between. During the next couple of days I found out that if I took the Yenshee I was all right, but if I forgot it I was in trouble. It dawned on me that I was hooked. I had to have it. Oddly enough, I wasn't bothered by the thought. It didn't seem to matter much one way or the other. I had to be sure to carry some Yenshee with me when I couldn't smoke, that was all.

I made the fix without difficulty and went back to St. Paul, where I sold medicine regularly. As a medicine woman was a novelty, I drew big crowds, and soon I was making more money than Will ever had. Far from being jealous, Will insisted on giving me my chance, as he phrased it. This meant that aside from introducing me he retired to a life of reading, drinking, and smoking opium.

Some weeks later I discovered I was pregnant. Will performed the abortion himself. I could have children later, he said. He infected me and I had peritonitis and went to a hospital for a minor operation. Before I left the doctor told me I could never have any children. I cried all that night, and for weeks my nights were frightful with terrible dreams. Two of them were especially vivid. I dreamed I was the mother of a beautiful baby and was walking up a hillside. The hill was covered with rattlesnakes, and they were all striking and hissing and rattling, trying to bite my baby. I tried to run, but my legs were so weak I could not. In the second dream I was on a train with my baby in my arms. I was sitting by an open window, and the baby was leaning out. We approached a trestle, and I could see the baby's brains would be dashed out against the wooden pillars. Hard though I struggled to draw the baby in, my arms lacked the strength. I would awake with a shriek. For months it made me feel faint even to look at a baby in the arms of another woman.

I went back to work as soon as I could, and Will kept me so busy I soon had no time to think. Among other things, I learned all Will could teach me about the manufacture of the medicines we used.

In those early years at the turn of the century medicine workers had a field day. There were no Pure Food and Drug Laws, and anyone could call himself a doctor. Most med workers sold a liquid of some kind, or granulated or powdered herbs. The most potent ingredient in their formulas was aloe, and consequently all med shows were called physic shows. Most liniments were concocted on a base of oil of capsicum—in other words, red pepper. Aloe was used so freely because it acted as a laxative and also made the medicine taste bitter. The natives always demanded a vile-tasting medicine. If the cure was savory, or even reasonably palatable, they didn't think it was any good. The reason for the liquid pepper in a liniment was that the natives believed if it didn't burn and smart to beat the cars it wasn't reaching the seat of their trouble. The skin had to get good and red, too.

We didn't put pepper in our salves, as they were advertised to cure anything from catarrh to piles, and unrestricted application would have caused severe repercussions.

The equipment of most traveling pitchmen consisted of a folding table, a banjo, and a gasoline torch. The torch was constructed of a round, rather thin container for the gasoline, to which was soldered a three-foot length of pipe. Another, shorter length of pipe was screwed into this at right angles, and a burner attached to it. The shorter length was removable, to make carrying the rig easier. The gasoline torch was the trademark of a pitchman. Charley Tryon was one who used it in the preparation of a medicine known as concentrate of sulphur. Whenever he hit a new town and wanted to mix up a batch he would take a bucket to the drugstore for some flowers of sulphur powder and proceed to a lumberyard for a quantity of unslaked lime. Back in his room, he would mix the lime and sulphur with water. It took only a minute or so to tie his torch to some article of furniture and light it up, and only a little while longer to get his bucket of medicine to boiling above it. Presently a clear orange liquid would appear. Tryon skimmed this off and poured it into four-ounce bottles. On went the label "Concentrate of Sulphur." Price, one dollar. Directions: three drops in a glass of water, drink at bedtime, put one teaspoonful in bath water. In very severe cases, bathe nightly.

Tryon never insisted on nightly baths unless the yokel thought he was in terrible shape. What a stench that sulphur mixture had. It was just like rotten eggs. The pitch was the old gag about the wise mother who used to give her children sulphur and molasses in the spring, and included a touching tribute to that dear gray-haired woman who "always knew best." This substance, however, Tryon informed the natives, was a more refined product. Taken internally, it killed all the germs in the body. Sprayed on plants, it destroyed bugs and germs with equal dispatch. A bath in water touched up with the Sulphur resulted in instant destruction for similar life on the surface of the body. Eczema, ringworm, and allied complaints succumbed at once to its potency. The one-dollar sales price permitted a handsome profit. The bottle and label cost more than the remedy.

The big shows had banners advertising their product. When they moved into a new town they would march up the street during the noon hour with the band going full blast. Perhaps they would give a concert at the largest school, passing out circulars which offered free admission for the night's show to the children, provided they were accompanied by both parents.

Our Tiger Fat had Vaseline as its base. We melted the Vaseline in a large bucket over a burner, adding gum camphor, menthol crystals, oil of eucalyptus, turpentine, and oil of wintergreen. We shaved paraffin into the mixture to make it set. Constantly stirring it, we got the medicine good and hot. The round tin boxes we spread out on a big table. Then we poured the hot mixture into a tin coffeepot for convenience in handling and filled the tin boxes. The labels described it as "Tiger Fat—to be used as needed." It was an effective remedy for every ailment the flesh was heir to.

Incredible as it may seem, some of the medicine men even got to believing the fantastic stories Will had woven around the medicines we sold. Arizona Bill once drove an express wagon up to the house where we were staying and started to unload packages and put them on the dining room table. Will watched him for a time and then asked what was in the packages.

"A surprise for you," Bill said proudly. "A tiger died out at the zoo last night, and I had them cut out the backbone to put in the Tiger Fat."

"You silly cockney ass," Will said. "You ought to be in our audiences instead of lecturing to them. Take that carrion out somewhere and dump it. Hog fat would have as much medicinal value."

For the Vital Sparks which assured masculine virility we bought a barrel of small hard black candy known as buckshot candy. We poured a quantity of it into an empty bureau drawer, sprinkled it with water, and shook the drawer back and forth until all the candy was damp. Then we threw in a handful of powdered aloes and shook it again until the pellets were covered with a thin coating of the bitter stuff. It took only a few minutes longer to transfer them to small pasteboard boxes. To our audiences, of course, they were always described as God's greatest gift to man—"they make old men young and young men stronger." The announcement that we were going to give them away free always held the yokels. A sucker never does get over the notion that he is going to get something without paying for it. They got the Vital Sparks free, all right, but only after they had laid out a dollar for the Tiger Fat.

Later, when I had graduated from Vital Sparks and Tiger Fat, I sold herbs. These contained Alexandria senna, cascara bark, Cape aloes, sassafras, sugar, baking soda, berberis root, and star aniseed. I bought these ingredients from wholesale drug concerns in a powder as fine as flour. This was strictly a matter of expediency. In the big cities our audiences were mostly men. Only at fairs and in country towns did we get women, and we didn't want them even there. If a man was convinced by the pitch, he would reach down in his pocket and buy. A woman seemed to have to talk it over with her husband and the whole family. A man could take a quarter of a teaspoon of powdered herbs in a glass of water and didn't have to bother boiling up the whole herbs. The one-dollar-size can of herbs was the regulation two-ounce spice tin with a plain lacquered top. The whole thing—herbs, tin, and label, together with any literature we passed out—never cost us more than ten cents. Still, the mixture was a darned good physic, and the natives got their money's worth. Our laboratory for mixing the herbs was the good old bathtub. I would have one of the men wash the tub with Lysol and water and dry it carefully. He then dumped in the sacks of different herbs, rolled up his sleeves, and mixed the powders together thoroughly with his hands. Ten or fifteen minutes of that and the stuff was ready for the boxes.

In the early days the word "cure" could be used indiscriminately. There were some cough syrups advertised as a cure for consumption. By way of legal restrictions, the only things that hampered us were the shakedowns by local officials. This, of course, could be decided on and paid privately, but when the Pure Food and Drug Laws got around to us we were flirting with the United States Government. Before we knew it, we could no longer use the word "cure" in our literature. By this time I was handling all our affairs, and I hired a lawyer to keep me posted on new legislation that was passed. I made him write me a letter whenever a new drug law went into effect, and kept a file of them to show that my intent was to remain within the law.

Pretty soon we had to put the weight of the medicine on the label, and then the formula. Next we had to list the diseases for which the medicine was intended. Instead of saying mine was a physic I described it as an "intestinal eliminant," and below that I added, "In case of sudden illness, call your doctor." Next came a law which stipulated that the medicine must be manufactured by a reputable drug firm. So I had one of the largest drug mills in the country put together my herb formula and ship it to me sealed in compound drums. My private formula was on file, and I could wire or write for a barrel of it at any time. The interest of the firm ceased when the stuff was shipped, as they were manufacturing druggists only. The lawmakers kept after us. Their next effort was a regulation requiring that medicines be boxed in sanitary quarters under the supervision of a registered pharmacist. Evading this one was easy. We would just get some drugstore clerk who was a registered pharmacist to come down to the office and relax while the herbs were boxed. Then he would sign a statement testifying that he was present while the medicine was boxed in sanitary quarters. Perhaps it should be mentioned that forty years or so ago some registered pharmacists possessed less feeling of responsibility than is normal today.

Subsequently things got even tougher, and a pitchman's stand had to be plastered with insurance policies. One protected him if anyone suffered ill effects from the medicine, provided the medicine had been taken according to directions. The joker in this, of course, was the difficulty a yokel would have proving he had followed directions to the letter. Another policy guaranteed the medicine was harmless. This was usually true, and an overdose would cause only the inconvenience peculiar to any laxative. A third protected the natives in the audience, in case they fell down or suffered bodily injury inflicted by other listeners.

Insurance policies for pitchmen, however, were unknown during that first summer I worked in St. Paul as Princess Lotus Blossom.

Busy as I was, there was still time to enjoy the town. St. Paul took a free-and-easy attitude toward members of the underworld. So long as crooks didn't make trouble in St. Paul, they weren't molested. All they had to do was report to police upon their arrival in town, register their address, and refrain from breaking the law within the city limits. You could rob a bank in Minneapolis and, if you avoided being caught, turn up as a law-abiding citizen in St. Paul the next day. The red-light district was an established part of the community, although its residents were not allowed to go into restaurants until after eleven o'clock in the evening. They were allowed to shop only during a couple of designated hours on certain days of the week. Dressed in their best on these occasions, they rode downtown in open hacks. The men naturally knew when this parade was coming off and lined the streets to inspect any new recruits.

We were all proud of the souvenirs—silverware, napkins, and towels—we picked up in trains, restaurants, or hotels. I still have twelve square butter dishes I collected from different railroads. Probably the worst scare I got during the period of acquisition was in one of St. Paul's leading restaurants. Our meal had included lobster and a demitasse. The lobster forks were odd in shape, with long tines, and the coffee spoons were tiny. My friend and I each had taken three pieces of silverware and stuffed them into our stockings under our long skirts. When the waiter came with the bill, Will handed him twenty dollars. The waiter ran short of change and looked around abruptly at us, demanding courteously, "Have you ladies got any silver?" We thought he meant what we had in our stockings and would have dug down after it if Will hadn't spoken up.

Will always let me do anything within reason that came into my head, so long as it didn't interfere with his pattern of life for me. He supervised my clothes and my smoking and was with me all the time except when I was working. He had never let me get acquainted with any of the other women, but in St. Paul one of the other med workers began seeing a telephone girl who was about my age. She knew even less about the world than I did, and we were both young and full of energy. I would do my mind-reading act, deliver my lecture, hand the money to Will, and away Gladys and I would go for some fun. Riding a merry-go-round was still one of my favorite pastimes.

We were always planning jokes we could play on men. When we couldn't think of anything else we got a telephone book and called up a dozen or so lawyers at random. Our story was that we had heard them in court and admired them so much we wanted to meet them. After a little conversation we arranged to meet them on a designated corner at a certain time. For identification, we explained, the lawyer was to wear a carnation in his buttonhole, and we would have one pinned to our coats. When we had a good assortment hooked we hired a hack and pulled up at the corner to observe the expressions on the faces of the town's leading dandies as, carnation-marked, they tried to explain their presence to each other.

Other medicine men drifted through St. Paul, and among them was Prince Nanzetta, who stopped in the same rooming house we did. The Prince was responsible for a lesson I never forgot.

If there was anything Will despised, it was gossip. One evening we were preparing to lecture from a large stand set against a billboard. Just our head and shoulders were exposed above the cloth-draped shelf on which we placed the medicine grips. Another pitchman had been lecturing, and a small crowd still loitered in front, waiting for the next performance. We both stooped down to get our Chinese hats.

"Oh, Will," I murmured, "Nanzetta's door was part way open, and what do you think I saw him doing?"

Will didn't say a word. Bang! He gave me an uppercut on the nose. The blood flew.

I didn't scream or make a noise of any kind. I was too well trained to let anything drive me out of character. Nor was Will the least embarrassed or at a loss for words.

"Damn you," he whispered, "get to a doctor and have your nose set. I think I have broken it." He stood up and said, "An unfortunate thing has happened. The Princess has a nosebleed." He handed me a handkerchief and very kindly added, "Sister, the audience will excuse you."

I went to a doctor and he stuffed my nose until it was all out of shape. When I got back to the apartment Will said, "Vi, I hate to hit you, but you must always do exactly what I tell you to. I don't give a damn what anyone does or says. Don't gossip about it, even to me."

It used to make me pretty mad sometimes when Will hit me, but if I complained he would threaten to take my jewelry and pretty clothes away and send me home. That threat always persuaded me. After one of these sessions Will always bought me a present, or bought me something to send to my mother or sisters. Sometimes he took me out for an especially nice dinner. During my farm days we had had chicken on Sundays, but by the time Dad, Mother, the hired man, and the other children had theirs I was confronted with a choice of the back or the neck. I used to dream of a coat of arms formed not of diamonds or lovely clothes, but of the breast of a chicken garlanded with fried oysters.

In the fall it came time for us to move again. Will, as usual, selected our destination, and this time it was Seattle, which still was experiencing the tag end of the Alaska gold rush. Will gave a farewell dinner for our friends. Complete with champagne, it cost more than fifty dollars. The memory of it was still on our lips when Will obtained some calling cards bearing the name "Rev. Darien Brown." I asked him what they were for, and he told me ministers and their families got rates on the railroads.

"But you're not a minister," I protested.

"What difference does that make? I'm entitled to the rates just as much as they are."

→» CHAPTER SEVEN «←
THE
YOKOHAMA
MEDICAL
INSTITUTE

IN 1906, Seattle was virtually a two-street town. First and Second Avenues punctured the red-light district of King and Jackson Streets to the south and wandered up to Pike Street on the north. Beyond Pike Street was what amounted to a wilderness. To the east houses clung to the hillsides like swallow nests on a barn; residents had to climb long flights of steep stairs to get to them. To the west of First Avenue was the water front. The ferryboats and steamers nuzzled in so close to the hotels and business houses that it looked almost as if they were tied up to their back entrances.

The skid roads of all West Coast towns were pretty much the same, but Seattle's was the skiddiest of them all. "Skid road" was originally a logging term, used to describe the road or trail down which logs were skidded from the woods to the railroad. It came to designate the area in a town where loggers gathered in the off season when winter weather made logging impossible. Such areas, likewise, became the wintering place or the general hangout of all men who worked in the woods, the construction camps, the harvest fields, or the far-ranging fishing fleets. Seattle's skid road picked up shiploads of men who had worked all summer in the canneries or mines in Alaska, lumberjacks from the big Douglas fir timber country of Washington, and farm hands who had been laid off for the winter. San Francisco had its lumberjacks, too, but it also got miners from the Mother Lode country, sheep shearers and herders from Nevada, and deep-sea sailors from the ports of the world.

Skid roads were rough-and-tumble places, but there was a kind of tough honesty to most of the men who temporarily called them home. They worked hard, played hard, drank hard. They didn't expect decent women and didn't look for them, but they respected one when they found her. They had a kind of sixth sense about that.

In Seattle, as in other cities, street lights got less attention on the skid road than anywhere else. Just the same, there was always boisterous movement, a raw feeling of restless action. Streetwalkers roamed the area. The rooming houses were full of prostitutes, whose names and addresses would be whispered by bartenders as whisky gurgled out of the bottles.

The heart of a skid was always same and always different. Every evening its song began, drifting out in broken, blending fragments: the jingle of a tambourine… Fellow workers, we must organize…No matter how bad your condition is, Vital Sparks will restore your vitality...He was a damn scab, so I knocked him out. . . . Jesus saves…I know she gave me knockout drops; when I woke up my money was gone...Bound to the wheels of capitalism's chariot… Buy a War Cry…Gimme two bits for something to eat…Her name is Tillie; turn left and it's the third room…

Gamblers who had made their fix operated games in back rooms and took the shirts from the backs of the cash-loaded men from the mines of the North and from the forests which crowded downhill to the shores of Puget Sound. Death walked along the skid road with an easy indifference. Some died of illness, some by accident, others by violence. Knockout drops administered in saloons brought death, and the bodies were carted down to the docks and tied beneath a pier, where confederates could discover the corpses the next morning and collect the twenty-five dollars paid by the city for such finds. It was not uncommon for a thug to take a drunk for a walk and push him off a pier. An associate waiting below in a rowboat took good care that the victim drowned, and then tied the corpse where it could be handily located on the next day.

Prostitutes did well at their trade, but the big money lay in getting a man drunk and rolling him; that is, lifting his wallet and any loose cash. Skid-road men seldom complained. If they had a woman and plenty of liquor for a few days, they didn't expect anything else. Complaint to the police, of course, with everyone paying off handsomely, would have been useless. The only time a skid-road man went to police headquarters of his own free will was when he was drunk and in a fighting mood, and he never won.

The skid road always boasted a wonderful assortment of secondhand clothing stores and a few which offered new clothes of the cheapest caliber. Street signs calling attention to these stores always described them as the "Workingman's Friend." There were pawnshops which would make a loan on anything from a pair of lumberjack's low-topped boots to a twenty-five-thousand-dollar diamond necklace. Greek restaurants were invariably named the U.S. Café or the American Restaurant, and there was usually an American flag in the window. All of the establishments, from shooting galleries to barbershops, were clip joints.

One of the Seattle barbershops had worked up a gag which was better than most. The barber had manufactured a lot of pink hair tonic which he had named "Nice Day Hair Tonic." Sales of this preparation were heaviest in the spring, fall, and winter, particularly when it was raining or cloudy, which was a good deal of the time. After giving his patron a haircut and shave the barber would pick up the hair-tonic bottle, making sure that the label was hidden from the customer. "Would you like a Nice Day?" he would inquire. The sucker invariably answered, "Sure," or stated grumpily that it was "about time for one." The barber then doused his head with the mixture and gave him a vigorous scalp massage. The patron thought this was just a little extra service until he got his bill. The shave, haircut, and Nice Day came to five dollars. The squawking that followed was tremendous.

Very much injured, the barber would say, "Well, you ordered it." Ordered it? The patron would begin to yelp again. "Didn't I," the barber would say, "ask you if you wanted a Nice Day? Here's the bottle. Look at it." "Oh hell," the disgusted patron would reply. "I thought you were talking about the weather."

Skid roads were notable, too, for the employment offices which lined them. Each employment office had a blackboard facing the street, and on it were scrawled the jobs which, from hour to hour, were open. Skid road employment language exists nowhere else on the face of the earth. "Gandydancers," for example, are railroad section hands. A "bull cook" is a logging-camp flunky. A locomotive engineer is a "hog's head," and a "tallow pot" is the fireman. A switchman is a "snake," and a "king snipe" is a section boss.

Years later, in 1920 I worked the Seattle skid road again, but times had changed. This was the era of the Wobblies[16], the I.W.W.'s.

The workers, those who carried I.W.W. cards, were in revolt, and Seattle was branded as a town in which no pitchman stood a chance. Even Curly Thurber—a pitchman who was a former I.W.W. organizer—had been badly mauled when he tried it. During the last few nights, before he quit Seattle, he carried a sponge saturated with oil of mustard. If a man made a move toward him Curly would jump forward and press the sponge against the man's nose. Tears would begin to flow, and the man would be all but knocked out.

I decided to try it anyway. I was working from the front seat of an automobile then. My driver drove up and parked the car on the same corner I had worked years before. Figuring there would be trouble, I told my driver to get out as soon as I had a crowd. When the crowd got wise to the pitch all hell broke loose. Men began to shout, "Capitalist! Capitalist!" Others yelled, "We don't need a physic! What we want is something to eat. Let's take the car away from her. That's the only way we'll ever get one!" They started their famous Wobbly song—the one about "pie in the sky." I stood pat. Finally I was able to make myself heard.

"You dumb fools," I said, "I'm not here to exploit you, but to help you. You workingmen are the backbone of the nation. I'm here because you men can't afford a doctor or medical care. That's for the rich. That's for the people who live in fine houses. But you men get sick too, don't you? Pain means as much

---

16   The Industrial Workers of the World (IWW), members of which are commonly termed "Wobblies," is an international labor union that was founded in 1905 in Chicago, Illinois. The union combines general unionism with industrial unionism, as it is a general union whose members are further organized within the industry of their employment. The philosophy and tactics of the IWW are described as "revolutionary industrial unionism," with ties to both socialist and anarchist labor movements.

to you as it does to them. If something is wrong with you it hurts just as much. Well, that's why I'm here. To tell you why you're ill and what you can do about it. You can take this car if you want to, and you can do anything else you want to, because I'm not here with a flying squadron of mounted police ready to run you down when a whistle blows. But if you have any brains—and I think you have—you'll listen to what I'm going to say. I'm down here to say it because I think it will keep some of you from getting any sicker than you are now and maybe cure you if you aren't too far gone."

They quieted down, and I went into my pitch. One of the toughest of the objectors had been a peg-legged man who claimed to be a cousin of John L. Sullivan[17]; by about the third night he was selling medicine for me. They finally did me the honor of asking me to join and talk and organize for them— an invitation I declined because there didn't seem to be enough money in it.

Another pitchman who made his pitch stick during those hectic days was Sam Sault. Sault was the founder of a private religion. His disciples wore their whiskers and their hair long. When it came time for Sault to go into his pitch he sat down on an apple box on the curbstone and began to ring a bell—one of those things with a handle teachers used to call pupils in from recess. His religious patter came to me in a somewhat disjointed form, as he would be lecturing on one side of the street while I lectured on the other. I did gather that only a limited number of persons were to be saved, and that the uncut whiskers were to make it easier for St. Peter to separate the sheep from the goats.

Sault didn't take up collections. He wanted live ones. When people joined his band of disciples they turned all their money and property over to him. He in turn guaranteed to feed and bed them for life. Actually, the reason he rejected barbering in any form was that it saved him money for shaves and haircuts. Sault lodged his followers in a tenement of the meanest sort. They had sworn to become vegetarians, and he prowled the markets for slightly spoiled fruits and vegetables. Each morning the poor devils would file out to jobs Sault had found for them. They had to turn over their pay check to him. They also took

---

17   John Lawrence Sullivan (October 12, 1858 – February 2, 1918) was an Irish-American boxer recognized as the first heavyweight champion of the gloved boxing era. He held the title from 1882 to 1892. He was also a bare-knuckle champion prior to the change in rules requiring professional boxers to use protective gloves. He was one of the highest-paid athletes of the era.

an oath to live a life of chastity. Sault had taken a similar oath, but apparently it failed to work with him. He and one of his ministers fell out over a girl in the office, and Sault drummed the minister out of the organization. The minister was a good convincer who later pitched for me. At the time he thought I was wasting my talents pitching medicine and tried to persuade me to start a religion similar to Sam Sault's. "I've got it all figured out," he told me. "There's a place in the Bible that says, 'And her name is Wisdom.' That's the Holy Ghost. I can show you just how to do it." I told him I wasn't interested in playing Wisdom but preferred to stick to physic. Sam Sault's semi-biblical empire collapsed when several of his disciples brought suit against him for fraud, but when he died his estate amounted to two or three hundred thousand dollars.

Sam Sault and the Wobblies belonged, however, to a later era. During that first year Will and I pitched together in Seattle there was nothing to worry about but separating the natives from their money. We lined up a couple of shills and went right to work. Shills, or shillabers, were a necessary part of nearly every pitchman's performance. They were used in two ways—as the subject in demonstrations, and as bellwethers to lead the sheep over the edge of the cliff. The shills were always the first to buy; when the pitch was over they sneaked the product back to the pitchman and got fifty cents or so for their trouble. Some of them worked for two or three pitchmen at once, timing their visits to coincide with the last few minutes of each pitch.

While we were in Seattle we had a chance to watch one of the best of them in action. He shilled for a pitchman who sold catarrh salve. Before the performance opened the shill would go up to the pitchman's room and pack one nostril carefully with either custard or cornstarch pudding, made a little stiffer than usual. Breathing gingerly or holding one finger against the packed nostril, he would work his way up to the front of the crowd as the lecture drew to its close. Concluding his remarks, the pitchman would invite any catarrh sufferer in the crowd to step forward and be shown the miracle-like action of his famous salve.

The shill stepped right up.

"My friend, have you catarrh?"

"Yes, sir," the shill snuffled.

"Please put a small application of this salve in each nostril."

The pitchman handed down the tin. The shill obediently stuffed a dab of the salve into his nostrils.

The pitchman waited, tapping a finger on the lid of the tin salve box. At this point silence was the best of all pitches. The shill just stood there, and people began to crane their necks to get a look at him.

Finally the pitchman drew a spotless handkerchief from his pocket and passed it down to the shill. "Now blow your nose hard."

The shill blew hard enough to be heard half a block. "Now hand me the handkerchief."

The evidence that relief had been immediate and complete was overwhelming. The suckers were convinced that if such an advanced ease could be cured by the salve, it probably was the most potent medicine ever compounded. They bought lavishly at fifty cents a tin, the contents of which had cost about five cents to make. The shill got a dollar for his trouble.

Will and I also discovered a honey of a shill in Seattle. He was an old ex-con who had had a paralytic stroke and walked on crutches. Will found he could stagger three or four steps without his crutches, so he arranged with him to buy the Vital Sparks and Tiger Fat the first night. Four or five nights later he came hobbling up on his crutches, full of enthusiasm, to tell us that since using the remedies he had discovered he could take a step unaided by the props. Very dramatically he handed his crutches to the nearest yokel and took the tottering step. At intervals he would add another step, until he had reached his limit of four.

Everyone knew him, as he had begged for a living ever since his stroke. He shilled for us a long time and made a good deal of money for us. He was an odd mixture of ruthlessness and idealism. I was talking to him one day when an outsize thug came up to me and began to whine for a handout. Crippled though he was, old John spoke up without a moment's hesitation. "You rat, if you need some money go up an alley and knock some sucker on the head, but don't let me catch you begging from a woman." He was proud of the fact that he himself begged only from men. He had a muscular or nervous ailment which caused his hands to tremble continually. He came up to me one after-noon with an expression of injured helplessness on his wrinkled face. "Oh," he wailed, "if God would just give me the use of my hands for fifteen minutes!" What, I wanted to know, would he do? He shook his head miserably. "There's a drunk sleeping in back of the saloon, and I could roll him."

Another part of John's story we learned from a detective who was a mu-tual friend. John's wife had died some time before he had his stroke, leaving him with a baby daughter. Together they had saved a considerable amount of money. Old John was a dope addict and knew his own life was finished. He went to a judge in Seattle and told him to use the money to board the child out and eventually send her to school. She was to grow up, he insisted, never knowing who her father was. When he had his stroke the judge wanted to turn some of the money back to him, but John wouldn't take it. He went to the county hospital with the other charity patients. He never saw his daughter and never let her know he was alive.

The license to sell medicine in Seattle was twenty dollars a day. We were doing well, but we were losing the big money by not operating an office. Will had been thinking about it, and when a friend of his from the East dropped into town and asked him if he needed a case taker Will made up his mind. His first move was to send me around to the police chief to make the fix. A fix wasn't necessary if we simply wanted to sell on the street, but on an office operation a lot of kicks got back to headquarters.

Walking in on a police chief, even if you know he takes graft, requires some finesse and usually a few letters of introduction. I got my audience, all right, and told the chief we would like to run an office. He didn't nibble. I told him I would like to call again. He said I could. I called several times, and we talked about the weather, and about conditions in general, and national politics, always steering clear of the office topic. At last, after I had been there on a half-dozen different occasions, he reached into a drawer of his desk and pulled out a picture of a corpse. "This man was killed prowling a hotel room last night," he said casually. "Do you know him?"

I looked at him disdainfully and threw the picture down on the desk. "You don't think I'd tell you if I did, do you?" That did it. From then on he trusted me. The price was named, and we went to work.

We rented all but one room of the first floor of the Interurban Hotel. We had been doing our lecturing beside the California Saloon. Directly across the southeast corner of Washington and Occidental was the famous saloon, Our House. We cleared out a couple of rooms in which we had had girls pasting labels on the boxes of medicine. Will had some cards printed. They advertised the "Yokohama Medical Institute" and promised "free consultation and advice." That "free consultation and advice" always brought the natives to the office in droves. A sucker has a quaint idea he is going to get something for nothing, and no matter how many times he gets stung that word "free" will always start him over again.

The office always had to be close to the place where you made your street pitch. You had to be able to point to it and say, "My office is right over there," or "Turn around, everybody. Look over there. That is my office. I am going to that office as soon as I finish this lecture. Follow me there for free consultation and advice." This had to be repeated two or three times during the lecture, and the lecture always closed with another invitation to get something for nothing. If this wasn't done, half the natives wouldn't be able to find the office, and probably the other half would be dissuaded by some half-wise chump who would tell them we were grafters and advise them not to come to the office.

The case takers were always people particularly skillful at separating the yokel from his money. They had different ways, but a good one never failed to get whatever loose money was available. Will told me to watch this friend of his from the East, whose name was Ed Carlyon, and see how he worked.

First Carlyon fixed up his private office, where he took the suckers to land them. He had the room papered with a solid-colored wallpaper. He wouldn't permit a picture to be hung. Then he had drapes hung over the windows so the chumps could see nothing that would distract their attention. The room had to be lit by electricity; kerosene lamps, with their colored flame, gave a man something to look at. There were only three pieces of furniture in the room—a chair and desk for the case taker, and a chair for the chump. The chump's chair was the softest, deepest upholstered chair money could buy. That was to make the chump relax. He had to fairly wallow to get out of that chair.

I asked Carlyon why he didn't have more furniture.

"Vi," he said, "never let a third person in the office when you're landing a sucker. If there are only two of you, and it ever comes to court, your word is as good as his. If there is a third person present, say a friend of the sucker's, he can testify for the sucker. If one of the med bunch is in the room, a smart lawyer might frame a conspiracy charge against you, and that's a felony. Otherwise you're just practicing medicine without a license, and a hundred-dollar fine is probably the worst you would get—one or more suckers will make that up fast enough."

When we operated from a med store, or on a larger scale from the street, we kept lecturers going from nine o'clock in the morning until ten o'clock at night. Traveling medicine men would work for us, varying their pitches to sell our medicine. In Seattle we built up to the point where we required two case takers, a waiting room, and a room where the lecturers could hang out while they were waiting their turn to pitch.

One of our case takers called himself an "iridologist." He persuaded the chumps he could diagnose their diseases by looking closely at their eyes. This man was so crooked that we had a concealed listening post between the office and my room so we could hear how much money he got. After he had got as much money as he could out of some miner or lumberjack and had given him his medicine, he would take him by the arm and escort him to the door.

"Now, my boy," he would remark in a fatherly way, "I want you to make me a promise."

"Yes, Doctor," the chump would invariably answer.

"I want you to promise me that while you are taking this treatment you will not eat any quail on toast or lobster or porterhouse steaks—and be sure you do not drink any champagne."

The yokel always gawked at him and said, "No, Doctor, I won't." When the chump's funds were exhausted the iridologist, of course, wanted to get rid of him before he started to squawk. He had a method that never failed. His equipment included a large syringe, which he loaded with diluted capsicum (red pepper) ointment. At his request, the cashless customer would lie face down on the operating table. The iridologist always explained the treatment before he administered it, as he never had a chance to afterward.

"Brother," he would say, "there is only one thing that will do you any more good, and that is this injection I am going to give you now. You must come back three times a day for this treatment."

He then proceeded to administer the rectal injection of red-pepper ointment. Strong men jumped off that operating table and ran down the hall with their trousers around their knees. No patient ever returned for the concluding installments of the cure.

Medicine men would gyp each other as quickly as they would a sucker. Case takers held out part of their fees if they could. Lecturers stole medicine from the stock room and sold two or three packages from their pockets while they were selling through an audience.

We had one lecturer, Charley, whose wife had run away with a long-haired Indian-scout medicine man from the East. This loss was consequential, but not nearly so much so as the loss of Charley's spitz dog, which the couple took with them. The spitz had been trained to do tricks, and Charley had used him for ballyhoo. Charley long and sincerely mourned the canine half of his bereavement and became so useless to us that Will had to fire him.

At the head of the stairs in the Interurban Hotel was one dark little room we had not rented. Our office was at the end of the hall. We noticed Charley hanging around the hotel but thought nothing of it. After a couple of days, though, business in the office began to drop off. There was a sign on the door of the little room—"Office. Walk In"—but we assumed the manager was using it for his private office. Investigation disclosed that Charley was sitting in there, like a cat at a rat hole, picking off our clients as they stopped in to inquire if they had come to the right place.

As I gradually got the hang of the work I began to do a little case taking myself. I laid down two rules—never doctor a sick man, and never doctor a woman, sick or well. I talked to the women who came in but asked such tremendous fees that they walked out. Women are harder to fool, in the first place; in the second, they aren't too shy to kick up a fuss when they figure they've been gypped, while most men are. So far as the first rule was concerned, there were too many young men and middle-aged men who wanted their vigor and vim restored to bother with men who were really sick. When one came in actually ill or in need of a minor operation, I would collect the fee and send him to an ethical physician or surgeon. We, of course, paid these ethical croakers a portion of the fee we had collected. One of them almost got me in a jam.

The incident involved the largest fee I ever got—one thousand dollars. One of the men case takers was working the office at the time. He came back to our apartment with a certified check, made out to the patient, for the thousand.

"Will," he said, "this man is willing to pay two hundred dollars for his treatment. How can we cash this?"

"To hell with two hundred dollars," Will said. "Vi, go back in there with Herbert. Discharge Herbert and get the full thousand."

I followed Herbert back into the office. I was very haughty and sharp with him, while the yokel sat looking on, his jaw sagging open.

"Pack up your things," I said. "Get them out of here. I can't conceive of a man calling himself a doctor who could make such a grave mistake in his diagnosis. This man is sick, and you've failed completely to find the cause of his trouble. If he had followed your advice he might have died. Go on. Get out. Take your instruments."

The yokel's eyes were bugging out of his head. Herbert, looking very abashed, picked up his things and left. I got out my box of colored crayons, a leather-padded hammer, and a stethoscope. The yokel was stripped to the waist. I went over him fore and aft, marking a red X here, a yellow circle there, and a green check mark somewhere else. When I got through with him he looked like a tattooed man in a circus. I tapped him all over with the hammer and listened. Then I let him tell me all his symptoms. It was clear that what he needed was a minor operation.

I stood there looking at him for a time, shaking my head and pursing my lips. Then I took his check and handed it back to him.

"I'm sorry this mistake happened," I said. "It's a reflection on the reputation of the Institute. You're in serious trouble and you need far more medical attention than you can possibly get for two hundred dollars. We can help you—and you need help badly, my friend—but it's going to cost you more than that."

The yokel said he wanted to be cured and how much was it going to cost? At last he agreed that if he was in such bad shape a thousand dollars wouldn't be too much to pay. While he was dressing I went back to Will.

"Take him over to the bank," Will directed. "Have him deposit the check in his name and then write you a personal check. Have him write on it in his own handwriting, 'For value received.' Then have the banker put his stamp on it. Ask the cashier to make the necessary entries and give you the check with the sucker's consent."

We stood in well with the bank, as one time there had been a small run on it and we had been able to help them out. While people stood in long lines waiting to draw their money out, I went in with a large sack of silver dollars three or four times a day, thumped it on the counter, and asked in a loud voice to have it deposited.

I took the sucker over to the bank, and everything went as scheduled. We went from the bank to the office of one of the best surgeons in town. When I told him what was required he consented, after making his own examination, to perform the operation for two hundred dollars. I didn't, of course, mention the fee I had collected.

A few days later Will and I were lying on the couch, smoking opium and talking. Will previously had put all our property in my name because he thought it would be easier for me to fix with the authorities in case we got into trouble.

"I think you had better turn over the property and the smelter and mining stock to a friend of mine I'll introduce you to," Will said. "That fee was pretty high, and it may come back to us."

Sure enough, as soon as the sucker was out of the hospital I was served with papers notifying me I was being sued for one thousand dollars. The surgeon had found out how much I had collected, had got peeved, and had talked the yokel into bringing the suit. Scared stiff, I turned to Will.

He always had things figured out two or three laps ahead of anyone else, and he wasn't disturbed now. "Here is what you must do, Vi. I'll get you a law-yer. He won't ask you more than one or two questions, and I'll tell him what they're to be. You're going to have to do this alone. Never bring me into it. The yokel will tell all about being examined by you. Don't get frightened. The bank cashier will identify your check and testify that the words, 'For value received,' were written on it in his presence."

The case came to trial and went as Will had predicted. When I was put on the stand my lawyer asked me if I had received the money. I said yes. Then he asked me what I had received it for.

"For value received," I replied, "and what he got at the time he thought was worth a thousand dollars."

I looked the judge straight in the eye as I said it. The yokel began to squirm in his chair, and his face got very red. The judge's face screwed up a little, as if he had just found out about being swindled in a horse race.

The yokel and his lawyer were whispering frantically, but it was too late. I couldn't help remembering Carlyon's instructions about witnesses. By the time the yokel's lawyer got to his feet he couldn't have persuaded anyone in the courtroom, much less the judge, that nothing but a simple medical ex-amination had occupied us the day the yokel visited the office. The case was dismissed.

But for the rest of my office career I was satisfied with fees from ten to one hundred dollars. Collecting ten one-hundred-dollar fees caused less wear and tear.

As our stay in Seattle wore on I became sort of official fixer for the thieves, gamblers, and what have you whom Will knew. An acquaintance of Will's had been caught prowling rooms in the Tourist Hotel. When he got out on bail he came to us to see if we could fix his case. I went to police headquarters, and for fifty dollars they returned a gun, a blackjack, a can of opium, and a pass key, which were being held in the safe as evidence. The case eventually was dismissed for lack of evidence.

There were three classes of people in Seattle—the residents, people who came to town with a bank roll, and crooks who were after the bank rolls. In San Francisco before the earthquake you could always find pennies in the street; people threw them away when they got them in change. In Seattle they didn't throw dollars in the street, but they might as well have. A high police official went to the penitentiary later for taking graft. A few police officers were dismissed as a result of graft charges; others didn't get caught and became rich and respectable. Missions began with one smart talker, a drum to catch the money, and one room below the level of the skid-road sidewalk; they wound up with costly churches, while their originators waxed wealthy and lived in expensive houses. Prostitutes married rich men and snubbed their less lucky sisters; some of them founded families whose names became important in the town's history. There was money aboard every ship putting in at Seattle from Alaska. Newspapers carried the names of the big mining men, the amount of gold theywere bringing down, and the hotels at which they were stopping. The cheechakos[18] usually stayed at the Rainier Grand Hotel, while the sourdoughs preferred the Butler or the Northern. The Butler got the sourdoughs who had acquired a little polish. The Northern got those who didn't worry about having a crease in their pants; they had hearts of gold, or at least their pockets were stuffed with it.

We were reaching up for the big money, and I did less and less lecturing. I was becoming too valuable as a fixer, for one thing; for another, Will was getting other ideas. He hired a Japanese cook and a maid for me. I got more diamond rings and more clothes. I had squirrel furs, mink wraps, and an ermine neckpiece. It wasn't long before the politicians and moneyed men began to notice me in the restaurants and hotels and tried to meet me.

"You are missing a lot of money," Will said kindly one night. "Someday you may get tired of being an old man's darling, and if that time ever comes I want you to be protected."

When he said this he reached across past the brazier and squeezed my hand.

---

18   Cheechako is a derogatory slang term used in the Pacific Northwest, especially in Alaska, to describe newcomers to the region.

It is derived from Chinook jargon, from chee, "new" (from Lower Chinook čxi, "right away") + chako, "come," from Nootka čokʷa· come, imperative.

"If you should ever tire of living with me," he continued, "we'll split the bank roll fifty-fifty. You can go your way and find happiness, while I will go mine as best I can."

I began to cry. "Will, I couldn't ever leave you."

He stroked my hand. "More than likely, dear child, I will be dead and gone before you are, and all our money will be yours."

He sounded so sad and noble that I was brokenhearted. I was sure he was dying slowly and was keeping the fact from me. He wrote out a will, leaving everything to his beloved wife Vi. I was overcome with gratefulness, forgetting that it was I who was making the money.

"I want you to be clever, my dear, so always pay attention to what I tell you," Will went on.

Weeping, I swore to follow his instructions to the letter.

"These men you will meet don't love you as I do," Will said. "They are out after what they can get. Have no sympathy for them. Always remember men are more romantic and sentimental than women if they are handled right. Now listen carefully, because I am going to tell you the things you must remember if you are to become a smart woman.

"Never try to trim a young handsome man; all the women will be running after him. Your best bet is a man over forty, and the homelier, the better. Don't be vulgar or too talkative. If you listen a person will always betray himself. Don't smoke. If a prospect asks you to have a drink, say yes, and then order lemonade or milk. It will knock him over. Never let a man paw you. He can get all that rough stuff in the red-light district. Never have physical relations with a prospect, no matter what he promises. A woman's body is the cheapest commodity in the market. Always use 'New Mown Hay' perfume in the daytime and lilac at night. Nine-tenths of our rich men came up via the spittoon and office-boy route or are the farm boys who came to the city and made good. The office-boy man doesn't want to be reminded of the past, and the farm-boy man won't realize he is attracted to you because you smell like a stack of hay or the lilac bush on the front lawn at home. It will merely remind him of his carefree youthful days on the farm, and he will feel more kindly toward you. Always go for money the first week. If the prospect doesn't come across, drop him. If he does, get hard-boiled when you've cleaned him. Never let him think circumstances have kept you apart. He might brood and kill you. Make him disgusted with you and ashamed of himself. Never feel sorry for a chump, even if he cries."

Will watched the papers for the arrival of miners from Alaska with gold dust. The newspaper accounts always recorded the miner's plans to stay over a few days in Seattle before going on home and named the hotel at which he was stopping. These miners were among the easiest prospects in the world. After months or years in Alaska they were ready for a free-wheeling blowout in the first big town they hit.

When we had picked our prospect I dressed in plain but attractive clothes, went to the hotel, and asked for him. People weren't so hard to see in those days. The prospect always came down to the parlor to find out what I wanted. I told him I had a brother who had gone to Alaska a couple of years ago. Mother and I had heard from him regularly until about eight months ago. The last letter we got was mailed in Fairbanks or Dawson—or whatever town the paper had reported the man came from. Did he know my brother, or had he ever heard of him?

If the prospect was interested in my looks and wanted to get acquainted he stalled and said he didn't know my brother personally, but it seemed to him he had heard the name. Would I come back in a day or so, after he had had time to inquire among his friends? By way of identification I always told them I was the office girl at the Yokohama Medical Institute. The next time I called the prospect would be on my brother's trail. He thought he had found a man who knew him. Meanwhile, would I have dinner and go to a show with him? During the next few days, while we were giving each other the run-around, Mother would come. She was an ex-shoplifter who had lost her nerve. I would introduce Mother. The prospect would grow very sympathetic. He had been unable to find out about my brother, but if I would go back to Alaska with him in the spring he was sure he could locate him.

That was the time for the touch. Mother had to go back home, but neither she nor I had enough money for the trip. Would he lend me one hundred and fifty or two hundred dollars so I could buy her some clothes and a train ticket? It was a touch that never failed. The touches were small, but Will didn't want me to make them so large the miners would talk to each other about it. Sourdoughs were a clannish bunch, but to them a few hundred dollars tossed away weren't worth mentioning.

All told, I promised to take a good many trips to Alaska. If I had had to make good on the promises I would have been on the water for years.

Another angle of our Seattle activities that summer involved Vancouver, Canada. We didn't lecture there at that time because there was no fixing or squaring anything in Canada. When Will found a live prospect he sent him down to Seattle for treatment. Will accompanied the sucker to the depot in Vancouver, where I took over, riding down on the day coach with him to Seattle to make sure no one talked to him. I tailed the prospect to the door of our Seattle office, then telephoned to give the case taker the low-down. Afterward I would catch the night boat back to Vancouver.

Vancouver in those days was a strange and foreign town to find within a stone's throw of the United States. A newcomer stepping off the train found himself in the center of Chinatown. In the gutters of the streets opium was cooked in large pots suspended over charcoal braziers. The fumes smote the nostrils with a stout and immediate pungency. The opium cooked in Canada was called Fook Lung, a first-grade product imported from China. On the streets were to be seen such varied nationalities as East Indians, colorfully turbaned, and Doukhobors[19], who were members of a Russian religious sect. It was, and still is, the troublesome habit of a small clique among the Doukhobors, known as "The Sons of Freedom," to disrobe in public whenever matters did not go to suit them.

Between my trips to Canada and my activities in Seattle, my education in the medicine-show business was advancing speedily. I had become a big

---

19   The Doukhobours (literally *"Spirit-Warriors / Wrestlers"*) are a Spiritual Christian religious group of Russian origin. They are one of many non-Orthodox ethno-confessional faiths in Russia, often categorized as "folk-Protestants," Spiritual Christians, sectarians, and/or heretics. They are pacifists who live separate from mainstream culture as they reject personal materialism, work together, and have a tradition of oral history and memorizing and singing hymns and verses.

The modern descendants of the first Canadian Doukhobours live in southeastern British Columbia, southern Alberta and Saskatchewan, where their ancestors settled. Today, the estimated Doukhobour population is 40,000 in Canada and about 5,000 in the United States.

Beginning in 1902, a faction of zealots began using arson and nude marches to protest against a breach of trust by the Canadian government about registration for citizenship. Though the number of zealots soon diminished, they were the main focus of media as "Freedomites."

money-getter. I could make more money on one pitch than any of the men, but I still was not a finished artist.

Will had bragged about how well I could do, and inevitably the time came when it was demanded that I prove whether or not I was tops. It was traditional among medicine men that this proof could be presented in only one way. A beginner who was getting a little big for his boots or an established pitchman who began boasting about what a powerful lecturer he was had to deliver what was called the Lucy and Johnny lecture. This wasn't a medicine pitch. It was simply a tour de force in which the pitchman painted a horrible picture of the results of self-abuse. It was, of course, the most unadulterated bunk. The object of the test was to deliver the lecture with enough dreadful emphasis to make at least one of the listeners faint. If the pitchman failed to make one of the natives topple over, he lost face among the other road people; if he succeeded, his reputation was established, and the scoffers had to pony up for a champagne supper.

The place picked for my attempt was on Twelfth and Pacific in Tacoma, which is about twenty-five miles from Seattle. It was the heart of the skid road, and the audience would be lumberjacks, miners, fishermen, and smelter workers. There wouldn't be a cream puff in the lot, and nobody was going to make them faint away by talking about indigestion. Every pitchman working Seattle at the time went over with me. We rented a hack, drove to the corner, and lit our gasoline torch. Will and I did our mind-reading act, and then Will stepped down and left me alone.

I started in telling about the Vital Sparks and how they had restored the happiness and virility of the Chinese. I reached over and turned the gasoline light down so it revealed nothing but my face, which took on an eerie aspect because of the changing shadows. I made my voice low and dramatic.

"But, gentlemen, it is possible to wait until it is everlastingly too late. Don't delay until Johnny's fate befalls you.

"Johnny and Lucy were brother and sister. Lucy was a lovely girl, and Johnny had just reached man's estate. It was with pride and joy he escorted Lucy to parties, where he was a favorite with both girls and boys. He was the head of his class during his last year at high school.

"For no discernible reason Johnny began to fail in his lessons. His teachers and parents excused it by saying, 'He is growing too fast.' Before long Johnny was staying away from parties. He wouldn't go out with his sister any more. He shunned companions and skulked by himself. Gentlemen, need I tell you the vicious habit into which this poor boy had fallen? Need I describe in detail the reason he sought to be alone and unseen by any other human being? Or does every man of you listening to me now know the vice to which he had become addicted?"

I paused. There wasn't a sound. Rigs rattled along the street, but no one looked at them. I went on, pulling my voice out with a hushed sadness.

"At last Johnny's parents became alarmed and took him to the family doctor, who discovered his secret vice. He advised Johnny to get married. Fear already was creeping through the boy's heart, and he took the doctor's advice. He married a beautiful girl he had known for years. In a short time she left him in loathing and disgust, and her last words to him were: 'May God forgive a man such as you who blasts a trusting girl's love!' Terror-stricken now, Johnny tried to break himself of his terrible vice. He failed. At last his parents moved him out to a hut on the edge of a dark swamp. Neighbors reported that the boy, who had grown hideous to look upon, wandered about aimlessly and talked to himself. They followed him to his hut and peered through the windows. They could hear him muttering gibberish like an ape. The neighbors complained to the authorities, and Johnny, screaming and struggling, was taken to an insane asylum in a straitjacket. There he remained until one night a shriek rang down the iron corridors, and the next day a rude pine board in the asylum graveyard marked the last resting place of what had once been a bright and promising career!"

There was a moment of quiet, then another, before a groan came out of the packed ranks of the crowd.

My man hit the sidewalk, and I was at last a bona fide member of the medicine show profession.

So far as I could see, I was sitting on top of the world. I couldn't go two blocks without calling a hack. I dressed like a queen and looked forward to making entrances into the theater boxes. Nothing made me prouder than to have theater audiences level their opera glasses on me.

By hook and by crook we made sixty thousand dollars in Seattle that year and we decided it was time for a blow-out in San Francisco. In San Francisco it was possible to spend money faster than in just about any other city in the world.

Violet McNeal. This photo is the only purported photo of Violet as a younger woman, c. 1915.

Will Archambault, aka William Davis, a.k.a. Tiger Fat Davis.
Violet's common-law husband, c. 1900.

Will Archambault, aka William Davis, a.k.a. Tiger Fat Davis.

TIGER FAT FAILS TO CURE

Laborer Who Spent Earnings for Alleged Miraculous Remedy Now Asks Court to Give Back His Money.

Samuel Hillbury, a laborer, appeared in Justice George's court this morning in a suit against Frank Myers, Charles Walden and William Davis, of the Yokohama Medical Company, to recover $15 which he paid them last August for alleged remedies.

Hillbury went to the "doctors" and complained of pains in his head and back. He alleges he was told in glowing terms of the medicinal value of "Tiger Fat," a concoction said to be made from the marrow of the tiger's bones and which was guaranteed to cure anything that came along, but its strong point was its miraculous cures of the very complaint which ailed the patient.

Hillbury paid the price asked by the "specialists" and got a written guarantee to refund his money. If his cure was not effected within a reasonable time. The wording of the first contract did not suit him so he went back and was given a second paper with the offending clauses stricken out.

Late in September, Hillbury says, he went to Walden and asked for the return of his money, as "Tiger Fat" had failed to give him any miraculous relief and it is alleged Walden, with his two associates, beat him and took both papers away from him. They were fined in Judge Gordon's court for assault and battery and later were put out of business by the police as quacks and fakers.

Hillbury is now suing for the return of his money and the case was continued until this afternoon to give the plaintiff time to get witnesses necessary to prove his story concerning the contract, which he says was stolen from him.

News article about a lawsuit involving Will Archambault, a.k.a. William Davis, that "Tiger Fat" and the Yokohama Medical Company are fraudulent. *Seattle Daily Times*, June 19, 1907.

TIGER FAT
Oriental Salve, 50c.
Cures Catarrh, Deafness, Sores, Eczema, Piles, etc.
VITAL SPARKS,
Oriental Nerve Tonic For Men.
Sample Box by Mail $1.00.

Oriental Medical Inst., 314 E. 5th st., City.

ARRESTED ON SUSPICION OF STEALING DIAMONDS

"Tiger Fat" Doctors Taken Into Custody—Prisoner Promises to Produce Jewels from Safety Deposit Vault

William Davis, George and Bob Meyers, the "Tiger Fat" doctors who have been holding forth at Fifth and Main streets for several months past, were arrested last night by Detective Thomas Zeigler and taken to the central station on suspicion.

According to the story told by the police, a Mrs. L. M. Cline, who is stopping at the Hotel Rosslyn, lost a small chamois bag containing diamonds valued at $300 several days ago. This bag was found on the street by Bob Meyers, who turned it over to William Davis. The latter says he deposited it in a safety deposit vault at a bank, but which bank he did not say.

George Meyers, who seems to have had nothing to do with the case, was released from custody, and Bob Meyers was released on depositing $250 cash bail for his appearance.

Davis was committed on suspicion, but today he promised to go to the safety deposit vault, take out the lost diamonds and turn them over to the police.

News article about Will Archambault, a.k.a. William Davis, arrested on suspicion of diamond theft. *Los Angeles Times*, c. 1905.

DR. ARCHAMBAULT'S
PARIS
VITAL SPARKS

Make Men and Women Strong and Powerful! Ten Thousand $3.00 Boxes Free.

SEND AT ONCE FOR OUR $3.00 BO /
—LAST A FULL MONTH—THOSE
WHO SEND AT ONCE GET A BOX
FREE—SEND BEFORE THE
TEN THOUSAND ARE
ALL GONE.

PAINLESS PARKER, DENTIST

THE ORIGINAL OUTLAW FROM ETHICALVILLE STILL AT LARGE WITH A PRICE ON HIS HEAD!

State and Commercial Streets, Salem, Phone 296

Portland, Ore., Tacoma, Wash., San Francisco, Los Angeles, Oakland, San Diego, Fresno, Sacramento, San Jose and Bakersfield, Calif., Brooklyn, N. Y.

Advertisement for Painless Parker Dentist. *The Tacoma Times*, Tacoma, WA, December 15, 1916.

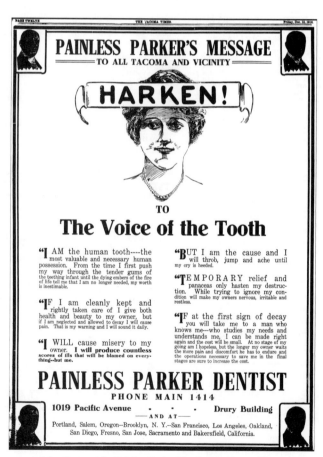

Advertisement for Painless Parker Dentist. *The Tacoma Times*, Tacoma, WA, December 15, 1916.

HELPED SCHOOLFIELD BOY.

Earl York, a Schoolfield Boy, gives the following testimony, regarding Dr. Nanzetta's Remedy:

"After suffering with rheumatism for nine weeks, I was unable to walk without assistance, could not work at all, and suffered terrible pain in my back, legs and hip. I had tried several things and everything failed to do me any good, until I tried Nanzetta's Remedy and, after taking it for five days, I could walk without assistance and I am now able to work.

(Signed)   "EARL YORK."

When you are suffering with rheumatism so you can hardly get around, just try Nanzetta's Prescription. It frees the blood circulation and breaks up congestion, filters the kidneys and causes your liver to act normally and so the rheumatism is soon gone.

Nanzetta's Remedy is sold by all leading druggists at the regular price. Nanzetta's Prescription, $1.00 per bottle; Indian New Discovery, 60c and $1.00.

Before Taking Nanzetta's Remedy

After Taking Nanzetta's Remedy

NANZETTA MEDICINE CO.

219 MAIN STREET.

Advertisement for Prince Nanzetta, 1923

The Great Nanzetta

Will be in Anderson for ten days, commencing Monday, near Equinox and Twine Mills, with his big Vaudeville Show, and Free Lecture.

Everybody Welcome.

Respectfully,

**J. H. NANZETTA,
The Indian Doctor.**

Advertisement for coming appearance by Prince Nanzetta.

A Wandering Prince.

Prince Nanzeta Montezuma, a wanderer and practically an exile from Mexico, is traveling some where in the West. He claims to be the only lineal descendant of the great Montezuma. The Prince is described as a man with delicate features, a striking face, of polished manners and well read.

A small news note about Prince Nanzetta. *The Star*, Reynoldsville, PA, c. 1904.

PRINCE NANZETTI'S TIGER FAT WORKS NO CHARM

Dispenser of Oriental Remedies Is Found Guilty of Practicing Medicine Illegally

After a consultation of less than fifteen minutes yesterday afternoon a jury in the case of the people against Prince Nanzetti, charged with practicing medicine without a license by the state board of medical examiners, returned a verdict of guilty and "the prince" will be sentenced Saturday morning.

The case against Nanzetti has been the hardest fought of the crusade against illegal practitioners by local representatives of the state board and a determined effort was made by the Oriental Remedy company, of which Nanzetti was an employe, to test the case. Attorney Dockweiler defended the prince.

At the examination of witnesses yesterday Nanzetti confessed that he went under the names of Nanzetti, Dias, Van Sant and Hodji. He explained that his true name was Harry Nanzetti and that, he was born in India. He also explained that his mother's maiden name was Dias Van Sant and that he belonged to the clan of Hodji in India, thus explaining his multitude of names.

Dr. Price W. Hughes appeared for the defense and testified that he was the physician of the company and attended to the examination of patients, but the prosecution proved that Hughes did not attend to the case of the prosecuting witness.

A bottle of herb tonic for rheumatism and a box of tiger marrow fat with some black nerve balls and vital sparks were introduced as evidence in the case.

Article from *Los Angeles Herald*, c. 1905 detailing guilty verdict against Prince Nanzetta for practicing medicine without a license.

WHO IS HE?

HE CURES PEOPLE GIVEN UP TO DIE!

To the People of St. Paul and Vicinity: TAKE NOTICE—That the Oriental Remedy Co., of "PEKIN, CHINA," and San Francisco are now in St. Paul. They guarantee by means of their Chinese herbs and remedies to cure people of diseases given up in this country as hopeless and incurable. Consultation and advice absolutely free. Call in person if you can, or write us a letter. We will send a valuable book about China.

ORIENTAL REMEDY CO.

6th and Wabasha.   St. Paul, Minn.
Room 2, Sherman block.

Advertisement for "Oriental Remedy Co.," *St. Paul Globe*, St. Paul, Minnesota, c. 1904.

Advertisement for "Hal the Healer," *The Gazette*, Colfax, WA, c. January 1902

Pitchman Owen Stratton dressed as a Quaker to sell "Quaker Medicine," c. 1899.

Silk Hat Harry was a soap pitchman who did his own ballyhoo act featuring comedy and rope tricks. His legend grew to such an extent that other pitchmen and performers adopted his nickname of "Harry the Hat" or "Silk Hat Harry." Most famously in the modern era, actor, comedian, and magician Harry Anderson made appearances on the television show *Cheers* as a character named Harry the Hat from 1982 – 1993. Image above is an early 20th Century tavern named for the pitchman.

The Kickapoo Medicine Show troupe c. 1900.

FEMALE PICKPOCKETS.

Dene Smith and Kittie Fitzgibbon, two of the most notorious female pickpockets in the country, were arrested last night by Policeman Regan and charged with vagrancy. They were in the act of robbing a stranger in front of the Palace Hotel when recognized by the officer, and he placed them under arrest. The Smith woman has a charge of grand larceny pending against her in Judge Conlan's court.

Several weeks ago she was arrested for holding up a bucolic stranger on Stockton street and robbing him of $65. She was caught by Police Officer Fennel, after an exciting chase, and was formally charged at the City Prison. For some reason no effort has been made to prosecute the case against her.

Captain Spillane is determined to prosecute the women on the vagrancy charge, notwithstanding their boast that they have a "pull" with the Police Judges.

San Francisco newspaper clipping about women pickpockets Kittie Fitzgibbon and Dene Smith. *San Francisco Call*, December 31, 1898.

Pete "Kid" Herman, bantamweight boxer, active 1899 – 1913.

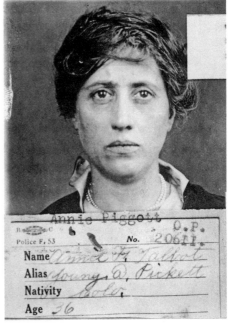

Annie Piggot, a.k.a. Annie Talbot, a.k.a. Young Pickett, a.k.a. Gertie Young, the infamous San Francisco pickpocket.

A medicine pitch in Huntingdon, TN, c. 1910s. The ballyhoo performers, a ventriloquist on stage and a black-face performer leaning against a pole. The man in the "Indian Headdress" standing near the ventriloquist is the "doctor" or pitchman.

A performer ballyhooing the crowd in preparation of the pitchman's spiel, c. 1890s.

Example of a medicine show traveling wagon c. 1900.

Advertisements for patent medicine from the early 1900s.

Example of a pitchman's license. Burlington, Vermont, August 9, 1922.

Violet McNeal, publicity photo from the original release of her autobiography, c. October 1947.

Advertisement for Violet McNeal book signing appearance.
Seattle Daily Times, October 14, 1947.

'Oriental Princess' Hunts for Golden Lizards Here

Main St. Quest of Medicine Show Woman Brings Nostalgic Memories, but No Rarities

Down to Main St. yesterday went an "Oriental Princess"—otherwise known as Violet McNeal—in search of golden lizards, an orangutan, some flea powder, a bottle of Vital Sparks and a can of tapeworms in alcohol.

She didn't find any of them, but she did find a lot of memories—and she wasn't suffering from delirium tremens.

Violet McNeal—otherwise the "Oriental Princess"—was revisiting the scene of her greatest triumphs as America's premiere "Medicine Show Woman," triumphs which took place more than 40 years ago. All the items listed above, including the flea powder and tapeworms, figured in her hilarious achievements. Her adventures have just been divulged in a book, "Four White Horses and a Brass Band" (Doubleday,) and Mrs. McNeal is here on a visit from her Oregon home in the interests of that publication. She will part with a copy if urged.

Nostalgic Memories

Yesterday on Main St., she conjured up nostalgic memories of the time when William Desmond was the leading man at the Burbank, and gas torches cast their flickering shadows over the medicine shows on the vacant lot at Fifth and Main.

"The glamour's all gone now" she mourned. "All they ·peddle these days is alfalfa tea or some other calf food. We gave the suckers their money's worth in entertainment, even if they didn't get it in the medicine we sold 'em."

She was speaking of her career as medicine woman during which she did "mind reading" for her employer—who, incidentally, thought so much of her as a young girl that he had her drugged and hired an artist to tattoo a dragon on her left hip to match the one on his arm. Later despite the tattoo, she broke away from this admirer and set up her own medicine show business. She

PAST REVISITED — Violet McNeal has nostalgic memories of medicine show days. *Times photo*

went scientific and adopted the name "V. Pasteur" because the great Frenchman then was in the public eye. But in her early experiences she was the "Oriental Princess," selling "remedies" made of sugar pills, vaseline and wintergreen.

Vital Sparks Popular

The two most popular items in the medicine line were Vital Sparks and Tiger Fat. Vital Sparks reputedly was made from the glands of a golden lizard and was responsible for the rising birth rate in China. Tiger Fat cured anything from acute broken bones to corns. The orangutan and the flea powder were standard items in the entertainment and nostrum departments of the shows. Everybody in Los Angeles scratched for fleas in those days.

The exhibits included chameleons and a ripe mummy, but the most popular display with the yokels was the pickled tapeworms in alchohol. Only trouble was that the show had a drunken stagehand who continually drank all the alcohol off the tapeworms.

"There are just as many suckers now as ever," Mrs. McNeal believes. "But nowdays they just get their money taken away in other ways."

Mrs. McNeal is very frank about why she went into the medicine snow business.

"I was so poor in my job of copying records at the Courthouse at 50 cents a day that I couldn't afford any kind of a room but one with bedbugs," she confides. "As an 'Oriental Princess' I left the bedbugs behind."

Mrs. McNeal—or the "Oriental Princess"—parted from Main St., yesterday with a sigh.

"It's not the same," she mourned.

She didn't say whether she still wears the tattooed dragon.

News article about Violet McNeal upon release of the original edition of autobiography. *Los Angeles Times*, November 30, 1947.

Medicine-Show Suckers—
But Seattle's Different Now

Violet McNeal returned to Seattle yesterday. She came back to the city of her triumph, of a sort, 41 years ago, when she cashed in on the tag end of the Alaska Gold Rush by relieving "suckers" (her description) who attended her medicine shows of $60,000 in a year here.

When Mrs. McNeal was in Seattle then, she found "virtually a two-street town." She confined most of her activities, selling "Tiger Fat"—"an effective remedy for every ailment the flesh is heir to"—to the Skid Road.

"Beyond Pike Street was what amounted to a wilderness," Mrs. McNeal recalled. "The skid roads of all West. Coast towns were pretty much the same, but Seattle's was the skiddiest of them all.

"There were three classes of people in Seattle—the residents, the people who came to town with bank rolls, and the crooks who were after the bank rolls."

Mrs. McNeal is in Seattle this week to appear at department stores and bookstores and autograph copies of her book, "Four White Horses and a Brass Band," which just has been published.

Mrs. McNeal said she has been working ten years on the book, in which she tells her life story, assisted in the final draft by Robert Mahaffay, former Times reporter now living in Portland, Or.

Mrs. McNeal said she plans to buy an automobile and trailer and tour the country gathering material for another book, the subject of which she did not disclose. Mahaffay will be her collaborator.

VIOLET McNEAL

News article about Violet McNeal upon release of the original edition of autobiography. *Seattle Daily Times*, October 12, 1947.

→ CHAPTER EIGHT ←
"FOR MEN ONLY"

SAN FRANCISCO was well fortified in, among other things, museums of anatomy. Most of these museums were run on the same pattern. Situated on the skid road, they preyed on the fears of uneducated men to whom houses of prostitution were no novelty.

Usually the first ten feet or so of the corridor leading from the street would be lined with cages containing monkeys, snakes, and birds. Yokels always stopped to have a look at the wild life and automatically drifted on in for a quick inspection of the other displays. A sign reading "For Men Only" did nothing to decrease their interest.

The remainder of the store space was lined with glass cabinets about eighteen inches deep. These contained wax or papier-mâché replicas of portions of the male anatomy which had been attacked by venereal disease. They started with the early symptoms and progressed to the point of depicting the most dreadful ravages. Above the cases were engravings which contributed to a graphic portrayal of the various ailments. A card beneath each engraving and a wax figure added a printed explanation for the benefit of the morbidly fascinated.

The atmosphere in a museum of anatomy was always hushed. A floorman was in attendance, but he never approached the sucker until he was nearly at the end of the store. Only then would the floorman step forward and hand the yokel a card which assured him he could obtain "free consultation and advice." A famous doctor, the yokel was told, had his office right there, and it happened he was exceptionally proficient in troubles of this kind. In went the sucker to be fed a hair-raising story which relied more on honor than on medical accuracy. The sucker was generally good for whatever he could raise in the way of cash.

One of the museums of anatomy had an individual twist to the pitch. The store was lined with a lot of wax heads, and the floorman advertised himself as a phrenologist. For ballyhoo they used a strong man who tore up decks of cards and telephone books and bent horseshoes and iron bars. Then the phrenologist would get up and announce that he was going to tell members of the audience all about themselves free of charge. One yokel after the other would climb into the chair on the platform. The phrenologist would begin fumbling with the bumps on their heads, talking to them as he did so. The conversations were enough to tell him whether the yokels thought they had something wrong with them. If they did, he told them he had discovered something important which he would prefer to discuss with them privately. He would be glad to give them more information free of charge, he said, if they would come back to his office after the demonstration.

I knew there must be some kind of squeeze, but I thought the phrenologist must be kind of simple and probably was getting a dollar or so from the natives who stayed for the private conference. One day, however, a friend came to tell me he was doing right well by knocking me and my office. We were just guessing at things, the phrenologist said, while his diagnoses were scientific and accurate. I sent a shill over to get the low-down, and he went through the works like any other sucker. When he got into the back room after the demonstration, the phrenologist, sure enough, discovered he had a disease. The phrenologist explained, however, that he was not a physician. It just happened that there was a famous doctor in the building across the street. The phrenologist waved aside all offers of payment; he was only too glad to help humanity; the doctor had once cured him, and it was a small enough favor to be able to recommend others who were equally in need of treatment. A shill then escorted the sucker across the street to make sure he didn't get off the hook. Meanwhile the phrenologist telephoned the doctor to tip him off on the sucker's fancied ailment.

My man let himself be led as far as the doctor's door and then broke away with the excuse that he had to go after his money. When I got the report

I didn't even wait to put a hat on but headed straight for the doctor's office. I barged right in with fire in my eyes. The doctor was far from pleased, as he knew me by sight. He had a gaunt face, and the hollows of his eyes were so deep that his eyes looked as if they had been set in the bottoms of coffee cups.

"Look," I said. "I don't like you and I don't like museums. Quit knocking me or I'll put you out of business."

He placed the tips of his fingers together the way a preacher does and said, "Go to hell. A museum is legal. It pays for a license. Just what do you intend to do about it?"

"I intend to put you and your skull-fondling friend out of town," I said.

"Try it."

"I will. When your shill drags a native across that street you're skipping the law. That's steering, and the three of you are a party to it. Steering is good for a stretch in the bucket; you know it as well as I do."

"I didn't say we couldn't talk it over," he said. "Stop shouting and sit down."

The phrenologist and the doctor, of course, split fees. It was quite a setup, as there seemed to be no connection between them. After our little talk I had no more trouble with them. Museums of anatomy were a good racket while they lasted, but they were made unlawful many years ago. Too many men fainted or had heart attacks while adding to their medical education.

We had too much of a bank roll during those first months in San Francisco to spend any more time than we had to trimming chumps.

Our chief diversion in the evening was hiring a Pope-Toledo[20] or a Winton[21]. There was more noise than speed to them, and the price was five dollars an hour. A favorite night spot was Mike Shean's, whose saloon, restaurant, and dance hall was a gathering place for pitchmen, race-horse people, gamblers,

---

20 The Pope-Toledo was one of the makes of the Pope Motor Car Company founded by Colonel A.A. Pope, and was a manufacturer of Brass Era automobiles in Toledo, Ohio between 1903 and 1909. The Pope-Toledo was the most expensive of the Pope range.

21 The Winton Motor Carriage Company was a pioneer United States automobile manufacturer based in Cleveland, Ohio. Winton was one of the first American motor car companies.

con men and women, madames, jewel thieves, and prize fighters. The elite of the city visited Mike's on the theory that they were going slumming. Beside the piano was a large horn which served as a receptacle for contributions from the customers. The money, gold or silver for the most part, made comedy noises going down the gullet of the horn, striking drums and ringing gongs. Special requests demanded a tip of from two to five dollars. A specialty singer would go among the tables and ad lib verses about any famous people who happened to be there. At our table the singer would stop to mention "Tiger Fat Davies," "with a box of Vital Sparks in his pocket," and warn the customers to guard their thinking, as "Diamond Vi" could read their minds. This, of course, always meant a minimum of five dollars for the horn.

Along about twelve or one o'clock the hopheads would leave to get back to their favorite hop joint to smoke. We usually smoked until three or four o'clock in the morning. Most of us had our forenoon smoke in our rooms; the night smoke was more of a social event, like a cocktail party.

Sundays, if the weather was favorable, we always went to the beach. The first entertainment started at the end of the streetcar line, in front of Sutra Gardens. People leaving the cars immediately encountered a pockmarked man with a handlebar mustache who pitched with a cage full of canaries. "Come over and see the little canaries perform," he used to yell. Only two of the canaries actually worked, although he had several in the cage. He talked to one of them and had it trained to sing what sounded faintly like "The Star-Spangled Banner." In the cage was a miniature cannon with a string tied to the trigger. One of the canaries got in front of the cannon; the other pulled the string; there was a small click, and the canary in front fell over as if shot. After this demonstration the pockmarked man took off his derby and announced he was taking up a collection to buy birdseed for his little canaries. Those who neglected to contribute five or ten cents were given an unrestrained tongue-lashing. It was a horrible thing to hear. He called a spade a spade. We always contributed lavishly for the privilege of watching the nickel-savers hurry out of range with crimson faces.

There were more canary pitchmen working the beach. One of them had an out-and-out clip joint. A woman named Lottie ran it. She had trained her canaries to pick out with their beaks certain cards bearing numbers ranging from one to ten. Her hoarse voice rolled out over the sand, urging the natives to draw near and watch the little birds pick out the number of their choice. She bet anything from one to ten dollars the canary could pick out any number the chump selected. She worked with a shill who led the parade, invariably losing. Lottie shook her head dolefully. "I guess my babies aren't feeling well today," she announced, "but I'll give them another chance. They're sick, poor dears. Who wants to outguess the sick canaries? Who's next?" Some yokel would step up and offer a two-dollar bet. Lottie was an expert with a scornful look. "Don't be a piker, my friend. You know my birdie isn't feeling right. I'll bet you five dollars and take my chance." The canary, trained to select the individual cards in response to certain commands, took the chump's money like a shot.

Gypsy fortunetellers had a field day on the beach. The yokels got about as much as they ever got from the inside of a crystal ball, although at intervals one of them got a little more. We were strolling on the beach one afternoon when a yokel bolted out of a fortuneteller's tent, yelling that he had been robbed. Raw egg mixed with eggshell was dripping from his face. He had gone in to have his fortune told, he explained, and the gypsy had asked if he wanted to have the money in his pocket doubled. He had replied in an enthusiastic affirmative. The gypsy had instructed him to place the money in her hand and close his eyes while she invoked the increase with a short incantation. He observed the egg she was holding but assumed it was to play some mysterious part in the ritual. In a way, it was. As soon as his lids were tightly shut she smacked him between the eyes with it. While he was clawing at the sticky mess she departed under the rear wall of the tent and was seen no more.

Just before Christmas we met The Great Ferdon again, He had switched his pitch and wasn't a "Quaker" doctor anymore. He had a big Negro show and traveled in special railroad cars with his name lettered on the sides. Jim Ferdon, one of the best medicine men who ever lived, was also uncommonly close with a dollar. Will and I went over to visit him in the tent where he was lecturing. He was lounging on the platform where the show was to be given, and we pulled up chairs and began to cut up a few jack pots. This was a term to describe a favorite occupation of the medicine bunch—seeing who could tell the biggest lie about a night's pitch or a season's take.

Ferdon was to close his show the following night, and he had advertised as a publicity stunt that he was going to give away baskets of food to the poor. Piled on the stage were dozens of baskets; each one bulged with a long loaf of French bread, a bunch of celery, carrots, and some cranberries. It made a noble-looking sight, and of course the yokels expected a chicken or duck to be tucked under all this shrubbery. If they had known Jim Ferdon better they would have expected nothing but more shrubbery, which was what they got. Even Jim's performers collected nothing but trouble when they went to him about money matters. For example, while we were chatting one of Ferdon's Negro performers stepped up. "Excuse me, Mr. Ferdon," he said in a very humble voice. "Mr. Ferdon, tomorrow is Christmas, and could I get twenty-five dollars of my back wages?"

"What?" boomed Ferdon in his most benevolent tone. "I'm surprised at you. Don't you get your food and a place to sleep in the car? I can't let you have any money now."

"Please, Mr. Ferdon, can't I have ten dollars? I'm ffidn' to buy a Christmas present for my gal."

Ferdon shook his head sadly. "Now you know what you would do with that money if I gave it to you. You'd get into a crap game and lose it all."

The performer stood for a while, scratching his head and debating this. Finally he said, "Please, Mr. Ferdon, can I have one of the poor boxes?"

"Certainly not," said Ferdon instantly. "They're for poor people."

So far as Will and I were concerned, we had money to spend and we spent it. We used to start our evenings at the Bank Exchange, located in the wholesale district back of the Hall of Justice, which was famous for its Pisco Punches. The walls were lined with signs reading, "Three Pisco Punches are the limit for each patron," or "Do not ask for more than three Pisco Punches." That was their story, and they stuck to it. I always drank my three and sat around waiting for something to happen to me or the other customers. Nothing ever did. We always had to go somewhere else for a cocktail. That somewhere was usually the Barbary Coast. We started with Spider Kelly's, moved on to Red Kelly's, and then the Thalia. We always saved Purcell's for the last. Purcell was a Negro, big in stature and big politically. The moment you opened the door of Purcell's a primeval atmosphere of suppressed violence took hold of you. The only time I had ever felt the same was just before a cyclone in the Middle West. With the prickling quality that was singularly Purcell's pouring out at me, I felt as I had then—tense, anxiously watching, every nerve on the verge of screaming. The sensation of fierce excitement never left me.

The dances put on by the performers were unrestrained and uncivilized—routines that belonged in a jungle clearing, danced in the moonlight to the beating of drums. The drums hipped up excitement into a froth. There was a flimsy partition dividing the dance floor and the bar. While we were sipping our drinks at a table one night a mulatto couple came out on the floor and began an extremely suggestive dance. Before they had danced more than a minute or two there were three ripping explosions. I didn't see the gun or the man who had shot, but across the room was a haze peculiarly unlike tobacco smoke. Quiet for an instant; then the rumbling rush of a stampede to escape. The door was too small; the crowd surged toward the saloon. Down went the partition. The crowd noise broke up into individual screams, shouts, oaths. No more shots came. We stopped, looking foolish. When we got back, the male dancer was lying face down on the floor. His partner was kneeling beside him, gently shaking him and moaning in a low voice. Two of Purcell's bouncers were carrying a third man; one had his hands, the other his feet. A bartender with his apron stuffed under his belt walked behind them, kicking the man savagely in the head and jaw.

A woman with a silver comb in her hair went over to the girl kneeling beside the dancer. She pulled up his shirt, baring his back. The small hole opposite his heart was blacker than his body. She pulled down his shirt. "Let him rest, honey, let him rest," she said to the girl. "He's dead."

Somebody standing near me asked, "What's this all about?" The man next to him pointed to the man they were carrying out. "He's her brother. He's been showing up every night, trying to get her to quit dancing and come home."

It was only a matter of minutes before the orchestra was playing again. Memory of the murder was dimmed by the thunder of the drums.

It cost money to go to Purcell's but nothing to go to the skid road, where we made ours. The heart of the skid road was at Third and Howard. Years later I pitched on Third and Natoma. Across Natoma from my stand was a vacant lot where habitués of the skid road spent their nights around a fire, drinking denatured alcohol. This beverage was known as dehorn[22] and came in bottles marked with a skull and crossbones and the word "Poison." Also consumed was Jamaica ginger and canned heat[23], which could be melted and drunk. On many a foggy morning a man who lay curled up beside the ashes of the fire would be found to be dead.

For all their roughness, I liked pitching on a skid road best. And there was more to skid road manhood than dehorn drunk and Museum of Anatomy chumps. One night after I had made a good sale I happened to be feeling cheerful and for the fun of it began to recite verses from the *Rubaiyat*. When I finished the audience shouted for more. I was hooked. From then on I had to recite some poetry after each pitch.

When it came to appearance and modesty, the men of the skid roads were my sternest critics. For a long time I had worn my hair done up in a French knot. In the early twenties, when women began having their hair bobbed, I went up to Stockton to pitch over the week end and got a boyish bob. Back in San Francisco Monday night, I could feel the disapproval of the skid road boiling up at me. Several men stayed for a private word with me after the pitch. It was immodest, they said, for a woman to have her hair cut short. They hadn't believed I was that kind of woman, and I would be well advised to let it grow out again.

---

22   Wobbly slang for denatured alcohol or homemade distilled spirits.

23   Sterno ("canned heat") is a fuel made from denatured and jellied alcohol. It is designed to be burned directly from its can.

There are many instances of people drinking Sterno to become intoxicated. Since the alcohol it contains is denatured, Sterno is poisonous. Bluesman Tommy Johnson alludes to the practice in his song "Canned Heat Blues" recorded in 1928. The practice is said to have become popular during Prohibition and during the Great Depression in hobo camps, or "jungles," when the Sterno would be squeezed through cheesecloth or a sock and the resulting liquid mixed with fruit juice to make "jungle juice," "sock wine," or "squeeze."

San Francisco's skid road, like Seattle's, had an individual array of queer characters. I had to split time there with the Peniel Mission[24] people and a religious pamphleteer. "Splitting" time meant simply that we arranged beforehand to take turns so we wouldn't all be talking at once. The Peniel Mission representatives were more than friendly. Every night one of them would step up as I got off the stand and say, "Good evening, sister. We covet your voice for the Lord." The other party was pretty much of an individualist. Distinguished by long hair and a beard, he went bareheaded and barefooted winter and summer. Over his suit he wore a long robe. He had once been a lawyer, but I could never decide whether he was wacky or smart. He was backing a religion of his own which mingled spiritualism with three or four more or less obscure forms of worship. He held his audiences with accounts of trips to graveyards, where spirits appeared to him. When asked to describe these encounters in a little more detail, be always replied that the spirits "came quick and went fast." Most people, he confessed, couldn't understand what he was talking about, so he had decided to write a booklet. This project was hampered by his lack of money, and he carried the matter to the Lord with a directness which brought results. "Lord," he said (according to his pitch), "I want to write a booklet explaining what I am talking about, but I can't pay for it. What shall I do, Lord?" And the Lord answered at once, "Let the people pay for it." Acting on this divine instruction, he offered his pamphlets for sale at the modest price of fifty cents a copy.

We all used animals a good deal for ballyhoo, and it was only to be expected that their performance at times would take unexpected turns. While in San Francisco we went down to Chinatown and obtained some dried liz-

---

24   The Peniel Missionary Society was an interdenominational holiness missionary organization that was started in Los Angeles, California in 1895 by Theodore Pollock Ferguson (1853–1920) and Manie Payne Ferguson (1850–1932). The objective of the organization was: "Mission work, as God shall lead, and as means shall be provided." The Mission operated on the faith mission model, with workers unsalaried, and guaranteed no financial support. It was merged with the World Gospel Mission in 1957.

ards. These were extended on small strips of bamboo and made an intriguing display. We also obtained a lot of dried herbs in their natural state, and what we called blood balls. These latter were round masses of slightly moist herbs encased in white wax. Some of the balls bore Chinese lettering in red and some in gold. They were intended for office use, but audiences like to look at things, and, like the dried lizards and herbs, they helped arouse the curiosity of the natives. I had trained a monkey to hand out the office cards which carried the office address and the offer of "free consultation and advice." The monkey's unusual emotional warmth led me to name her Sappho. During my pitch Sappho sat on the edge of the stand which held our various exhibits.

One night I had picked up one of the blood balls and was extolling its virtues, describing the ailments for which it was beneficial. The Chinese take a whole one at a time, for whatever they take them for. We got ten dollars for the balls lettered in red and twenty-five for the balls lettered in gold. I cracked the wax on the ball I was holding and began to explain that the ball had to be cut into sixteen pieces, one of which was to be taken each night at bedtime. So powerful were the ingredients, I asserted, that it would be highly dangerous to take more than one small portion each day. I had made this point with a good deal of emphasis when the audience suddenly began to laugh. I was forgotten, and their attention was riveted on the exhibits. Sappho was happily cracking the wax on the remainder of the blood balls and devouring them whole.

I called that pitch off. The only way I could get off the stand without being hooted off was to announce that Sappho would be at death's door in a matter of minutes and it was imperative that she be got to the office at once for medical attention.

Gila monsters were always good ballyhoo. After my performer or performers had attracted a crowd I couldn't just leap to my feet and go into a serious physic spiel. So to ease the crowd's mind into more serious channels I would take an eighteen-inch Gila monster out of a grip and hold it up.

"Gentlemen," I said, "this is a Gila monster. Notice how beautiful he is. His body looks as if it were covered with beads. In fact, the Indians use the patterns on his body in their beadwork. Notice the beautiful orange and black colors. This is a poisonous reptile. He has no fangs, but I am going to show you his teeth."

I would start to pry open his mouth. This was the critical point. While the performers were ballyhooing, the natives stood back a little distance. You couldn't sell physic to a crowd that was scattered; you had to have them with their noses fairly touching the platform. If you had said, "Step up so you can hear what I have to say," they would have been gone like scared jackrabbits. To get them in you had to entice them with something to look at. Then they surged in like a bunch of sheep. I had Gus, as I called him, expose his teeth. Then I went on to say that the Gila monster was not only a beautiful reptile but a very useful one, as scientists were using its venom for nerve disorders. From there it was only a short step into my pitch. I held the Gila monster where they could see it until I had gained their attention. With the pitch in full swing, I casually dropped Gus back into the grip.

Gus eventually died, leaving me in a hole for ballyhoo. It took about ten days to get a replacement from Texas. When we ordered we specified the size and the color—either light or dark. As all Gila monsters look pretty much alike, the audience never knew there had been a change and consequently didn't learn they were easy to acquire.

I kept the dead Gus well wrapped up in a saloon's icebox when I wasn't pitching so he would keep. I told the saloonkeeper the package contained meat. I handled him with a pair of kid gloves and told the audiences he was hibernating and would come to life in a couple of weeks.

My new Gila monster performed about as unreliably. After my pitch one night a man came up to the office and told me he had a friend, a lawyer, who was on the verge of having the d.t.'s. The lawyer had to try a case the following morning, and he had to be put in shape to make an appearance in court. I said I would try.

The lawyer came to my apartment in a pretty jittery condition, so I gave him a dose of bromides. My apartment adjoined the office, and I had him go into my bedroom, take off his coat and vest, and lie down on the bed. I went back into the office, leaving the door partly open so I could see into the room. Presently I heard a shriek. Out of bed came the drunk, and from behind some curtains came the Gila monster. I had forgotten that I always let him run loose in the apartment during the day. The lawyer went past me with his eyes looking like billiard balls. I took out after him, screaming that the Gila monster was real and not a vision conjured up by my medicine. The best sprinter in the world couldn't have caught him that day. A few hours later his friend came back after his coat and vest. That was one of the few cases in which I made no attempt to collect a fee.

Another ballyhoo of mine, which was even better than the Gila monster, involved a three-foot alligator. Where it came from I don't know. A stranger offered to sell it to me one night after my pitch, and I bought it. He showed me the trick of laying an alligator straight out on its back so it couldn't move or roll over. When an alligator is in this condition it requires only the slightest nudge to permit it to get enough traction to flop over on its belly.

In my ballyhoo I would call: "Come and watch me hypnotize the alligator!" When the crowd got in close I put the alligator on its back and let him lie motionless for a few minutes. "Now," I said, "I am going to bring him out of his trance." I talked to the alligator, telling him to awake. I stroked him gently, urging him to turn over. It was easy, while I stroked him, to give him the nudge that did the business.

I used to let the reptile stroll around at night in the offices. One night I neglected to close the window at the bottom, and the next morning there was no alligator. He had, however, made page one of the morning paper. A policeman who still doubted the entire incident had encountered him while walking a late beat. Although his impulse was to race off into the next county, the policeman stood still. The alligator advanced slowly toward him up the middle of the street. It did not seem possible, the bluecoat told reporters, but a man could not deny his own senses. After a period of consideration he placed enough reliance in them to capture the alligator and take it to headquarters. Disposition of their long-jawed quarry was a problem for the police. Eventually they found a place for it in a hotel window, where I tracked it down. Somewhere along the line of its adventurous travels, unfortunately, it had suffered injuries of which it died soon after.

Whether it was monkeys, Gila monsters, alligators, or something else, pitching was never dull. One night as I started my pitch a man in the audience began to talk right along with me in a foreign language. I tried to shut him up in a ladylike manner. No dice. I was furious but didn't dare let on. We had a nip-and-tuck race for the crowd's attention right through to the end of the pitch. I announced I was ready to sell. Beaming encouragement, the yokel who had been talking stepped up to the stand and picked up a handful of the medicine containers.

"What are you doing there?" I demanded wrathfully.

"I sell," he explained in broken English.

He had been interpreting my pitch to his fellow countrymen. He sold as much medicine as I did that night.

We had an established technique for getting rid of drunks who interrupted the pitch or simply mumbled annoyingly. Provided, that is, they weren't too large. One of the performers would get directly in front of the drunk and come down hard with his heel on the drunk's toes. The chump would automatically step back a few paces. The performer would then turn courteously to him and say, "Excuse me." A moment later he would again be grinding down on the drunk's toes and turning to beg the chump's pardon. By the time this happened two or three times the drunk would be edged to the outskirts of the crowd. The performer would then take him by the arm, suggesting apologetically that, to show there were no hard feelings because of his clumsiness, they go off and have a drink together. Off they would go, arm in arm, the performer steering a confusing course around a couple of corners to a saloon, where he would buy a drink and leave the drunk to find his way back if he could.

We also developed stock answers for the interruptions which were most likely to occur. They weren't very sparkling, but they served to turn the laugh on the talkative chump and shut him up.

Some smart aleck would pipe up, for example, with "We know all about our bodies," as I started my pitch. "Oh no, you don't," I would reply. "You don't know any more about your bodies than so many children. And to prove it, I'll give you an illustration. A schoolteacher once told her class she was going to find out how much they knew about their bodies. 'Johnny,' she asked, 'where is your heart?' Johnny put his finger over his heart. 'Here, Teacher,' he said. 'Right,' the teacher declared. 'Charley, where is your spine?' Charley indicated his back and said, 'It runs up the middle of my back.' 'Right,' the teacher said. 'Herbert, where are your bowels?' Herbert thought a moment and answered, 'I don't know. They move every day.'"

Occasionally a sucker would speak up and say belligerently, "Men doctors know more than women doctors. You can always tell a real doctor because he has a Vandyke beard and a mustache." The answer to that was, "Brother, if a long beard was the criterion of a good doctor, we could educate billy goats, and they would be smart doctors." Another laugh, and a crisis passed. I always tried to avoid talking about doctors, or knocking them, as they sometimes got hostile.

I had two rigid rules for my pitchmen and myself. The first was never to bawl out an audience. Some pitchmen did this if they failed to make a good sale. I told my men if they missed fire it was their fault; if they had put up the right arguments and the sucker had the money, he would buy. Second, a pitchman should never lose his temper in front of an audience. The thing to do was kid a heckler and get the audience laughing at him. If the audience got to laughing at the pitchman he was lost; he might as well pack up and go back to the office until time for the next pitch. I broke these rules only twice, and I broke them with a vengeance.

The first time I was building up to my pitch by telling the crowd what women of history had accomplished. A drunk down near the front kept interjecting, "Women don't know much," or, "Women haven't done so much." I was standing on the back seat of a hack, and the hack doors were open. I really got mad. He was spoiling my pitch. I said, "I'm going to show you what one woman can do," and jumped out the hack door. I leaped right on his chest, and we both went down in the gutter, with me on top. I grabbed him by the ears and pounded the back of his head on the cement pavement. They pulled me off or I guess I would have beaten his brains out, if he had any.

The second time I was well into my lecture when a maudlin drunk wandered into the audience. The chief of police was one of my listeners. The drunk began a loud mumbling. I tried to quiet him in a polite way. He simply wouldn't shut up. I asked the chief to take him away, but the chief refused. The audience was beginning to titter, and I got so furious I picked up a tin box full of powdered herbs and threw it at the drunk's head. Thank God it missed and broke against the building wall behind him, as it might have cut him severely or blinded him. I must have looked like a plain she-devil to the chief when I whirled on him. "Get hold of that drunk and get him out of here!" I said. "If you don't, I'll prefer charges against you in the morning. Your city issued me a license to lecture on this corner. I paid for it and I'm entitled to protection." By the time I had finished the chief was hustling the drunk off. Still boiling, I gave it to the crowd next.

"I'm now going to have the luxury of telling you what I think," I said. "I think you're the most ignorant swine I've ever had before me. You're the kind who would run a mile to see a dogfight or a drunken brawl."

There wasn't a peep out of that crowd. They just stood like rocks and gaped at me.

"You're the kind," I went on, "that laughed and taunted Jesus on the cross. You're the kind that put the Frenchman in a madhouse for discovering photography. You're the kind that said anyone believing ships could be run by steam was crazy. Because of people like you, anyone who makes a scientific discovery is met with ridicule and hostility. You'd rather stand in a bar guzzling beer than learn anything about your bodies." I snapped open the grip. "Here's my medicine. Come up and buy it if you want to. Personally, I don't care."

They surged up and bought lavishly.

Most pitchmen used gimmicks of one kind or another. The theory behind them was the old saw, "Seeing is believing."

When I was lecturing on catarrh, my gimmick equipment consisted of a glass graduate, a glass drinking tube, some vinegar in a tiny vial, and a bottle of limewater. To the uneducated eye the pitch appeared scientific and convincing.

I lifted the bottle of limewater and said, "This is water. I am going to take a swallow of it to prove it is plain water and nothing else." After the swallow—which, of course, proved nothing except that a drink of the fluid was not instantly fatal—I poured some of the limewater into the graduate and put the drinking tube in it. "Now," I said, "I want someone in the audience who desires to find out if he has catarrh to step forward." There was always a native who had catarrh or thought he had. It didn't matter which. "Take this graduate," I instructed the volunteer, "and blow through the tube into the water. If you have catarrh the water will turn a milky color." The brave native bubbled the water briskly, and, as limewater always will, it turned milky. "This man has catarrh, as you can see for yourselves," I told the audience. "He may not have known it before, but he knows it now. I am now going to show you, simply and clearly, so all of you can understand, how a purified concentrate of V. Pasteur's Herbs will sweep catarrh from your body." Most medicine men used acetic acid to clear the lime-water, but I used vinegar because I was afraid some chump would want me to take a taste from the little vial to prove it was harmless. I held up the graduate into which the yokel had blown, letting everyone get a good look at the milky color. "Observe the reaction," I said, "when even a tiny amount of the herb concentrate is introduced into the graduate." I poured in a few drops of the vinegar; the smoky limewater turned clear. "You see, gentlemen, what happens to catarrh when you take the right herbs?"

We used approximately the same gimmick in selling herbs to clear up the bile. As in the case of tapeworms, the stockyards were our source of bile, and a horrid, yellowish fluid it was, too. We made a reasonable substitute with tincture of iron chloride and salicylic acid.

We displayed the real bile first, putting it casually out of sight on a shelf beneath the exhibit stand as we worked into the pitch. Next we put on view the good old clearer, the "herb concentrate," which in this case was citric acid. Then we brought out the bile bottle again, but this time it wasn't the real bile but the gimmick bottle, which turned clear when poured into a graduate containing a few drops of the citric acid.

→ CHAPTER NINE ←
THE
TATTOOED
DRAGON

NO MATTER HOW WELL a pitchman was doing in a town, his natural restlessness made it pall after a time. San Francisco was glamorous, but spring was coming, and other fields beckoned. The lure of the mining country had been growing on us. We didn't mind exchanging San Francisco's night spots for desert, sagebrush, and crudity. Will, Charley Tryon, and I headed for Goldfield[25].

Will and Charley rented a tiny cabin, a primitive affair without running water. I went to the Casey Hotel to see if I could pluck a few live ones. The hotel was full, but a mining engineer gave up his room to me. In those days, especially in boom towns, chivalry was rampant, and men would sleep on the floor in the hall to give a lady their room.

The dining room at the Casey was jammed with millionaires as well as mining engineers in wool shirts and high-topped boots. One of the most col-

---

25   Goldfield is an unincorporated community in Esmeralda County, Nevada. Goldfield is located 247 miles southeast of Carson City, along U.S. Route 95.

Goldfield was a boom town in the first decade of the 20th century due to the discovery of gold—between 1903 and 1940 Goldfield's mines produced more than $86 million at then-current prices. Much of the town was destroyed by a fire in 1923, although several buildings survived and remain today, notably the Goldfield Hotel, the Consolidated Mines Building (the communications center of the town until 1963), and the schoolhouse. Gold exploration continues in and around the town today.

orful of the big operators was George Wingfield[26], who used to take a handful of twenty-dollar gold pieces out of his pocket, stack them in front of him, and aimlessly and ceaselessly shuffle them back and forth as some men do poker chips.

The first night I came down to dinner dressed in a white embroidered wool dress with white hose and slippers and long kid gloves. My hat was white lace faced with pink rosebuds and was turned back a little from my face. A knot of pink chiffon, with long streamers, fastened under one ear. Mrs. Casey seated me and went from table to table, speaking to all the patrons. In about twenty minutes she came back and sat down at my table and started to talk.

She said it would be so nice, since I was a stranger in Goldfield, if I could meet some of the leading citizens and that she would vouch for anyone she introduced to me. I graciously assented. It was right up my alley. All the big shots were to be presented to me without my making a move. She introduced two or three men to me that night, and before long I was being wined and dined.

At night I sneaked down to the cabin to tell Will whom I had met and what they had said. He never failed to amaze me. He listened carefully. He had a queer habit when he was concentrating. He lay beside the opium tray with the lamp burning. He had a tiny pair of tweezers, and he pulled the hairs out of his beard and passed them over the flame in the lamp and smelled the odor of each separate hair. As he shaved every day or so, they were short. Then he would begin to talk and tell me what the men I met probably would say or ask me the next day, and tell me in a general way what answers to give. He was so right in his guesses it was uncanny.

In Goldfield I disobeyed Will's orders about drinking with a prospective victim. The reason was that I didn't have to make a move to get anything out of the men. They gave me money, jewelry, or large blocks of stock in their mines just for knocking around with them.

Some of the stock was not valuable at the time, but Will cashed it in for thousands of dollars afterward. Another reason I let off steam was that the

---

26   George Wingfield (August 16, 1876 – December 24, 1959) was a Nevada banker and miner. He was considered to be one of the state's most powerful economic and political figures during the period from 1909 to 1932. Wingfield rose from faro-dealer to the position of richest man in Nevada in less than five years.

town was so exciting it made a person feel reckless. Goldfield was the champagne town of the era. After dinner we usually went for a drive around town. We always toured the red-light district. There was a mile-long row of cribs occupied by prostitutes of every race and color. The women sat just inside the open doors. Some wore short dresses, like school girls, with their hair hanging in curls or braids and tied with ribbons. Others wore evening dress. They didn't care much for the female sight-seers and more often than not took the opportunity to give them a foul tongue-lashing. Near the cribs were the higher-class places with drawn curtains.

During the drive we stopped off at one or more Box Houses. These were saloons with a dance floor and a small stage. The Box House women did a turn, singing or playing an instrument on the stage, and then danced and drank with the customers on a percentage. Most of these women were decent; some were married and had children. Their favorite stunt was to start a man out on champagne and then, when he got drunk, keep on charging him for champagne while they served him cheap wine. A clever Box House woman could make as much as one hundred dollars a night. The roughnecks who had struck it rich were fed up on the red-light district and would be more than generous to a ladylike person. Going to one of these places with a man didn't diminish his admiration for you, but you lost his respect if you smoked or told a smutty story.

When the men at the Casey Hotel got wise that the evening stopped at the door, and I had got all I could out of them, I moved down to the cabin with Will and Charley Tryon. We went to selling medicine, and after I did my mind-reading act I answered the two questions burning in every man's mind: what was his lucky day to dig for gold, and in what direction should he go to dig? Charging five dollars for the information, I tossed in a horoscope for good measure. I was doing a land-office business.

Will took me down to Tex Rickard's[27] place, the Northern, to gamble. It

---

27   George Lewis "Tex" Rickard (January 2, 1870 – January 6, 1929) was an American boxing promoter, founder of the New York Rangers of the National Hockey League, and builder of the third incarnation of Madison Square Garden in New York City. During the 1920s, Tex Rickard was the leading promoter of the day, and he has been compared to P.T. Barnum and Don King. Rickard also operated several saloons, hotels, and casinos, all named Northern and located in Alaska, Nevada, and Canada.

was big and peppered with housemen. Floormen roamed among the tables with short guns on their hips or in shoulder holsters. On each side of the room were lookouts perched on elevated platforms; they wore revolvers and sat with sawed-off shotguns across their knees. By some queer coincidence most of them had handle-bar mustaches. Every twenty minutes or so a bartender came around to the tables to take orders for drinks on the house.

One night at the faro table I ran twenty dollars up to eighteen hundred. I had heard about breaking the bank at Monte Carlo, and I thought it was my night. I sent for the manager, who made an exception and removed the limit for me. They also removed my bank roll in short order.

A little to my surprise I found that Will had been gambling every night after I had smoked at the cabin and had gone back to the Casey Hotel. A week or two later Will asked for the manager and said, "Vi, give me that diamond ring," indicating the biggest one I had. He asked the manager what he could borrow on it and got a third of its value.

He kept on playing, and when we got home about dawn Will told me we were broke. I couldn't believe it. We had made a small fortune in San Francisco and had had most of it when we hit Goldfield. I had made money at the Casey on the live ones, and we had been selling medicine every day. I pleaded with Will not to gamble anymore, but I might as well have argued with a stone. Night after night we went back to the Northern, and my diamonds were stripped off one by one and the money lost. Finally all my jewelry had been pawned. Will tried to borrow money and couldn't. There was nothing left but to get out.

Charley Tryon had fifty dollars sewed inside his waistband. Everyone carried money planted in their clothes. They called it "fall" money; it was hidden so it wouldn't be found if they were arrested and searched. With the fifty, and a little more we got by pawning two ballyhoo guitars and my seal-skin coat, we got away from Goldfield and as far as Reno.

Reno meant hard work. We ran into a magician who was out of a job, and Will hired him to teach me some tricks. I lectured at night and worked in the hotel room with the magician most of the day. He taught me three tricks.

One was to make a silver dollar walk off a man's hand without my touching it. The second was to make a card selected by one of the yokels walk out of the deck and come to me without my touching it. I wore a tailored dress to do these tricks. I had to have buttons as low as my waist. As the tricks were done at night on the street by the light of a gasoline torch, they were impossible to detect. Before going out to pitch I pulled a long hair from my head. To each end of the hair I attached a tiny piece of shoemaker's wax. One end I stuck to the back of one of the buttons at about the level of my waist; the other swung loose until I was ready to attach it to the dollar or card. While giving my talk I would pick up the bit of swinging wax under my nail and stick it swiftly to the pasteboard or the coin as I held it up to show the audience. I would stall and talk for a time and then draw in my abdomen and move back slightly. Drawn by the hair, the article would move toward me. When I picked it up to display to the audience, I turned loose the wax.

The third trick involved a small cabinet with a drawer which the magician built. My equipment consisted of some envelopes and a sponge saturated with alcohol. I let the audience pick out an envelope and examine it. Some yokel then wrote a question on a slip of paper and placed it in the envelope, which he sealed. I took the envelope from him and put it in the drawer, giving it, as I did so, a swipe with the alcohol-loaded sponge. The alcohol made the paper transparent for a moment or so, and I could read the question. I closed the drawer to let the "spirits" work. After a bit I took the envelope out and held it against my forehead—stalling, of course, to allow the smell of alcohol to dissipate. After a reasonable interval I took the hand of the person who had written the question, and we would both concentrate. Then I stated the question and answered it. I had to hand around the envelope to prove it hadn't been opened or tampered with. To the bewildered natives this was black magic with a vengeance.

Little by little we were getting a bank roll together again, and we headed back to Los Angeles, where we worked for the next two years. Most of the time we pitched on the corner of Fifth and Main, where the Rosslyn Hotel now stands. In those days the Beaumont Café, which resembled an old residence, stood on the back of the lot. There was an immense space in front of and on one side of this café. This space was sublet to medicine men and hawkers of all descriptions. There was even a mummy and a snake pit on it. Hawkers peddled the traditional razor-strop dressing as well as spot remover, soap, and Gummy-

Ga-Ho, the cement for gluing together broken dishes and pieces of wood. One woman was selling chameleons; each chameleon had around its neck a tiny chain to which was attached a pin. Women bought them to pin to the front of their waists. They were more of a nuisance, however, than the profit in them warranted. They ate flies, which was a disadvantage, as the dealer had to put sugar or syrup on a windowpane and spend his time waiting around to catch enough of the insects to keep their chameleons alive.

Not the least among the hawkers were the purveyors of flea powder. The flea was Public Enemy Number One in Los Angeles just after the turn of the century. If a woman darted suddenly into a doorway and discreetly lifted her skirt she was not being immodest; she was merely trying to catch a flea. Local residents were inured to them, but they used to eat up the Eastern tourists.

The lot was a strategic point, as the tourists had to walk past it as they went to the Arcade Depot at the foot of Fifth Street. Many of them passed it as well on their way to the Interurban Depot at Sixth and Main. The place was going full blast from eight o'clock in the morning until after midnight. Tourists had to be caught early. They were up and looking around by eight o'clock, and the town was so small they seldom took a streetcar. The tourists were easily distinguishable from the home guard. As a general rule they had a sack of oranges in one hand; peeling the oranges and throwing the peels on the ground, they would stand around sucking the fruit and listening to us. We got many a laugh out of those old yokel farmers from the Middle West. We were smart enough to talk them out of a few dollars, but meanwhile they walked around with an orange in one hand and a few thousand dollars pinned to their underclothes and picked up real estate buys that made them richer than any of us dreamed of being.

Will, as usual, took over the leadership of the bunch. He got together Prince Nanzetta, Arthur Hammer, Charlie Tryon, and Arizona Bill. Will paid for the location and also paid one hundred dollars for the California itinerant vendor's license. He furnished the medicine and took half of what they made and everything I made. We took turns on the stand all day and evening. We made money so fast it was no time at all before we were able to send back to Goldfield for all my jewels. I got new clothes and a new fur coat.

That lot was the most glamorous spot I've ever seen, especially at night. As darkness fell the pitchmen lit their gasoline torches. The lights would flare up and die down, casting mysterious shadows over our lovely Chinese costumes. Prince Nanzetta's dark olive skin glistened; he was wearing a new Chinese robe of deep red satin, lavishly embroidered with golden dragons and tiny mirrors. He seemed to be a shimmering Prince of Tibet in the flesh. Arizona Bill offered a contrast with his long hair and Indian-scout outfit. Will lectured only at intervals, wearing a mandarin coat and hat. His skirt was composed of panels of dark blue satin with exquisite embroidery running up each panel. He was carefully rouged to appear youthful, and his lectures about romantic, faraway lands were enthralling. Charley Tryon and Arthur Hammer lectured in frock coats and silk hats.

Of course I had the big build-up. Sometimes I would lecture garbed in full Chinese regalia, wearing pants instead of the skirt, and sometimes in evening dress. But whatever I wore, I was covered with diamonds. I had so many rings I wore one shaped like a snake on my thumb. When I lectured Will wore a tuxedo and carried an opera hat. I can still hear the click of the spring in the hat as Will collapsed it and put it under his arm and, with a deferential bow, assisted me up the steps to the stand. As he bandaged my eyes with a silken scarf an awed hush fell, and in the silence I began to tell people their names and birthdays, and identify dates and objects. Will introduced me with the most extravagant praise as a "healer of men" and a "benefactor of mankind." It was glorious to be a part of the lot's exciting pattern and to feel that you were holding an audience in the palm of your band. Even the papier-mâché mummy seemed to quiver to the voices of the barkers and the flicker of the gasoline torches.

By this time Will was again pinching the calves of my legs while I lectured. I had to stand the pain without a change of expression or without screaming, and often my legs were black and blue. Now he used the punishment to spur me to greater efforts when he thought the sales were going more slowly than they should have.

After we had been in Los Angeles some months Will bought a duplex in San Pedro. Part of the time we lived there, coming up to town on the streetcar each day, and part of the time we lived in rooms across the street from the lot. We had rented the second floor of a building there and had fixed up two of the rooms as offices. We got a case taker and hired an old doctor for twenty-five dollars a week as protection. We called him "Sugar-Foot" because he couldn't lift his feet when he walked. Two other rooms we fitted out as lounging rooms in which we could smoke opium. Our lecturers hung around there waiting their turn to pitch.

After a few months, however, I found it hard to recapture, except for brief moments, the old thrill of the medicine business. Happiness came in short bursts; most of the time I was dissatisfied and depressed. For one thing, the bunch didn't look or act the same. Some of them had begun to use morphine hypodermically and were acting queer. For another, I had discovered that the woman with whom Will had run away when he was seventeen was still in love with him. And although she was by that time fifty-five years old, Will's strange attachment for her persisted. Perhaps he loved her as much as he was capable of loving anyone, although he beat her, as he did me. Her name was Mary, and Will spoke of her as his foster mother. She was a simple, kindly creature whom he utterly dominated. She was old and hopelessly and helplessly in love with him. The discovery would have had a more profound effect on me if, because of the opium, my own married life had not virtually ceased. When I demanded an explanation of Will he told me his devotion to her was something he couldn't control. He pulled a sheet of paper from his pocket. It was a will, and he showed me that in it he had left all of the property and money we had made together to me. I didn't care much one way or the other. By this time I had an oh-what-the-hell attitude.

Up until now Will had always made me look for old men as prospects; he made the mistake of underestimating a young fellow in his thirties, good-looking and with plenty of money, who fell for me hard. I described him to Will, and Will said, "Go after him."

This young fellow fell for the old sucker game of advancing me enough money to get my diamonds out of pawn, but instead of asking for a date he asked me to marry him. I pretended to hesitate, telling him I was married but separated from my husband, adding that I didn't believe I loved him enough to marry him. He was broad-shouldered, with curly blond hair. His blue eyes were so honest and pleading that I wanted to cry when I looked into them. He said if I would just get a divorce and marry him he would be so good to me that I couldn't help learning to love him.

I told him I would think it over. I didn't mention it to Will at first, but the more I thought about it the better I liked the idea. It had never occurred to me before that there could be any other kind of life for me. The medicine business had been everything there was, and I had enjoyed it. Will had never let me talk to any of the other women or do anything unless it was done under his strict supervision. Now I began to dream of living like other people, of not being beaten or pinched, and of being married to a man who wasn't in love with someone else.

Finally I went to Will and said, "You remember you told me once that if I ever wanted to leave you we would split the bank roll and each go our way and be friends?"

He studied me for a long time, his solid jaw looking more than ever as if it had been chiseled out of stone. "That's right," he said. "Is that what you're after now?"

"Yes," I said, scared but stubborn. "I'm sick of living the way we do. I want a home like other people have."

He waited a while. "Who's the man?"

I told him. He listened thoughtfully. His eyes were so sad it nearly broke my heart to have him look at me. He wasn't angry. He began to talk softly, telling me how much he loved me and reminding me how much we had done together and how happy we had been in the past. He talked about little things, like the time after I had twisted my ankle while we were walking and he had carried me a block and a half in his arms. Each little thing he mentioned made me want to cry more than the one before, but I didn't cry. I had my mind made up, and nothing he could say was going to change it.

"That's all done," I said. "We can't bring that back now."

He shrugged his shoulders, but he did it in a hurt way. "If we can't, we can't. Have you told this man you use dope?"

"No."

"You'll have to."

"I know it. I'm going to. I can get off it any time I make up my mind to. I'm going home and get off the stuff and get my divorce at the same time."

"Very well, my dear," Will said. "That's a good plan. But I want your folks to see you in your best physical condition." He looked at me sadly for a moment or two and swallowed, as if his emotions were stronger than he wanted them to be. "I won't have another chance to show you how much I love you," he continued. "I want to do something, even if it isn't much. Your tonsils have been bothering you for some time. I'll have a doctor come to the office tomorrow and take them out."

My relief at his decision was almost more than I could stand, and his thoughtfulness almost drove me back to him. I had expected to be hit, or at least to have him go into a tirade, but he hadn't. He was kind and courteous to me during the rest of that day and that night.

The next morning the doctor came and I was given ether. When I came to I was in bed in the next room, and Will was sitting beside me. My throat wasn't sore, but the whole of one leg above the knee was paining me terribly.

Will leaned right over my face.

"You dirty, chippy slut! You thought you could leave me, did you? You damned ungrateful little tramp, you thought you could ditch me after all I've done for you!" He tore the bedcovers back. "Look at that!"

I looked; I screamed; I nearly fainted. A large Chinese dragon was tattooed on my left thigh. I closed my eyes.

"You're branded as mine as long as you live," Will said. "I'm going to have a dragon tattooed on my forearm tomorrow. We'll go to our graves marked the same."

→ CHAPTER TEN ←
"...THE FIRST MAN THAT COMES INTO THE OFFICE..."

FOR SEVERAL DAYS I could scarcely walk. I looked at the dragon for hours and wept as it got clearer. I could see where the claws were set. It looked as if great drops of blood were dripping on my leg.

One day Will caught me crying. "Have some sense," he said. "No one needs to know about this. No one will, unless you try to leave me."

I looked up at him, so choked with tears I couldn't speak.

"You may as well make up your mind to it," he said. "No man will ever marry you branded like this. People wouldn't believe the truth if you told them."

Will never again mentioned the dragon. If I did he merely said, "You made a mistake in judgment. I've settled it for all time."

The curly-haired young fellow with the blue eyes had been carved out of my life. I gave up all thought of being happily married. I started to drink a little more and to use more opium, trying to forget.

It was a month or two later that a medicine man came in off the road with wonderful news. He said his wife had got away from opium by using a new treatment developed in a New York hospital. I read over the literature he had on the subject, and it sounded good, so I told Will I wanted to take the cure. He looked at me, his hazel eyes blank, and I could feel he was trying to decide whether I would be able to do it or not. At last he said I could try it if I wanted to.

I wouldn't let him get the doctor this time. I went to the most reputable doctor I could find, told him I wanted to take this new treatment, and gave him the literature. He studied it and agreed to try. He told me quite honestly he had had very little firsthand experience with drug addiction.

As the first step in this particular cure, I was allowed to smoke all the opium I wanted. Then I went to a hotel room with a nurse and peeled down to the skin so she could make sure I had no dope planted on me. Will took away my clothes, and the nurse called the doctor.

At intervals the doctor dosed me with a combination of hyoscine and cocaine. Between these doses I took blue mass[28] and belladonna. This treatment was supposed to effect a complete cure in three days. At the end of seventy-two hours a bowel movement of a certain color was supposed to indicate that all the dope had been eliminated from the system. By the end of the second day I had broken out all over with a belladonna rash, and the blue mass had not worked. My gums turned purple. As a result of the abrupt withdrawal of the opium pain began to creep through my entire body. It mounted steadily until it became unbearable agony. Half crazed, I was no longer able to choke back the screams.

The nurse telephoned Will, who sent at once for the doctor. Very much alarmed, the doctor ordered the cure discontinued and let me have some opium. He had been on the square but knew nothing about drugs.

Will sent for my clothes and had me taken back to our rooms. My teeth got so loose they had to be wired together, and I had to take fluid foods for weeks. Will was tenderness itself, calling me his "poor brave little girl." It didn't

---

28   Blue Mass was the name of a concocted remedy for such widely varied complaints as tuberculosis, constipation, toothache, parasitic infestations, and the pains of childbirth.

It was compounded by pharmacists based on personal recipes or on one of several widespread variations. It was sold in the form of blue or gray pills, or syrup. Its name probably derives from the use of blue dye or blue chalk (used as a buffer) in some formulations.

The ingredients of blue mass varied, as each pharmacist prepared it himself, but they all included mercury in elemental or compound form. A standard recipe of the period:

33% mercury
5% licorice
25% marshmallow (the plant)
3% glycerol
34% rose honey

matter much now that he had foreseen what would happen. I was whipped. I was tattooed, and I couldn't get away from dope. The earlier experience in Winnipeg hadn't really got under my skin. In spite of it, I had believed I could quit opium any time I really wanted to. Now I knew how wrong I was. I hated Will and despised myself. I was like a little bird dog my brother had owned. When the dog disobeyed he would call and make her come to him. With her piteous eyes fixed on my brother, she would get down on her belly and crawl to him. She knew she was to be punished but didn't dare ignore his command. I felt like that every time Will spoke to me. It seemed to me I had been living an entirely different life when, only a few years before, I had knelt by the bed each night to say my prayers and thank God I had such a good husband.

By the time the wires were taken off my teeth, however, all the misery had been crowded back into my memory. It was more like a nightmare than an actual experience. I was young and I couldn't help believing in the future.

I went on lecturing because there was nothing else to do. One night after my pitch Will had gone out and I was sitting alone in the office. A man came in and asked for Will. I told him he could sit down and wait. While I went on making up a list of medicine we needed he began to whistle under his breath and ran a finger idly around and around the sweatband of his hat. I finally decided Will had gone somewhere to smoke opium and wouldn't be back. I asked if there was anything I could do.

He went on skimming his finger around the inside of his hat. "Guess not. I've got to serve some papers on him."

"What kind of papers?"

"Nothing to get excited about. His wife's suing him for divorce."

"What?" The words were as meaningless as if they had been in a foreign language.

"Suing him for divorce. Happens every day." He shrugged and clapped the hat on. I didn't say anything. I could see the words hanging there in front of me as plainly as if they had been painted on a wall.

He was turning toward the door when it opened and Will came in. The man said, "Davies?" and Will nodded and accepted the papers. The man went out and Will shut the door and swung around with his back to it.

"Am I married to you?" I screamed.

"No, you fool."

He stood there staring at me, and that burnt-umber color came into his eyes. I felt weak at first, as if my muscles had been tortured and were quivering after the pressure had been relaxed.

I said, "Why did you pretend to marry me?"

"Your crazy small-town ideas," he said. "You'd never have gone on the road with me if you hadn't thought you were married."

The weakness went away. I rushed at Will, trying to tear him with my fingernails, striking at him with my fists. "Damn you," I sobbed. "I'll kill you, I'll kill you, I'll kill you."

He caught my wrists and forced them up and back against my shoulders. He shook me savagely. "Shut up!"

I shut up. I was suddenly and desperately afraid he wouldn't marry me. I threw myself down and began to beat my forehead against the floor. I bit my forearms until they bled, to keep from screaming.

When I could talk again I said, "Will you marry me when you get your divorce?"

"Sure, if you behave yourself. I wouldn't desert you now. You couldn't make a dollar without me."

God, how I hated him. "Do all these people we're working with know we're not married?"

"Of course they do."

That thought was the worst of all. It explained, of course, why Will had never left me alone with any of the other women. My head was spinning madly with rage and hatred and a consuming fear that he might not marry me.

"Get up," Will said. He took my hand, and as I got to my knees I had a hemorrhage. A black curtain peeled down around me. The next thing I knew I was lying on the sofa and Will was chafing my wrists.

"Don't try to get up," he directed. "Just lie there." He began to read the summons, and a moment later he was cursing furiously. "Damn her, she can't get away with this. I'll fight her to the last ditch."

His wife had cut a connecting door between the two halves of the duplex

149

and was occupying the house as one dwelling, which she had asked for in the divorce petition.

Will hired a lawyer to contest the divorce, but when his wife learned of it she sent him a short note: "Don't fight the case or I'll take my marriage license into court and tell the judge everything there is to tell." Will stormed, but at last he said, "Then we'll have to play on her sympathy. She can have half the house, but not all of it. You'll have to go down and persuade her to give it up. Tell her you're sick and are going to have a baby and we have to have some place to live."

I didn't want to go, but in another way I did. I wanted to see what she was like. Will made me dress very simply and wouldn't let me wear any jewels. He explained he had married the girl before he met me and that they had been separated about a year when our fraudulent ceremony had been performed.

It was an odd thing—I could lie to a police chief and crooked mayors, but I couldn't lie to that woman. She was seven or eight years older than I was, a brunette and really stunning. Her eyebrows were very dark, and her eyes had a way of smiling even when her mouth didn't move.

"Come in, my dear," she said when I told her who I was. We sat down in the front room, and she smiled at me.

"Will sent you down, of course?"

All I could say was, "Yes."

She nodded. "You're Diamond Vi. I've seen you. I expect Will told you to put on your plainest dress and cooked up some plaintive story for you to tell me. If he didn't, he's losing his grip. You tell him he isn't going to get this house or any part of it. And if he wants trouble, I can make him more than he ever dreamed of. Now, is that understood?"

"Tell me," I burst out, "how did you get Will to marry you?"

"I wish I never had. I was a little fool who used to go every night and listen to him pitch. I hung around the edge of the crowd, adoring him. He noticed me, and because he needed someone he picked me up. I ran away from home to go with him, and he lied about my age to marry me."

She made some coffee, and we sat drinking it.

"I used to ballyhoo for him with a guitar," she said. "That is, I ballyhooed when he hadn't beaten me so I couldn't appear in public. Look here." She touched her upper lip. On it was a white scar about a quarter of an inch long. "He hit me with an opium pipe one night. I've forgotten why. He wanted something and I didn't get it fast enough."

She got up and went over to the mantel after some matches. She stood there, looking back at me over her shoulder.

"There was nothing I wouldn't do for him. There were times when we were really broke, and he used to bring home other men. Nothing cheap—it was high-class trade—but that's what it was."

She came back with the matches and lit my cigarette. She was smiling again. "That's gone and forgotten. Maybe you know how much a woman can forget when she has to go on living."

I said, "But Will—did he just let you go?"

"He didn't let me do anything. I just went. Nothing happened. Nothing big, I mean. Unless you'd call that foster mother of his something big. What's her name? Mary? I didn't hate her; I felt sorry for her. She was old when I knew her, and all she had in the world was that half devil of a man, Will, who hit her as often as he kissed her. She couldn't leave him. He was her food and drink and the blood in her veins. You've met her, I suppose?"

"Yes."

"I fought with her once. In Ogden. We tore out each other's hair on a street corner, and she wanted to kill me."

The light from the window made cool shadows in her hair. For some reason I felt like crying.

"It doesn't matter, my telling you all this now," she said. "As soon as the divorce is final I'm going to marry a man who loves me. It's different. Maybe someday you'll find that out."

After a while I got up to go. "Good-by," she said. "Tell Will I'm going to get what I want and never think of him again."

Deep down I was glad to see someone get the better of Will. It was the only time, to my knowledge, it ever happened. He didn't contest the divorce.

I went on working, ruled by the fear that he wouldn't marry me, turning hard and bitter. That fear became an obsession by day and a nightmare by night. Whenever Will became abusive I cringed. I was too wretched to realize that, whatever the cost, he wouldn't willingly release such a money-getter as I had grown to be. But while I was clever, I had only learned what he wanted me to know. I still didn't think I could make money without him.

Gladys, the telephone girl I had met in St. Paul, came to Los Angeles that winter, and she was some comfort to me during the long months of waiting for the decree to become final.

I made arrangements for a big church wedding—no petty-larceny ceremony would do—and issued invitations right and left. My triumph was going to be on as grand a scale as my deception. I had a matron of honor, a flower girl, a ring bearer, and a paid singer singing "Oh, Promise Me."

The wedding was something I had to have, but afterward I hated Will just as much as ever. On our wedding night twenty-four of us had a banquet at one of the best Los Angeles cafés. The owner came over to tell us a newspaper photographer was there to take a picture of our party. Will was so drunk he couldn't sit up straight, and they shoved him under the table. I put my feet on him to hold him down, and a guest sat by my side in my only wedding picture.

Gladys was the only one I cared to associate with. I asked Will if we couldn't take her on the road with us that season. He was glad to see me interest myself in something, so he consented.

After the wedding I refused to look for any more live ones. I ran the office and lectured. Something had happened to my appetite; I started to get thin. I had always wondered why drug addicts were unusually slim. Often, when I was sitting with them and had ordered ham and eggs for breakfast, they had been repelled to the point of getting up and leaving the table. For them a cup of coffee and some cup custard was a full meal. I found out that the hole in a doughnut was a banquet for an addict.

The three of us started working in a leisurely way through Arizona toward Colorado. I had given up any hope of quitting opium, and also, because of the tattooed dragon, of ever marrying anyone else. The opium I was taking left me without any physical desire.

Gladys, I discovered, had learned a great deal since our days in St. Paul. She wasn't brainy, but she was blunt. I had to have someone to talk to, and I told her everything about my life with Will. She laughed at the torture I had gone through to get married. Nothing was easier, she said, than picking up a man. It wasn't long before we were plotting a way in which I could make money without Will. It never even remotely entered my mind to go to work. After you have worn diamonds and expensive clothes and had a maid, a calico dress and a job haven't much appeal.

The three of us landed in Cripple Creek, Colorado, in June. I asked Will to let Gladys substitute for him in doing the alphabetical mind-reading code for my ballyhoo. He went instantly into a rage.

"Absurd," he said. "You wouldn't make a cent. It's our mind reading and my introduction that gives you prestige with the audience. If it weren't for me they'd laugh you off the stand."

But I was determined to try. A little while later I asked him if I couldn't go to Glenwood Springs for a few days. I picked Glenwood Springs because I knew he would have difficulty finding a place to smoke opium there. I told him the high altitude was bothering my heart, and he allowed Gladys and me to go alone. On the sly I had been teaching Gladys a simple code. I didn't dare take the Chinese costume I had been working in, so I packed a red Chinese kimono I wore around the room. As we packed our grips I slipped in a few labels from the office. We got to Glenwood Springs on Friday, but I was so convinced I wouldn't make any money that I didn't even invest in any medicine or pillboxes.

Scared but determined to go through with the test, I rented a hack the following night. Because we had no gasoline torch we parked it under a street light. Very much flustered, Gladys and I got out and started our mind-reading act. It wasn't as polished or as complicated as the act I put on with Will, but at least we got through it without trouble. I missed Will's lavish introduction, which always tossed me up to the audience on the crest of a wave. Lack of it left a hole which made me afraid the natives would simply turn around and wander away. They didn't. They were still there as I went into the Vital Sparks pitch, and by that time I was on familiar ground. There was no faltering or uncertainty about the way I gave the pitch that night. I warmed to it, and by the time I got through I was darn near believing it myself. I told the crowd to come to the hotel for the medicine.

The yokels swarmed in after us. I collected their money in the parlor and in the hall and told them to wait a few minutes for the medicine.

We had to work fast. I sent Gladys to the drugstore to buy pillboxes and ten cents worth of powdered aloes and to a candy store for some black buckshot candy. She ran both ways and came back panting. While she pasted labels on the boxes, I put the candy in a small top bureau drawer, sprinkled the aloes on it, and began shaking as fast as I could.

When I went out to deliver the pills I found we had sold more medicine than we had labels. I explained that the ingredients were rare and that we would be back in town later, and returned their money to those I couldn't supply. We could hardly wait to get rid of them. The money we'd missed didn't matter. We danced around the room and laughed and congratulated each other on our triumph. I had beaten Will at his own game.

We went back to Cripple Creek on Monday, never saying a word about what we had done. I wasn't ready yet to cash in on what I had found out. The idea that I could work on my own and make money was too new. I couldn't get used to it. I just let the knowledge lie in my mind, and each time I thought about it my confidence got stronger.

We worked around Colorado for a few weeks before heading west to Portland, Oregon. I made a fix which permitted us to work on a corner near the Labor Temple, and we rented offices in a hotel at Third and Salmon. We hadn't been working long when I caught a cold which developed into pneumonia. Will let me off for a few days, until I was on my feet again, but I was still hoarse and coughed and spit blood.

One night he came back to our rooms and said, "Get ready to go out and go to work."

"I can't, Will," I croaked. "I can hardly speak."

"All right," he said. "You do the mind reading and then slip away and come home. I'll deliver the lecture."

I finally agreed to that. We did the mind reading, and Will stepped up on the stand, clicked his opera hat shut, bowed to me, and turned to address the audience.

"The madame has a few words of great importance to say to you." He announced very firmly, "The madame is going to address you."

I had never made a fuss in front of an audience, so I coughed and spit my way through a short lecture. As I finished he doffed his hat and assisted me from the stand. His head was right near mine, and I whispered:

"You son of a bitch, I've had enough. I'm going to leave you for the first man that comes into the office tomorrow morning."

He didn't answer me. We went back to our living quarters and closed the door. Without taking off his hat or coat, Will walked over to the bureau. He picked up something and grabbed me and threw me on the floor and put his knee on my chest. The thing he had in his hand was a razor.

His eyes were flaming. "I'm going to cut your throat," he said.

I was scared, but not too scared to think. "The bulls will put you in the bucket and take your dope away," I said. The grip he had on me loosened a little. "If I've got to die, that's the best revenge I can think of," I said. "You'll get the third degree, and you'll die like a dog when they take your dope away."

He let me up. He was so furious his vocal cords were paralyzed. Nothing could have humiliated him more than the thought that I would live with any man in the world rather than him.

But I meant it. I went to Gladys's room and told her what had happened, then went to bed. The next morning I had had my coffee and was smoking opium when Gladys came in and said there were two men in the office asking for the lady doctor. I walked into the office and looked them over. One was a young, handsome six-footer with black hair and eyes and a light olive complexion. The other was a nice-looking blond, four or five years older.

"Which one of you wished to see me?" I asked.

"I do," the dark man answered.

"Which one of you came into the office first?"

"I did," the dark man said.

"Please step into my private office."

⇢ CHAPTER ELEVEN ⇠
THE
DAGO
WAS A
JEALOUS MAN

UNDER COVER OF ROUTINE office questions I learned all I could about the man.

He was twenty-three years old, two weeks older than I. He was an Italian, and he told me his nickname was "the Dago." He was a structural ironworker by trade and had come to see me about an attack of rheumatism in one elbow. I took eighteen dollars from him for remedies, just in case he had a wife and children and I would have to make a second choice.

The Dago came back every day—I told him he had to report progress—and I went to work on him, giving him quick glances and handing out the big-handsome-hero routine. I could see he was falling for it head over heels. Meanwhile, I kept running the office but told Will I couldn't lecture again until my cough was gone.

When I had the Dago thoroughly hooked I sat him down in the office one day and told him that even a doctor sometimes found it hard to remain strictly professional when such an emotion as love became involved in the diagnosis. I didn't let him make any mistake about how I felt and then asked him point-blank if he loved me. He blushed and stammered, finally blurting that he had loved me from the start but had been afraid to say so. That was all I needed. I told him to quit his job, that he and I and my girlfriend were taking the night train to Vancouver, B.C.

Will and I had a safe-deposit box, and in it were all my diamonds except seven diamond rings, my three-carat earrings, and a locket inwhich were set seven carats of diamonds. The box contained twenty-two diamond rings and several thousand dollars in cash.

I had three hundred and fifty dollars in my pocketbook, and I figured that would be enough until I got back and Will and I could go down and divide the bank roll. I told Will I was going away to think things over and that I would tell him what I was going to do when my mind was made up. In spite of his brilliance Will was a physical weakling and a coward. He knew I was going off with the Dago, but he made no move to stop us.

Going up on the train, the Dago and I talked about everything under the sun. I mentioned astronomy. His only knowledge of it was a quaint notion that if you saw a falling star you were supposed to kiss your sweetheart. To him ancient history was something that happened last week. He was devoted to me, and I became very fond of him.

I loaded up on morphine in Vancouver and, in secret, took it internally. The Dago didn't like my tattoo mark, but it was a case of take it or leave it. We went for horseback rides, went dancing and took walks, and did all the things I'd never done much of before. I quit drinking and cut down on the drugs and began to feel better. The Dago was as happy as I was. He'd never had many youthful pleasures. When he was a boy his father had taken him from Italy to South America. Later he had got a job as a cabin boy on a boat and eventually had got into bridge building.

After a couple of weeks in Vancouver we went back to Portland. I was afraid Will would kill me if I talked to him privately, so I arranged a meeting in a restaurant. I told him I was leaving him. He began to cry. The tears ran down his cheeks, and he kept brushing at them with his napkin. He begged me not to leave him, saying he was an old man whose only remaining aim in life was to see that I was comfortably provided for. I told him I would provide for myself and insisted that we go down to the bank and divide the contents of the safe-deposit box.

He finally consented. We went down to the bank, and he unlocked the box. In it was nothing but a piece of paper on which was written:

"I beat you to it."

I said, "Damn you, I haven't been near the box until now."

He wasn't the same man who had been weeping and pleading a few minutes before. "You're the biggest fool I ever knew," he said. "Did you really believe I'd ever let you have any of this money?"

I argued, and he changed his tune. "Half of it is yours, of course," he said. "I'm just keeping it safe for you. You've exchanged brains for brawn. When you get tired of the exchange and are down in the gutter, as you will be, I'll have your stake ready for you."

It was my turn to beg, but he refused to let me have a cent. Finally, as a matter of pride, I told him he was an old man who would need the money before I did, and left him.

I rented my old offices again and started to work. Gladys had been running around with an ex-convict, and I forbade her seeing him. She ran away with him, and the Dago and I were alone. I dressed him up in tailored suits, fifteen-dollar Stetson hats, and silk underwear and hung my diamond locket on his watch chain. He was proud as a peacock. We had decided we would get married as soon as I could establish residence and get a divorce.

We went to San Francisco, and I went down to contact the mayor, who was a labor man. There was no welter of secretaries to wade through; he was sitting with his feet on the desk, smoking a pipe. I showed him the Dago's union card and asked him if I could sell medicine on Golden Gate Avenue and Market Street at night.

"Sure," he said. "No good union man or his family will be refused a chance to make a living while I'm mayor."

I made good money, and we started to plan for Christmas. The Dago had never had a Christmas tree, and I hadn't had one since I was fifteen. We bought one and decorated it. We were so thrilled we woke each other up at night to go out and look at it. No more Purcell's. No more Barbary Coast. No more hop joints. The Dago taught me to play cooncan[29] and cribbage. Sometimes

---

29   Conquian or Coon Can is a rummy-style card game. It is an ancestor to all modern

the Candy Kid or Gin Fizz Smithy or some of the other bridgeworkers would come in for the evening. We began to discuss a home on Lake Washington, near Seattle. We made more plans that winter than the Russians have in ten years. I actually learned to crochet and was crocheting edgings for bath towels. I was as domesticated as a barnyard fowl.

A few days before Christmas a very well-preserved man of about fifty-five came into my office and said he had rheumatism of the shoulder. I told him the course of vibratory treatments would cost him fifty dollars and that an appointment could be made each week. He said he would rather pay me five dollars a treatment and come every other day. He was very anxious to be cured, he said, and thought more treatments, taken oftener, would be better. Of course that looked good to me. He told me he was a second mate on a boat. I was having such a good time with the Dago that I didn't pay much attention to him, but the day before Christmas an expressman brought the largest and most beautiful potted plant I had ever seen. On the card was the name "Mr. Larson," the name he had given me.

When he came to the office after Christmas I thanked him, and he asked me to go out to dinner with him. I refused, saying I didn't know him well enough. He repeated the invitation often, but I continued to refuse. Then, as I was hanging up his coat before giving him his treatment one day, I saw his name on the tailor's label stitched to the inside coat pocket. It was not Larson, but the name of one of the most prominent financial men in San Francisco.

Bing! Just like that a happy thought struck me. Here was corn in Egypt. Here was my first payment on that Lake Washington estate. I chided myself at first, but the more I thought over the idea, the better I liked it. Here was an old man who thought he was going to get the better of me. It was up to me to beat him to the draw. He was so rich he wouldn't miss the money, and he really ought to be taught a lesson. I talked it over with the Dago, and I actually felt quite noble when I had my plans all made. I would make this one touch and never do it again.

rummy games, and a kind of proto-gin rummy.

Some believe the game originated in Spain hundreds of years ago, and was then brought to Mexico. Others believe the game originated in Mexico in the mid-1800s. It was first described as Coon Can in 1887.

The next time he asked me out to dinner I told him I felt I knew him well enough to know he was a gentleman and began to lay the foundation. I pretended I had pawned most of my diamonds. We went to dinner a couple of times. One day he asked me about the dark man with whom he had seen me on the street. As we were both dark, I told him the Dago was my brother. The next time he invited me to lunch we passed an empty building. I told him I would like to start my brother in a pool hall there. When he asked me why I didn't I said it would cost twenty-five hundred dollars, which I didn't have.

"Come down to the bank," he said, "and I'll give it to you. And after we leave the bank I would like to go to your office. I have something to tell you."

When we got back to the office he sat down and proceeded to tell me who he really was.

"Now you've spoiled it all," I said. "You'll think I'm only being friendly because you're rich."

"No, my dear," he said. "You went out with me before you knew who I really was."

He went on to declare he wanted me to have anything I wanted and asked me my favorite recreation. I told him I liked to ride horseback. He bought me a beautiful riding habit and a number of white silk shirts and white stocks, with a horseshoe stickpin of diamonds, and made arrangements with the San Francisco Riding and Driving Club for a horse.

Not long afterward he supplied the funds required, according to my story, to get my diamonds out of pawn. Meanwhile, my brother had failed to get the right kind of lease and was looking for another location for his pool hall. I wanted to make another touch, but I wanted it to be a big one, and the last one, and I decided to leave town for a while to see what absence would do. He never tried to press an issue with me. He seemed to be satisfied to have me go out with him, on the theory that I was slowly learning to care for him. He was so much older than I that he didn't, he said, expect miracles.

I told him I was going to Stockton to find a location for my brother and that I was embarrassed about taking so much money from him. He tried to persuade me to stay, urging me not to think about money. I insisted he wasn't getting value received on his investment. I didn't feel right about it, I said, and he must allow me to do what I thought was right. He made me promise to telephone him every day, sent me a supply of Roederer's Brown Label champagne and a daily letter containing a twenty-dollar bill.

His demands for my return at length became so urgent that I told him he could visit me in Bakersfield, to which city I had moved in my supposed search for a suitable pool hall location. He came on the morning train. I told him there was nothing I would love more than a horseback ride if he would consent to join me.

While he was arranging for tickets for a play that evening, I slipped over to the livery stable, gave the boss a couple of dollars, and told him an old duck was going riding with me that afternoon. He was to give me a single-footer with a good padded saddle, but the old duck was to get the roughest riding horse he had and the hardest saddle. He agreed. After lunch the old man and I went for our horses. I galloped him over half of Kern County that afternoon. I came in fit as a fiddle, but he nearly fell off his horse.

He asked to be excused to take a bath and attend to some business, promising to join me for dinner. He got to the dining room, all right, but that was all. Before we were through he asked me if there wasn't someone in Bakersfield I would like to take to the theater. He had received an important phone message and had some important business to take care of.

The next day I pulled my Sarah Bernhardt act. Declaring I couldn't see him anymore, I began to cry. He became very excited. Why? What was the matter?

Haltingly I explained my brother had taken the twenty-five hundred dollars and had lost it playing blackjack. So my good friend must leave me alone with my misery. How much, he wanted to know, did I need? Three thousand dollars, but I couldn't trust my brother any more, neither could I desert him. I would have to earn the money to start him in business and send him home to start there.

My financier argued staunchly, and at last I permitted him to persuade me to a compromise. If I would return to San Francisco he would give my brother the money and buy him a ticket and see him safely off. For my part, I agreed to return as far as Oakland, where I would open an office. I didn't want to go back to Frisco. He would be too near me, and I was afraid he might get wise. Actually I wasn't taking much of a chance. I would rather try to trim a big butter-and-egg man any day than a ditchdigger who had got hold of some money quickly. A financial wizard may be a sharpshooter in business, but when it comes to his love life he is usually a sap. On the other hand, a laborer who comes suddenly into money usually demands a certificate of your virtue and your intentions at the first touch.

I packed up, and the three of us went back to Oakland that night. The financier brought the money over the next day. He handed the money to the Dago, and we went down and bought him a ticket to Chicago and solemnly put him on the train. The Dago, of course, got off at the first stop and went to a small hotel and holed up.

I knew this touch was too good to be true, and the next day I heard that Will was in town. I would have pulled out, but I had made too much of a fuss about coming to Oakland. I couldn't budge. Inevitably, I met Will. He asked me to go back to him, and I refused. He asked me where the Dago was and I said I didn't know. I left Will standing on the street corner, but he must have had someone follow me.

I had been meeting my financier every night for dinner and a show. One day he telephoned that he was coming to the office early. I would scarcely have known him, he looked so old and wrinkled and sad. The minute I saw him I knew the answer. I didn't wait for him to speak but with a woeful expression told him I was glad he had come early, as I had a confession to make.

I had a husband from whom I was separated, I admitted, while the man I had described as my brother was in reality my lover, whom I was afraid to leave because he had threatened me.

My financier said Will had been over to see him that morning and had given him the same information, adding that he, the financier, was keeping us apart and that he, Will, intended to bring suit for alienation of affection.

Still, he was glad that I had confessed before I learned that he knew, the financier said, and he would arrange matters if I left it all to him. He was not a man who lost confidence easily.

He arranged a meeting in my office, and there we all met, the Dago glaring belligerently and Will looking very sure of himself. My financier meant business. He offered to pay Will ten thousand dollars for an uncontested divorce and the Dago ten thousand if he would leave and never see me again. While they were to sign certain papers, he was willing to accept my word that they would never again enter my life. He had an elaborate scheme which involved hiring tutors and music teachers for me while my divorce was pending.

Will, of course, agreed, but the Dago wouldn't have any part of the scheme. I told the financier I would talk to the Dago and try to persuade him, but not to pay Will a cent unless I told him to.

That afternoon the Dago and I packed our things and took the train to Vancouver, B.C. Of course my financier was an old fool. He was fifty-five and I was twenty-three, but I felt sorry for him. I never saw him again.

In Vancouver I went to the mayor and obtained permission to give a series of health lectures on the street. Half a block away I rented an office and rooms. I discarded the Chinese-princess role and Americanized my lecture. The Canadians, I had observed, didn't have the touching faith in Chinese medicines that Americans had.

I set up my portable stand and began to do my magic. By the time I had got well into my lecture the street was so blocked that the streetcars couldn't get through. I begged part of the crowd to move on and not block traffic. Nobody budged. Hurriedly I told them where my office was and urged them to follow me there if they were interested. Before I could finish the mounted-police reserves came up and started riding through the mob. When they started to disperse a mob they dispersed it. But they didn't seem to blame me for the crowd. I went to my office; with the crowd following me, I was more like the head man in a circus parade than anything else. Soon the halls and the stairs of the hotel were filled, and the overflow was extending into the street.

The manager came fighting his way through the press. "What in the name of heaven is all this about?"

I told him the people were waiting to see me in my office.

Turning an apoplectic scarlet, he yanked a wallet from his coat pocket. "Office? Office? I rented you a room, not a hall. Take your money and get out of here!"

After getting the matter straightened out with the customers and explaining to the mayor about cluttering up his street, I arranged to pitch on a less congested corner and rented a two-story house next door to the Salvation Army barracks.

Meanwhile Will came to town and began to lecture a short distance away. Then Gladys and her ex-convict lover came to town. He had escaped, it developed, from the Walla Walla road gang. Someone had taught him a lecture, and he began to sell medicine not far from Will's stand.

The ex-convict hadn't been there long when the warden from Walla Walla paid a visit to the Vancouver police chief, bringing along a pocketful of pictures of criminals and escaped convicts. The chief spotted Gladys's friend at once and informed the warden he was selling medicine within two blocks of the police headquarters. The cops picked him up, but while he was waiting in the Vancouver jail he sawed his way out and escaped again. Although he made a clean getaway, he was caught soon after in Calgary, pitching in front of a billboard within a block of the police station. This time they didn't take any chances. They must have ironed him properly, because an hour or so after he had been arrested he had to call the cops into his cell to take a saw out of the front of his trousers. The saw was cutting his belly.

Will didn't bother me for several weeks. Then, about two o'clock one morning, there was a loud knock at our bedroom door.

"Who's there?" I asked.

"Get up, Vi, and put your clothes on and come with me," Will said.

"Nothing doing."

The door had a frosted-glass panel. Will stood in the hall, cursing us through it. The Dago got out of bed, and I followed him. Will was calling us all the vile names he could think of. He got so close to the door that we could see the outline of his head and shoulders, and suddenly the Dago, who hadn't uttered a word, lashed out with his fist right through the glass.

I crossed my arms and flung myself in front of the hole. Will was standing in the hall with a gun in his hand. He lifted it and shot, and the bullet nicked my arm. He turned around and started to run.

Someone had telephoned the police, and they arrested Will as he was dashing into the street. He raved that he was my husband and that the Dago had forced me to live with him. We were going to leave Vancouver in the morning, I said, and if they would hold Will until then I wouldn't bother to bring a charge against him.

I worked that winter in Seattle and Spokane and was never happier, although the Dago was beginning to act jealous. If a man came into the office to buy medicine and stayed a little too long, I noticed the Dago in the hall when I let the yokel out. Occasionally when I was downtown and turned around quickly I would spot the Dago dodging into a doorway. It didn't bother me much; in fact, I think I was flattered by his concern. It was during this period that my divorce from Will became final.

I had been hearing a good deal about Butte, Montana, and in the spring we decided to go there. By displaying the Dago's union card I got a permit to lecture from the mayor of Butte, and Saturday night I went out to pitch. I had rented offices and rooms, and I lectured on the street in front of the building.

When I finished my pitch I asked anyone who was interested to come up to the office. Not a soul came. This was something new, and it was several days before I found out the answer. My audience had been composed of Slavs, and they always talked things over among themselves before they reached a decision. In Butte they were called bohunks, and a finer or more honest race I have never met. I had told the audience my office would be open two hours on Sunday. Just as I was about to close up for the week end, feeling the Butte expedition was a complete failure, a bohunk came in. He had a baby, he said, with sore eyes. Would I go to the house?

I found the baby was in pretty bad shape. A bona fide doctor had been there, but no one had paid any attention to his instructions. I went out and bought some English Eye Drops, some witch hazel, and a boric solution. I washed the eyes thoroughly, put in some eyedrops, and put on a witch-hazel pack, repeating the treatment several times a day for several days. The child began to mend.

This bohunk turned out to be the boss Slav in Butte. He owned a saloon and set up one of the back rooms as a part-time office for me. I went there for two hours every afternoon, and he acted as interpreter for me. Butte was divided by Dublin Gulch; on one side were the Americans, on the other the bohunks. The bohunks who worked in the mines paid a monthly fee and were supposed to be cared for by the company doctors. As some of them had been neglected, they had it in for all staff physicians. Even the children were bitter; they sometimes stoned the company doctors' cars passing in the street.

The saloon business was tremendous, and the money began rolling in. I was riding the crest of the wave. The bohunks idolized me. I was having pretty good luck with my patients. Most of them needed nothing more than a good physic.

While I worked, however, the Dago began to gamble. We both were spending plenty of money, but it was coming in faster than we could spend it. Before long I was getting a little too optimistic. I was having such good luck with the people who were taking my medicine that I began to overstate the prospects somewhat. When these promises failed to materialize the patients took to viewing my medications with increasing doubt. I began to notice a chill in the atmosphere. The distrust came to a head one night when a bohunk I had been stalling along came to the office. It was pretty clear he wasn't there to idolize me. He looked hard and he talked hard.

"What time do I get well?" he said.

As I walked behind him I noticed the outline of a knife in his hip pocket. It was a big one that suggested business.

"Next week," I said, digging up some new pills.

That knife may not have been meant for me, but by this time I knew the bohunks were strong for direct action when matters didn't go to suit them. The Dago and I packed our things that same night and left, bag and baggage, for Seattle.

The Dago's jealousy returned, and our personal affairs began going from bad to worse. When I ate alone I would discover him nearby behind a palm or a pillar, taking a drink and watching me. Whenever a man came into the office the Dago would wait a few minutes, then open the door, peer in and say, "Excuse me," and walk away.

One day I told him I had to go to another part of town to get some morphine. He told me he preferred to stay in the rooms. An hour or so later I found him sulking along the street behind me. I didn't let him get away. After overtaking him I asked what had made him change his mind. He had decided, he said, to visit a friend. I knew he was lying and told him so. As I continued to prod him he grew sullen and at last burst out:

"I don't trust you because Will's right—you can't trust a woman."

"Will?" I demanded. "How did he get into this? What do you mean?"

Bit by bit it came out. He had met Will in a hotel bar, and Will had warned him—for his own good, of course—that I could be counted on to betray him if I wasn't watched. He had believed Will then, and still did, in spite of anything I could say.

I had to go on trips to work nearby towns, whether I wanted to or not. I always sent the Dago plenty of money, and each time I came back I added some to the bank roll we were accumulating in a safe-deposit box. After a trip to Canada I went to the box, as usual, and found the Dago had taken out several hundred dollars without letting me know. I went home in a rage and started a row. He had broken the code I had learned to live by. It was open season on the world but wrong to betray your friends or those close to you. He had lost the money at blackjack. We finally made up the quarrel, but from then on things were different. I was starting to break. I began drinking steadily and using more drugs.

The Dago, too, was drinking hard. The breakup came when I found he had taken all my diamonds from their hiding place. Luckily he hadn't had time to convert them into cash, but he refused to give them up. I offered to sell them and split the take. He refused. So I called the police, told them he wasn't my husband and had stolen my jewelry. They threw him in jail and kept him there three days before he weakened enough to tell them where the diamonds were. The cops gave me the diamonds and the Dago the bum's rush. We never saw each other again after that meeting.

I walked away from it with seven diamond rings, my earrings, and about fifteen hundred dollars. I was a drug fiend, and the ten best years of my life were gone. I was beginning to look haggard; my health was gone. My nerves were as frayed as a broken shoelace, and I simply went to pieces. I had no appetite and couldn't hold anything on my stomach. A pitchman friend of mine, an addict, met me on the street and took me up to his room.

"You're in tough shape, Vi."

"Don't I know it."

"The trouble is, you're taking too much dope into your stomach. Ever used a hypodermic needle?"

I'd always had a horror of the gun, as they called it, but he finally persuaded me it was the thing to do and gave me a shot.

The sensation of relief, comfort, and relaxation was wonderful. He got me a needle and showed me how to use it. I found the effect was quicker and more pleasant but that it wore off sooner. Previously I had taken the stuff twice a day; now, to get the same results, I had to take a shot several times a day.

→ CHAPTER TWELVE ←
COCAINE BUGS

AFTER A SHORT REST I hit the road again, but I couldn't get the money I had formerly. I was thin and growing more and more graceless. I used a little magic act to get my crowds, drifting around Arizona, New Mexico, Texas, and eventually into Denver.

I was about out of money. I had spent all I had when I left the Dago, and all I had made. Sometimes I didn't have more than five dollars in my pockets. I stopped at the finest hotels. I didn't dare stop at any other kind. I still had my diamonds and some nice clothes and put up a good front. More often than not I didn't have enough cash to pay my bill when I registered, but a big hotel never thought of presenting its bill if you had good baggage and good clothes and sported a few diamonds. I could sign for my meals and drinks.

Luck was with me. I always landed a sucker with money before the showdown came. Still, it couldn't last, and I knew it. Week by week the money was coming harder.

So when I met Will again I was in a frame of mind to fall in with his proposal. He and a friend named Charley were working Denver, and he suggested I throw in with them. The three of us together, he said, could make more money. I was too worn out to care about anything but release from the burden of responsibility.

Things began to pick up a little, and then one morning Will announced he was going to quit dope. I had two reasons for wanting to see him try—I wondered if it was possible, and I was anxious to see Will go through some of the torture I'd been through.

He began cutting down fast and before long was taking hyoscine and chloral as a substitute for the morphine. He went out of his head, and Charley and I took turns sitting up at night with him. A little of that—staying up all night and pitching all day—and we were both all in. Will finally gave up. He was feeling better, but he hadn't quit. He never did.

The couple of shots Will took put him back on his feet. Charley and I were the ones who were in bad shape. Will said he knew how to brace us up.

"I'm going to give you each a little shot of cocaine," he said, "and you'll be able to work."

It was sure dynamite. It picked us up and punched us out onto the street, ready for anything. An addict thinks nothing of using a new drug if he believes it will make him feel better. Opium is bad enough, and morphine is a little worse, but cocaine and heroin are the drugs that make the user lose his brain and imagine things. Cocaine users see strange things and strange people. We called these creations cocaine bugs.

Will persuaded me to obtain a narcotics permit from the federal authorities. You were supposed to use whatever narcotics you bought to manufacture medicine. I signed the drugstore slip for a lot of cocaine and morphine. Will said he would keep the drugs for me and I gave them to him, as I didn't want to get caught with them. Two days later a couple of men from the narcotic squad came to the office. I was there alone. One of them had a tic which made his left eyelid twitch continually. He did most of the talking. He asked to see the narcotics I had bought.

"Sorry," I said. "You can't."

"Why not?"

"I put them in some medicine."

He nodded. "Then we'll take a sample of the medicine. We're interested in the percentage of narcotics being used."

"You can't do that either," I said.

He straightened up in his chair. "Why not?"

"The batch I put them in didn't come out right. I had to pour it down the sink."

He stopped being courteous right then. His eyelid began to fly up and down like a window shade. "What in hell do you take us for, a couple of damned fools?" he yelped. He got up and began shaking his finger in my face. "You can't make that stick. You're a hophead, and so is that crooked husband of yours."

He was still talking when another cop brought Will in. They hustled us down to the chief's office. I told my story and stuck to it. Will hadn't trained me as long as he had for nothing. Even a bread-and-water diet couldn't have made me give cops the time of day.

They wanted to know if we were married.

"No. Divorced."

"But you're living together."

I looked like the devil, but I looked young beside Will's extra twenty years. I made an uncomplimentary remark which made Will squirm but persuaded the cops.

The chief came around his desk and tried oil. I was young and innocent and didn't know how serious this was. Will was a confirmed hophead who was trying to use me as a tool. I couldn't have used the quantity of stuff I had bought so soon. I knew it. They knew it. If I would tell them where it was cached they would let me go.

"It went down the sink in a batch of bad medicine," I said.

They were mad, but there wasn't anything they could do about it. They gave us until train time to get out of town.

The three of us went to Ogden, Utah. Will said he couldn't remember where he had hidden the drugs. We got up early the next day and were all sitting in Will's room. Will went out to sit on the fire escape in the sun. Suddenly he yelled, "I've got it!"

He came in, went to his grip, and pulled out an old woolly sweater that had a lining. He had planted the dope in the sweater.

The next day I got a license and a corner to work on, but the spark was gone, and we didn't do much. Will decided Charley and I were more of a drag than a help and that it was time to unload us.

"You hopheads make me nervous," he said. "I'm going to Montana. You and Charley work together."

He pulled out and I pawned some of my diamonds. Charley and I worked out a new angle to the medicine racket. We bought a microscope. Then we bought some clean slides and one phony slide with some horrible-looking microbes on it. We told the natives we weren't lecturing with the idea of selling them anything but that if they wanted to come to the office we would give them a free diagnosis and provide remedies should they be desired.

In the offices Charley listened to their symptoms and explained that the case would be studied according to scientific principles. He took a slide of blood, mucus, or urine, as indicated by the symptoms. A little sleight of hand was all that was needed to substitute the phony slide for the original one. Adjusting the light, Charley squinted into the microscope and looked very grave.

At this point I called him from the next room, and Charley asked to be excused for a few minutes. The anxiety, of course, was more than human nature could bear. The chump never failed to take a quick look into the microscope. Those bugs on the phony slide were honeys. They resembled prehistoric monsters of land and sea. By the time Charley came back the chump was landed. Charley studied the slide again and swung around with a professional air. Well shaken up, the chump would want to know if he could be cured.

"Certainly," Charley said. "There's nothing much wrong with you, my friend."

The sucker always knew better. Those microbes were convincing. The doctor, he was certain, was merely trying to keep him from worrying. All he wanted to know was the price of the medicine. He was ready to pay it.

It's a wonder anyone even listened to us, we were so full of cocaine and morphine, but we did well. Just the same, we couldn't save much. Dope was becoming harder to get. We were paying thirty-five dollars a dram for stuff that had cost sixty cents in any drugstore before passage of the Harrison Narcotic Act[30].

We began jumping from town to town with the microscope stunt. We were hitting the cocaine hard by now. We had been using it only a short while, and it still had a kick. Several times we saw a man with a gray suit and a gray cowboy hat. We changed towns, and he cropped up again. We began to see him nearly every time we pitched.

"Vi, that fellow's a bull," Charley said. "He's on to us."

I laughed at him. "We're just imagining it. He's a coke bug. We're getting as bad as the rest of the boys. The thing for us to do is cut down on the cocaine."

That was more easily said than done. We would cut down one dose and increase the next. We were on the jump most of the time now, and we still saw our coke bug. Charley decided he had better go home and try to get off the cocaine. We had to get together a stake, and we headed back for one of the towns we had worked before. On the train we got lower berths across from each other and went to bed. I awoke about two-thirty in the morning, and my brain was clear. Something was wrong. The train had stopped. The answer flashed into my head. Our coke bug wasn't imaginary; he was real; he was an officer and he'd turned us in. I woke Charley and told him. I had him take enough dope to last him until the next afternoon. He gave me his supply. I took an enormous dose and hid the rest of it where the cops wouldn't find it unless they had a smart matron. I put a kimono on over my silk nightgown and got back into the berth. The door at the end of the car slammed. Footsteps came along the corridor. A man jerked open the curtains of my berth. There were two other men behind him in the aisle, yanking at the curtains of Charley's berth. They

---

30   The Harrison Narcotics Tax Act was a United States federal law that regulated and taxed the production, importation, and distribution of opiates and coca products. The act was proposed by Representative Francis Burton Harrison of New York and was approved on December 17, 1914.

"An Act To provide for the registration of, with collectors of internal revenue, and to impose a special tax on all persons who produce, import, manufacture, compound, deal in, dispense, sell, distribute, or give away opium or coca leaves, their salts, derivatives, or preparations, and for other purposes." The courts interpreted this to mean that physicians could prescribe narcotics to patients in the course of normal treatment, but not for the treatment of addiction.

The Harrison Anti-Narcotic legislation consisted of three U.S. House bills imposing restrictions on the availability and consumption of the psychoactive drug opium.

were the sheriff and two town policemen. The train conductor was hovering beside them, looking worried.

"What are you doing?" I demanded.

"You're under arrest. Get your clothes on and come along." Charley began dressing.

"Where's your warrant?" I asked.

"You'll see it soon enough," the sheriff said.

I raised my voice. I wanted witnesses. "I won't go unless you show the conductor and me your warrant."

"You'll go, all right," the sheriff said.

I began to scream. "You're no officer. You're trying to abduct me." Heads were popping out of the curtains screening the other berths. "I want the names and addresses of these people," I yelled. "Conductor, what's your run and what days are you on it?"

"Shut up," the sheriff said. "Get started, or we'll take you the way you are."

"Don't go, Charley," I said.

One of the cops beside Charley hauled back his fist. "You come with me or I'll beat your head off."

Charley went. Not me. I braced my feet against the end of the bunk, and they had to pry my hands loose and carry me out kicking and screaming. The conductor brought out our grips, trying to get in a word of protest.

"Shut up and give your signal," the sheriff told him.

They had an automobile outside, but I wouldn't get into it. I fell down on the sidewalk and wouldn't get up. They lifted me into the back of the car. I slid to the floor and lay there. Charley was sitting in front. When we got to the jail I made them carry me in. They put me in a nice large room with a cement floor and an adjoining bath. The cell even had a push button I could use to call the jailer. The female population of that town must have been better than average, because I was the only woman there.

The next morning I asked the sheriff to send for a certain doctor, who had been furnishing us with dope when we were there before. The sheriff telephoned and reported the doctor had said he couldn't come at the moment. He had his calls to make and would show up at his own convenience.

I knew I was sunk if I ever gave up my hard-boiled manner. "Phone that bastard again," I said. "Tell him to get the hell down here as fast as he can or he won't be making calls or going anywhere at all for a long time."

The sheriff got wise and phoned the doctor, who reached the jail in nothing flat, giving Charley and me all the dope we wanted. When the sheriff came back later I told him I wanted to see his warrant.

"I'll have it," he said. "I'm going out now to get it."

"You'll have nothing," I jeered. "You haven't got one, and you can't get one."

"Don't kid yourself. I've got two or three men ready to sign it right now."

I laughed at him. "Don't be a sap. Your men will talk big, but they won't risk making monkeys of themselves on the stand against a woman."

After a while the sheriff came back, dejected. No warrant yet. He urged me to confess, promising he would do everything possible to get me off. "What in hell's the matter with you?" I scoffed. "You haven't got me on yet, and you're not going to." He told me Charley had confessed. I laughed at him. He went away, but I didn't give him any peace. I wasn't interested in medals for being a model prisoner. I refused to ring on the buzzer. Whenever anyone visited the sheriff in his office I took a tin pail and beat on the bars. One night I stuffed up the toilet and flooded the jail.

The next day they took us into court. The sheriff had given up on the dope charge. He said we would be charged with practicing medicine without a license. The trouble was, they hadn't prepared a case of that kind and had no witnesses. The prosecuting attorney knew that, of course. He and the judge talked it over.

Finally the prosecutor said, "Let's make them get out of town. They're both hopheads and are costing us money. We can't take the dope away from them because that damned woman has the goods on a doctor here."

The sheriff walked back to my cell with me. "Get your bags packed and get the hell out of here," he said.

I walked over and lay down on the bunk. "Nothing doing. I'm going to stay right here until the grand jury meets. I'm going to sue you and the county for false arrest and imprisonment. I've been disgraced."

He begged me to leave. I swore I wasn't going to. He used every argument he could dream up, and at last I compromised. I would leave, I said, if the sheriff would go to a veterinarian I knew about and bring me a half ounce of cocaine and a half ounce of morphine.

He was so mad he sputtered like an exhaust on a cold morning. Still, he knew I had him. What story he put up to the veterinarian I never found out, but he brought me the stuff.

When we left the jail Charley and I split up. He went home and I moved over into Idaho. I had plenty of dope, but I was nearly crazy. I was so sick and weak I could scarcely stand. It took me hours to dress. I couldn't eat; I drank eggnogs and cream fizzes. I lectured when I could muster the strength for it, and once in a while someone came to the office.

The doctor who was supplying me with dope at the time brought me up short. "Look," he said, "you can keep on taking this stuff if you want to, but if you do you'll be dead within six months."

I went back to my room and threw myself on the bed and wept for hours. I was only a little more than twenty-six years old, and I didn't want to die.

The doctor had told me it would take plenty of money to get away from dope. I had been pawning my diamonds to get the stuff, and I didn't have much left. One thing I wouldn't do was write to my family for help. I was too proud. Nor would I tackle any of the medicine bunch for stake. I had been at the top, and they would have loved to see me humbled.

I began to lay my plans carefully. They centered around a man who had been coming to the office for medicine. He had indicated in a tentative way that he was fond of me. According to the information I had pumped him for, he was a cowpuncher and miner and had a few thousand dollars plus some mining claims. He was bowlegged and far from handsome, but this time I couldn't be particular whom I married. He was elected. He pulled out for Nevada, but he told me to write to him, and I knew he was still on the hook.

He was the only hope I had left. The life I was fighting to escape was plain horror. I had seen addicts caught as I was, but somehow it had always seemed that it couldn't happen to me. You get the feeling that you're looking through a glass at specimens on public display. And then suddenly there isn't the glass between you anymore.

I'd seen addicts who were without a needle or who were afraid to carry their hypo with them. They took a safety pin or a nail and dug it into their arms, then loaded an eyedropper with their shot and pressed it into their bleeding flesh and held the hole together until the stuff had been absorbed. You do that, knowing it makes you an outcast, but you can't help it. There never was a sane addict who didn't want to get away from the stuff. Only a few do. The terrible, searching fear of every addict is that he will be caught and thrown into a cell, where his drugs will be abruptly withdrawn. That dread haunts him every moment of his waking life and every hour of his troubled sleep, because he knows it means horror and agony beyond the power of words to describe. A woman I knew, Break-of-Day Jennie, died in jail with hemorrhages. Women addicts were peculiarly susceptible to them. The dysentery, the vomiting, and the pain came in such sickening waves that an addict was willing to beat out his own brains.

So long as you could pay, you got your dope. It could come from a messenger office, a veterinarian, a doctor. The peddlers knew that the agony of an addict without his drug was so great he would chop his own mother's head open if he thought a dram of drugs was concealed in her skull. The peddlers didn't take any more chances than they had to. One druggist I approached was a stranger; I told him I was without morphine and wanted to buy some. He said he wouldn't sell me any, but he would tell me where it was; I could leave the money on the counter and steal it. He would report the theft to the police but would profess not to know the thief.

When I started to use opium the price was six dollars for a three-ounce can, which lasted a week or ten days. The price went up to seventy-five dollars a can and then to one hundred and twenty-five dollars a can. Morphine jumped from sixty cents a dram (one-eighth of an ounce) to one hundred and twenty-five dollars an ounce. Doctors demanded five dollars for a single shot.

It became gradually harder to make contacts for the stuff. In Salt Lake City I contacted a peddler for my daily supply. He was arrested. I contacted one or two others. They also went to jail. The peddlers became afraid of me and wouldn't sell to me. The addicts were sympathetic, but they had no dope to spare. My suffering became more and more severe. The last shot I got was of laudanum, and the pain of taking it was worse than if a knife had been ground around and around in my arm. It was so bad that some other addicts brought me a few marijuana cigarettes as a substitute. Marijuana, it seemed to me, was one of the most vicious drugs in the world. It didn't take the place of morphine, although it removed the sharp edge of suffering and set the brain to whirling. It also produced mad, vicious, murderous impulses.

Up to that time the only person I had ever felt like killing was Will. The marijuana changed that. Every morning about five o'clock a man passed my window on his way to work. He was always whistling or singing. I had a gun in my room, and the morning after I smoked the marijuana it took all my will power to keep from going to the window and killing him. Who was he to be so happy when I was enduring the agonies of the damned?

Only my inordinate pride kept me from descending to the lowest moral depths. Coupled with my pride was an unshakable belief that something would happen to save me. I used the last money I had to buy dope. At this time I was taking about thirty grains of morphine and twenty grains of cocaine daily.

As a last resort I wrote to the Nevada miner, whose name was Frank, asking him to send me fifty dollars. To my surprise he sent it at once. I never needed anything more. I was frantic. The doctors were afraid to write prescriptions for me. They were afraid I would die. I wrote Frank again, asking for another fifty dollars. Instead of sending it, he came himself.

When he arrived I played him as carefully as a fisherman does a trout. It was my life that was at stake. I didn't have any particular feeling for him. He was the only means I had of getting away from drugs. What bothered me most was the tattooed dragon and the blue hypodermic marks which were as thick on my arms as grains of salt on an egg. I had to keep Frank from seeing them. If he suspected what I was he would leave me. For several days I puzzled over the problem, and the day before the wedding I went to a department store and made a purchase. I was married with a suit of long underwear under my wedding dress, and I had it on when I went to bed on my wedding night.

Frank took my diamonds out of pawn and bought me some new clothes. The day after the wedding we went to Reno, Nevada. The minute we were settled I beat it downtown to arrange a contact for dope and to investigate the possibilities of getting cured.

I went to the city doctor, swore him to secrecy, and told him I was an addict who wanted to quit the stuff. Would he supply me with dope until I could take the cure? Even then, much as I wanted to get off dope, I didn't think I had a chance. There was one development I hadn't counted on. A half-wise relative of Frank's came to visit us. After looking at me for half an hour he knew the whole story, and the next morning he told Frank.

Frank knew I was going to see the city doctor that afternoon and that I had been to see him the previous afternoon. When I got to the office to keep my appointment, Frank had already arrived. Presently the doctor came rushing out of the conference room, asking to be relieved of his promise of secrecy. Frank was demanding facts and wouldn't be put off. There was nothing to do but face it. I asked the doctor if he could cure me. He said he could but that the cure would be costly. We went in to talk to Frank. The doctor told him I was an addict but that I wanted to be cured, and he could do it.

He was an optimist. I found out later that the only addicts he had cured had been criminals. His treatment had consisted of throwing them in jail and letting them howl it out. If they died that was too bad—they were too far gone to recover. If and when they stopped screaming they were turned loose and called cured.

I hired a special nurse and got a hospital room. The doctor knew how much dope I had been using. He had promised to reduce it. He did. He cut it in half the first day and kept cutting it every day from then on. At first my system was so soaked with the stuff that the pain caused by the reduction wasn't violent. My clothes and my private supply of drugs were in the hospital office. The doctor had assured me I would be cured without undue difficulties in thirty days.

About the fifth or sixth day I was in hell. I couldn't hold anything on my stomach. It seemed as if the marrow of my bones was burning up. The blistering agony centered in my knees. Observing that I had come to the end of my rope, the doctor gave me a shot of hyoscine. It caused me to have horrid visions. I lost the power to judge distance. My mouth was dry and as hot as a furnace. When during this period of pain and wild dreams I reached a moment of lucidness, I knew I couldn't stand any more. I told the doctor he was cutting me too fast.

He decided I was right and announced we would start the cure all over again. For a few days it was better; then the old round of torture began again. I tried lying in a hot-water bath for an hour three or four times a day. That doctor didn't have any idea what he was doing, and I was nearly as dumb. I knew I was suffering to the very limit of my sanity, but he had promised I would be cured in thirty days. As the time wore along it began to look as if we weren't getting anywhere.

I began to rebel at the torment, and the doctor threatened to put me in a straitjacket. I told him if he did he had better never let me get out, so he hedged and didn't—but he had me scared. I had turned in my hypo and my dope and was at the mercy of the hospital. The stories of old-timers who had been jailed and deprived of narcotics began to drift through my mind—stories of men whose agony had driven them to bite through their tongues, or gnaw at their own wrists in an effort to open the veins, or to drive their heads against cement cell walls. The straitjacket talk made me panicky and I had ceased to trust the doctor, but I stuck it out for thirty days.

At midnight of the thirtieth day I was walking up and down the hall with the nurse. I wasn't even close to being cured, and at the rate I was going I didn't figure I could stand it long enough to be cured. I had the nurse take me to a telephone and told the doctor I was finished. He argued, but it didn't do any good. They gave me back my hypo and dope, and I took a shot. The relief was so great that I didn't give a damn whether I ever got cured or not.

Frank had to examine a mine he had leased, but I was too ill to go with him. The first thing I did when he had gone was to make a contact with a messenger service for my dope. All I had to do was telephone them and say, "Have Eddy bring me up a chicken and a meat sandwich." Chicken meant cocaine and meat meant morphine. I didn't bathe or dress, just lay in bed and cried. I couldn't see any way out, and I went on a regular drug debauch, hoping it would kill me.

One morning I awoke—not so much from sleep as from a confused trancelike state—to find a large abscess on my right leg. In taking a shot I had infected myself. Since my arms had become too sore and hard to accept the needle, I had been using my upper leg. The abscess scared me.

I had three twenty-dollar gold pieces, and I telephoned three doctors picked at random from the telephone book to come to my room for a consultation that afternoon. Two of them were normal and pleasant in appearance; the third was a hunchback whose lips had a permanent sardonic twist. I told them I was an addict and exposed the abscess. One of the doctors lanced and dressed it. I was weeping and feeling pretty sorry for myself. The first two doctors were attempting to comfort me. Not the hunchback. He kept looking at me as if I were a snake.

Sniffling, I asked, "Do you think I can be cured?"

It was the hunchback who answered: "No. If you tried you'd go insane. Dope fiends like you are better off dead, anyhow."

I gaped at him, and then strength came boiling back into me. "You hunchbacked little rat! I wouldn't say a thing like that to a mad dog!" I was screaming. "Damn you, I'm going to get cured and come to your office and break you in two over my knee! Here's your fee." I threw one of the twenty-dollar gold pieces at him as hard as I could, yelling, "Get the hell out of here!"

I paid the other doctors and they left, murmuring sympathetically. I was so mad at the hunchback I was talking to myself. I would show him and the whole damned world I could beat it. I downed two or three drinks of whisky, took a big shot, and climbed out of bed. My reflection in the mirror was horrifying. My weight was down to eighty pounds. My hair was snarled, my face ghastly. I went downtown to a jeweler's and sold every one of my diamonds, replacing them with cheap brilliants. I still had my gun; this time I was going to make the cure stick or kill myself.

With a nurse I had hired I took the train to a small town near my husband's mine and rented a furnished house. I sent for a Dr. Kitchen, whom I knew.

He was a grand old man. I told him I wanted to quit and needed his help. By this time I knew how I was going to go about it. We were to cut the dope down a grain a day at first, then even less. If it got too tough we wouldn't cut it at all for a few days. But we were never to increase the amount of the last dose. He agreed. He was to bring me my daily ration each morning, and I was to have no more, even if I used it up in an hour.

I went to bed and didn't sit up for more than six weeks. I was so weak that if I tossed my head or raised a hand the bed would become soaked with perspiration. Some days I could hold nothing on my stomach but a tablespoonful of champagne. At the end of six weeks I had quit sweating and could take liquid foods. But when the sweating stopped I broke out with abscesses. After I took a shot an abscess large enough to lance formed within six hours. I had forty-two abscesses lanced in thirty days. By that time I was off the cocaine and had cut down on the morphine. We started to reduce the amounts in earnest. Although very weak, I was able to get out of bed.

To make very sure I wasn't fooling myself, I insisted that a sealed dram of morphine be set on my bureau. When the pains got really tough I wanted to feel I had a choice.

I started cutting fast. The suffering grew so acute that Dr. Kitchen moved out to the house to sleep. At night, when the outside world was quiet, things were worse. I cursed Will. I didn't want to kill him—I wanted to tear off his skin piece by piece. One night I asked the doctor to take me for a walk. Walking was easier, I said, on the railroad track. Pretending to be very gay, I waited until the Reno express came roaring toward us and tried to throw myself under the wheels. Dr. Kitchen jumped for me, knocked me down, and both of us rolled into the ditch.

Night after night no sleep would come. I walked up and down in my bedroom and looked at the bottle of morphine. "I'll wait just one hour," I said, "and if the pain isn't better I'll take some and then kill myself." The minute hand toiled around, and when the hour was gone I said, "You did that. Now try one more."

At last, after days and nights that blurred into centuries, I fell asleep. The sleep lasted two or three hours. I had been living on eggnogs and fluids, but when I woke up I was hungry. I told the doctor I wanted some corned beef and cabbage, mustard, pickles, and lemon pie. After an argument he ordered it for me. That meal was heavenly. I hadn't really tasted food for two or three years. The flavor of it on my tongue meant the end was in sight. I had started the treatment January 7, and this was April 20. I was still taking one-fourth of a grain of morphine a day, plus a few drinks of whisky to keep my strength up.

I paid off Dr. Kitchen and the nurse and arranged to join Frank, hiring a car to drive me to the mine. I took with me just one dose of morphine and a half pint of whisky. When we stopped for lunch I went over behind a clump of sagebrush and took my last shot and flipped the hypodermic syringe into the sand. I took my last drink and tossed away the bottle.

→ CHAPTER THIRTEEN ←
REJUVENATION

IT WAS TWO YEARS before I pitched again, and during those two years only two things of real importance happened: I earned and paid Frank every penny he had spent on my cure, and I fell in love with Mac, the man I was to marry and live with for twenty-eight years.

While I was cooking in mining camps and even taking in washing I was considering improvements in my medicine routine. I had been reading about Louis Pasteur and decided the scientific approach would be the most effective. I adopted the business name of Madame V. Pasteur. I never mentioned the name of Louis Pasteur, nor pretended I was related to him, but it's possible a few of the yokels had heard of him and drew their own conclusions. Such a noble name required a change in appearance too. From a masquerade store I rented a college cap and gown. The audience reacted so well, listening with increased respect and attention, that I took the rented attire to a tailor and had a duplicate made to order. From then on I wore it whenever I pitched.

San Francisco had dealt with me so agreeably in the past that I headed there. Paying off Frank had taken my last ready cash, and I had to go to work. I met another medicine man who had two small children. He also wanted to work, and we decided to work together. The only location available was south of Market Street—"south of the slot." We had to make a fix, of course, even to work there.

By making the proper inquiries I found that the man to make the fix was a shyster lawyer I had known casually years before. Finding him in his office, I asked how much it would cost for a permit to sell medicine on the street.

"Fifty dollars a week to you," he said.

"I can't pay that much," I told him. "Ten dollars a week is the best I can do."

He threw back his head and roared. "Save your act for the yokels, Vi." He got out a handkerchief and dabbed at his eyes as if it were the best joke in the world. "What's the pitch this time? I'm not blind. You've been living in cream up to your chin. You've got fat on it. You look as respectable as a schoolteacher. No diamonds, no rouge. You must have cooked up a scheme that will knock the suckers for a row. Fifty iron men for the fix, my dear."

"Damn you," I said, "I told you ten was the best I can do. Either I fix with you or I skip you and make the fix on top. Take your choice."

He grinned. "Take it on up if you want to. Ten bucks is too thin to fool with. But make your story good. To him it's all money, and all it will buy is groceries."

The man I had to see was a top-level city official who was running San Francisco at the time. I took my partner's two children with me when I went to his office. Boosting them up on a couple of chairs, I said, "Now be quiet, children. Mother will be through in just a minute." I walked over to the man and told him I was broke and had to have a permit to sell herbs if I was to get money to feed the youngsters. I had the permit in a matter of five minutes.

Not many weeks afterward I ran across Ray Black, he of the long-winded pitches, and he went to work for me as lecturer. To ballyhoo the crowds I hired a blackface comedian who played and juggled a banjo. Ray's duty was to introduce me. I always sent him out at six o'clock, as it took him at least two hours to get around to presenting me to the crowd.

His act consisted of unbuttoning his shirt and displaying to the crowd an enormous scar which puckered the skin of his chest. How he acquired it, I never found out. In a hushed voice he informed his listeners that it was the result of a venereal disease caught because he had carelessly taken a bath in a hotel bathtub. Leaning forward, Ray whispered, "Syphilis!" For the next hour or so he led the audience around the world as he sought out famous physician after famous physician in a futile effort to be cured. At least, he asserted, his case was referred to a famous Midwestern sanatorium. Blessed with no mean imaginative gift, Ray fabricated in detail the exhaustive tests which were given him at the sanatorium. When all their efforts had proved vain, they called him into their private office. "My boy," he was told, "we are sorry, but we cannot cure you. You have only one chance of escaping death. You must find a woman named Madame Pasteur. We wish we could tell you where she is to be found, but we cannot. If you can find her she will cure you."

Ray embarked then on a search which took him into every corner and cranny of the United States. Worn out and discouraged, he at last reached "this very street corner" and sat down to rest on "that very fire hydrant there!" He heard a woman's voice and lifted himself wearily to his feet to investigate. And there, lo and behold, was the woman "I had searched the United States of America over to find!"

The fire hydrant was my cue to start walking toward the stand. I arrived just as he finished, and he swung around to me with a dramatic sweep of his arm. "And right here beside me tonight, gentlemen, is the woman who cured me and saved my life. I have consecrated my life to telling suffering humanity what she did for me. Gentlemen, I want to introduce Madame Pasteur, the woman with the brain of a Daniel Webster!"

He tenderly assisted me to the platform, and I went into my pitch. We were selling herbs, and I had had a rejuvenation pitch written especially for me by a college professor. The rejuvenation pitch was perhaps the last of the great pitches. A new crop was coming along. I began to feel a little out of place.

A new pitchman was urging the consumption of spinach and vegetable broth. Another was extolling the benefits of alfalfa tea. Cattle, it appeared, flourished on alfalfa, and a brew of the plant could confer equal vigor upon mankind. Another pitchman loftily displayed a picture of himself, his wife, and several children arranged around a table which supported bunches of celery and carrots and a few nuts. Although he was sixty-five and his wife only twenty-seven, he asserted, his diet—which was available to the public at a moderate price—was responsible for a vigorous and happy married life. He intimated that the looting of a vegetable store would invariably result in the production of a prize family. Their pitches in general gave rise to the suspicion that the human race would soon be dining in a rabbit hutch or a stable. It was alkalize this and irrigate that, but it was the same old game, played along more genteel lines.

I was getting tired of the business, but for a while at least I had to keep on at it. I had to wait a year before I could get my divorce from Frank and marry Mac.

At intervals I saw Will. He looked like an old man now, but there was still an indefinable air about him. Though he was wealthy, he had become a miser. He was still living with Mary, the ancient flame of his fourteenth year. She told me he had become so penurious that he wore his underwear until it was a mass of patches and bought his clothing only at secondhand stores. His stinginess, however, didn't extend to his personal comforts. The best prescription whisky cost him about twelve dollars a day, and he was paying one hundred and twenty-five dollars a can for opium, and a can never lasted more than ten days.

Once when I was down on my luck I asked him for some of the money I had earned while I was with him. He gave me two hundred dollars and swore the rest had been invested and that I was to receive it all when he died.

When I told him I was going to marry again a trace of the old power came into his faded hazel eyes.

"If I can't have you," he said, "I don't care how many men you marry. You're mine as long as you live. You're the child of my brain. You may drift along for years without thinking about me, but when you get in a tight pinch, even if I'm dead, you'll start to figure with my brain."

He was right. He had taught me more than I was ever able to forget. I fell ill as an aftermath of dope taking and had a series of operations. They took all my money and left me heavily in debt. I wrote Will, asking him to pay the bills, which were a fraction of the sum he said he had invested for me. He replied with a promise to send the money if I would provide him with a statement assuming the blame for our separation. The pill was a bitter one, but I swallowed it.

At once he wrote again, begging me not to work lest I overstrain my health. He himself was very ill, he said, and didn't expect to live long. When he died everything he owned would go to me.

When Mac and I were married Will wrote us tenderly:

MY DEAR CHILDREN:

I hope you will not be offended at this letter, or at my addressing you in this way, but Vi has always seemed like a daughter to me, and I hope I may regard her husband as my son. I am an old and broken man, so let bygones be bygones, and accept my friendship. I hope to give you a token of it for the new life you are starting. Please telephone me. I wish to send or give you a belated wedding gift.

It was all a good pitch, as carefully thought out as the others Will had created.

Not long after he had written the letter Will shot himself, spurred to the act by Mary's death. I felt no sentiment. A part of my life was over and done with, that was all. I didn't discover until a few days later that, like any open-mouthed chump, I had once again bought Will's medicine.

I received a copy of his will, and the sentence in which I was interested read:

"And to my former wife, Vi, I leave the sum of one dollar."

Oddly enough, I wasn't angry. That was Will. He had planned the build-up, planned the twist. He had meant it as something which would leave me bitter, chained to him by resentment the rest of my life. It didn't. It broke the chains. I was able to murmur:

"May God rest his lying, ruthless soul."

→» APPENDIX I «←
PITCHES, SPIELS, AND BALLYHOOS

CERTAIN PITCHES were pretty well standardized. As a general rule a pitchman memorized his spiel and gave it with the most minor variations for years. It was perpetuated when he passed it on to a friend or trained other pitchmen to work for him.

An exception to the single-pitch rule was Curly Thurber, the ex-I.W.W. agitator. There was no telling in what disguise Curly was going to crop up next. One week, dressed in Indian costume, he would be Chief High Eagle. The following week would find him decked out in turban and flowing robes, posing as a swami, and the week after he would be plain Curly Thurber, exhorting his "fellow workers" to buy. Curly had such a way with crowds that he could get away with murder. One day in Portland, Oregon, I was passing his store on Burnside Street and stopped to listen. "Buy this medicine," Curly was insisting. "Don't go to the doctors. What do they do when you go to them?" He paused. No one answered. "I'll tell you what they do," Curly continued. "They cut open your umbilicus and take out your tweedium." This revelation had such an alarming ring that the crowd stampeded up to buy.

Most pitchmen, however, stuck to the proven routines. Actually, only a few of them, like Will, were clever enough to improvise new pitches. Three of the basic pitches, used by scores of pitchmen throughout the country, dealt with soap, mineral salts, and herbs. Echoes of them are to be found in the spiels of many a traveling "health lecturer" today.

One of the most famous soap pitchmen was Silk Hat Harry. If he had a last name, very few people knew it. He was a small, trim-looking man who wore a silk topper and clothes of a youthful cut. He ballyhooed with clever card and rope tricks. He had his own soap put up at a soap factory. His picture, with the identifying headpiece, was on the wrapper. He never used the soap himself. As a matter of fact, he never had to buy a cake of soap of any kind for his personal use, making it a practice to pick up the well-known brands discarded by members of his audience during his pitch.

His pitch, the model for all soap pitches, went like this:

"My dear friends, a lifetime habit of men and women is the habit of washing. As everyone knows, the skin attracts dirt. It is a well-known fact that water alone will not dissolve the dirt and oil. Therefore, we must use soap. And when you stop to think how often we use soap and how little we know about it—how it is made, and from what it is made; the materials, I say, used in manufacturing this soap for our skin and hair—then you can get an idea of how valuable my lecture on the hair and skin and scalp really is.

"To start with, here are a few popular brands. I'll begin with this one, a brand everyone knows. This one is advertised the world over. This, like most all other soaps on the market today, is made of cheap fats and cheap oils, bleached with acids, et cetera, and saponified with lye, caustic soda, and potash, and made to smell good. Some of you may say, 'Why, I have never heard of this before.' Let me ask you this: Where does the refuse go that is gathered up at night in big barrels from your hotels and restaurants—the garbage, as you call it? Do they throw it away? I should say not. It goes to the soap factory. What does your butcher do with the ends and scraps of meat and fat that you don't want? Does he throw it away? Oh no. He throws it into a barrel under the counter, then sells it to the soap manufacturer. And how about the cows, steers, and sheep that die in the pens of the stockyards? Do they burn them up? Oh no. They remove the hide, and the rest is sold to the soapmaker.

"Pick up a newspaper and read the miscellaneous department. You will see ads like this: 'Highest prices paid for dead horses.' Who buys them? The soapmaker. When the dogcatcher gets your dog and you refuse to pay the fee to redeem him, what do they do with poor Rover? They kill him, then skin him. The skins are made into fur coats for women, the fat and bones into soap. Why, only recently in the East the Board of Health of New York stopped the garbage pickers who sort over the garbage on the dump heaps from selling the bones which they picked out of the muck and which the soapmaker calls benzene bones. Stopped them, made them cut it out! Is it any wonder, my dear friends, that your skins are hard, harsh, dry, and scaly? And that some of you have pimples and blackheads? Is it any wonder your hair falls out when these dyes, caustic sodas, and potash eat up the oil out of your scalp and rob the hair of its life and its luster?

"Here is a brand you all know well. It keeps you healthy, kills germs. If it does kill germs, why doesn't your doctor, when he is about to perform an operation, why doesn't he stick his instruments in a cake of this soap? Oh no! He boils them in hot water. You may say, 'But it's got carbolic acid in it.' That is a phenol odor you smell. If it had anything in it strong enough to kill germs it would be strong enough to blister and scar you for life. The proof is that it's full of lye and cheap fats.

"Now you are thinking, 'What's to be done?' Look at this. No, it's not a soap. Call it that if you wish. It's a cleansing compound made of pure vegetable and edible oils such as coconut oil, palm oil from flowers, and the whites of eggs, saponified with soap bark that grows in the highest altitudes of Colorado. It is pure enough to eat. It contains no poisons, acids, dead dogs, cats, or other dead animals that have died of some disease. Let me show you how to use it for pimples, blackheads, and falling hair, for the scalp, skin, and complexion. What do you usually do for pimples and blackheads? You take your fingernails and squeeze until you get black in the face to remove one blackhead.

"Here is my method. Take this bar and soak it in some water, either hot or cold. Put it to your face and rub it in like this. Then take your hand and massage it into your face as you would vanishing cream. It goes right into the skin. Allow it to remain there about thirty minutes, then rinse your face in lukewarm water. All the soap will come out and bring all impurities out of your face. As you notice, the soap has disappeared into my hands. Notice that here is a pan of water, cold water. Watch the impurities that will come out of my hands [washes hands, using soap-loaded sponge], and notice the lather it will bring out. For shampooing it has no equal. Massage it into your scalp the same as I did into my hands. Rub it good, then rinse your hair good, and repeat it again and rinse your hair in two waters, then comb your hair and go to bed. When you get up in the morning your hair will have a natural luster and it will be naturally curly and fluffy.

"For men who shave yourselves, this soap has no equal. Just rub your brush in it, then put it on your face. Rub it on good, and you'll get the best shave you ever had. If the soap you are using on your skin burns you or itches after your bath, try this. For eczema or itching skin it's wonderful. If your feet perspire or ache, put your feet in hot water, then massage this in as I did into my hands. Let it stay there for a while, then put your feet back in the water and soak them good. When you get up the next morning you'll swear to God you have a new pair of feet, you'll feel so good.

"When your wife bathes the baby, the baby cries. Why does that baby cry? Babies all like water. Do you know why it cries? I'll tell you. The soap that Mother uses burns the poor baby's skin, that's why. Try this soap and it won't burn because it's pure. I told you it was pure enough to eat. When you go home try this with your own soap. I promise you it will make you sick. Look, watch me eat this soap. Why can I? Because it's pure. It contains no animal fats, acids, or poisons. It's light as a feather and will outlast any two bars of ordinary soap. These cakes of the most extraordinary soap in the world, gentlemen, sell for only twenty-five cents."

Silk Hat Harry kept up a drumfire of talk as he sold the soap.

"People come forward every day, my friends, and tell me how this soap has cured them of skin diseases. . . . Yes, twenty-five cents. Thank you. . . . I was talking to an audience in Durango, Colorado, about a year and a half ago when a young man came up to me. His face was covered with scabs and sores. He said, 'Doctor, will your soap or cleansing compound help me?' He was a pitiful sight. 'Yes,' I answered, 'but you had better buy three cakes of it.' I left town and thought no more about it. I happened to be lecturing there about a month ago. I noticed a clean-cut-looking man and a woman standing at the edge of my audience.... Twenty-five cents out of a dollar. Thank you.... The man had his hands on the handle of a baby buggy in which were two babies the same size. As soon as they could push the baby buggy through the crowd they came forward. 'Doctor,' the man said, 'do you remember me?' For the life of me I couldn't place him; it didn't seem to me I'd ever seen him before. 'I was in your audience,' he said. 'My face was a mass of sores. . . .' Two bars? Thank you, sir. . . . 'All the girls in town were ashamed to go out with me. I used the three cakes of soap. Now I would like to have you meet my wife, Doctor, and these are our twin babies. That's what your soap has done for me.'"

Harry beamed out at the audience, adding, "But, gentlemen, I do not guarantee this same result for everyone who buys my soap."

The audience laughed, as if to say Harry couldn't fool them, and crowded up to buy more soap.

Mineral salts were a great favorite among pitchmen because they provided an opportunity for the use of colored charts which diagrammed the organs of the body and constituted an irresistible lure for the natives.

The salts pitch was equally effective in a store, its windows crammed with tapeworm jars and huge colored globes of salts, or on a street stand with torches to cast an eerie light over the drawings or the wax figure which was sometimes used.

The traditional salts pitch, given by the lecturer after performers had ballyhooed a crowd, was this:

"Our objective in asking you to stop and listen to the entertainment was not so much for the purpose of entertaining you as it was to instruct you for the first, last, and only time, thanks to the U.S. Government, in a subject that always interests every intelligent man or woman. There is no subject more fascinating than that which says, 'Man, know thyself,' and in order to teach you as much as we possibly can, we use this manikin here before you, which is a representation of your body just exactly as you are formed and made; and in looking upon it I desire you should do so as you would your own body in a looking glass, for each and every one of us is constituted exactly as pictured here before you.

"I further wish to state that, contrary, perhaps, to your expectations, I am not a doctor, nor do I pose as such, nor do I have any medicine of any class or character for sale at any price. But I do intend to show you every organ in the human system, both in health and disease—how they break down and how to take care of them without the use of medicine. This information will cost you absolutely nothing, only your time spent, and I doubt if any one of you could spend your time to better advantage. I am going to eliminate a long portion of my talk, which, although interesting, the back view of your lungs, your intestines, thirty-six feet of them, the large colon, and the manner and method Nature has of picking up the food after it has been digested. Now, these organs that I pass over so quickly you have no control over whatever, but the organs you do have control over are the ones you abuse. They are consequently the seat of every disordered condition of the human system.

"Now, the first organ that breaks down in your body is your stomach. Here is an excellent view of your stomach supposed to be cut open here and pulled apart so as to show you the inside mucous membrane of your stomach in perfect health. That is as it should be. Depicted here is the first stage of disease known as indigestion or dyspepsia, and nine out of ten of you standing right here suffer from it. How do I know? Ah! That is easy, because every living soul of you indulges too freely in that one great American habit of eating too fast, and all of you are guilty. That makes your stomach work overtime. This overwork causes an inflamed and irritated condition and enlargement of the blood vessels due to the strain on these organs. Now you don't do anything for that, naturally, because it doesn't lay you up. You let it go, but the one who lets it go long enough brings on a condition which is known as ulcerated stomach.

Say that's the time you get a move on for help, but it's too late then; you had your warning and your chance and you lost it and in the end; friends, to make a long story short, it then develops into complete ulceration of the stomach, which means cancer of the stomach, and that means death.

"Now many of you standing here now would like to know how to take an ulcerated stomach and bring it back to its healthy condition without the use of medicine. Well, if you will listen to me just five minutes I will teach you so you will all know. Now the first organ that breaks down in your body is your liver, and the first stage of disease of the liver is that backache which so many of you complain about right across the small of your back. Now all a man or woman does for a backache is kick about it and let it go. If let go long enough, it brings on a condition which is known as sclerosis of the liver, better known as hobnail liver, and there is no power on earth which can straighten out your liver for you when once it gets in that condition. I am going to teach every one of you to keep your liver out of that condition without the use of medicine. Now the organ that breaks down in your body is one you are all interested in, and that's your kidneys, so let's take a look at them. [Points with pointer.] There is one and here is the other. Notice how closely they are connected together. They look like two boxing gloves, don't they? Now the kidneys not only have to take care of all the liquids and fluids, but they must neutralize all the poisons and acids of the entire system.

"When kidneys cannot do that work they then throw what is known as uric acid into the circulation of your blood. Then your troubles commence because this uric acid is the strongest poison in your body. That acid searches every part of your body and finds every weak spot in it. The first weak spot it finds in nine out of ten of you standing here now is right across the small of your back. That acid settles there. That in time causes your backache and lumbago and afterward, mind you, that same uric acid settles upon your muscles and different parts of your body. That causes rheumatism. Then it settles around your heart, in time causing apoplexy or heart disease. If it settles upon your nerve centers it first produces neuralgia and in time paralysis, and you all know what that means. If there is any hereditary weakness of your lungs, it settles there, causing tuberculosis; in other cases it may form a so-called blood clot resting upon the brain, which means headache, epileptic fits, and insanity.

"But one would say to me, 'Suppose I had no weak spot in my body? Where would that acid go then?' Watch that! Acid would pass directly into your blood. In time it would be brought straight back to the action of the kidneys upon either side. Now as that acid could not pass off through the proper channels into your bladder, it would remain right there in your kidneys and in the course of time cause that dreaded of all diseases known as Bright's Disease of the kidneys, which means consummation of the kidneys and which is fatal, there being no cure for it. In other words, my friends, the sum of all I have said is the first true cause of every disordered condition of the human system. It is first brought about by the presence of that uric acid in the circulation of your blood. Some of that acid which I have right here in this bottle, and with which I am going to perform for you some of the ocular demonstrations and experiments that will interest every intelligent man or woman standing here, and I don't want any of you to miss what I do with the contents of this bottle.

"Now to those of you who have listened carefully, this is what you are saying: 'Here is a man with a different argument than anything we have ever heard before.' You bet it is, but you know it is the truth. You have heard of this uric acid before. You have read of it in your newspapers, magazines, medical advertisements, et cetera. But this is the first time you ever had an explanation of it so you can thoroughly understand the damage it does to the human body, and the question that arises in your mind here and now is: 'How am I going to get that uric acid out of my system when once it gets there?' My friends, it is your right and privilege to know, and if you will listen to me carefully I will teach every one of you.

"Now common sense tells you the time to take care of your health is while you have it and not wait until it is gone. Is there any medicine that will reach those cases? Well, if there is you have never found them. There are more than one of you standing here right now that have spent many a dollar for medicine. I want to say to you, my friends, very promptly and plainly, that medicines do not cure. Rather a startling statement to make, but nevertheless I will prove it to you. If medicines cured as they claim they do—and God knows there are enough of them on the market—if one per cent did as they claim they do, why, we would all live forever, for except the simple fact, you understand, there is none of us that wants to die.

"At least the rich man would live as long as his money held out and the poor man would have to die because he wouldn't have enough money to buy medicine to keep him alive. How does that argument strike you? Did you ever give it a thought?

"The other day while lecturing a man came up to me at this point in my lecture and said, 'Say, can I ask you a question?' I said, 'Surely, if it is relative to what I am talking about?' He said, 'Do you remember a few years ago when the flu was raging throughout the country? Well, I was considered a very sick man then and I took medicine and became well. I thought the medicine cured me. Now if your argument is right and medicine does not cure, will you kindly tell me what cured me?'

"I looked at him a minute and said I would try. I said, 'Did you ever cut your hand severely?' He said yes, when he was a little boy he wanted to become a butcher, and every time he would go to cut meat he would invariably cut his hand. Sometimes clear to the bone. 'Well, you didn't put any medicine on it—you just wrapped it up in a clean rag and let it go, didn't you? It got well, didn't it? Will you kindly tell me what helped it? You didn't doctor it; you didn't put medicine on it; now what healed it?' He said, 'I don't know as I have given that a thought.' I said, 'Well, seeing that you don't, I will tell you. The natural action of the laws of Nature, that power contained in your own body, is the only healing power on earth for any one of us from the day we are born until the day we pass on. A man may fall on the sidewalk and break his leg. The surgeon is called, and he sets the bone because he knows how they go together, and that is as far as he can go. He possesses no power of magic, no medicine, that will make those bones knit together if Nature doesn't do it for him, and you know it as well as I do.'

"He said, 'That's right, I never thought of that. Now may I ask one more question and then I will leave you alone? If your argument is right, will you kindly tell me why every doctor that I know uses medicine?' I told him that he was wrong because there is not an up-to-date doctor in America today that uses one drop of so-called medicine for the purpose of curing anyone. He said,

'You must be mistaken; here is a prescription right here.' I said, 'I don't doubt that you are taking it, but did that good kind doctor that gave you that prescription tell you that it would cure you of anything?' He said, 'Well, I wouldn't swear to that, but he told me to take it.'

"I said, 'That's all right. Let's you and me come to a showdown, my friend. There isn't a man in the world that understands the healing power of the human body so well as the man that makes a study of that work, and that's your doctor. He takes advantage of that knowledge at all times for your benefit as well as his own. Whenever there comes a time in your case that he administers anything to you in the way of medicine to take into your body, he does not give it to you as a medicine, nor with the hope or intention of healing you or curing you of anything. But he does give it to you for the sole and entire purpose of stimulating some spot or crisis, as it were, in the case. Then if you have the vitality and willpower in your body you will get well; if you haven't you will die. And there is no power, no medicine, no doctor that can cure you; if he could he would because a live man is more valuable to a doctor than a dead one ever dared to be. Unfortunately for you, my friend, that's where the undertaker gets his work. And believe me, if there was anything known to materia medial today that could keep you here on this earth after the vitality of your body is gone there wouldn't be any funerals in this man's town for many a day to come and all the undertakers would go out of business. Now think that over.' But he said, 'Well, is there a treatment that can be given in these cases?' I said, 'There is, but, thank God, it is not a medicine. Now let me ask you a very simple question, one that you can answer, but you have never given it a thought. What does any good doctor do with all the cases that come under his hands for treatment that he fails to cure after he has given a man everything he knows of medicine indicative to that particular case? They are all advised and sent to some mineral-water springs. If it is a bad case of rheumatism, a case that is a last resort, mind you, he is advised and sent to the Mount Clemens Mineral Water Springs of Michigan. Just above the city of Detroit, where they drink of the water and bathe in it, thus neutralizing the uric acid in the circulation of their blood, and come home cured, and never a failure. Your consumptive cases are sent to the Glenwood Springs in Colorado. These springs are ten thousand feet above the level of the sea. That rarefies the air, takes the strain off the lungs and the action of breathing, and gives those lungs the rest they require. Then they simply drink of the mineral water and bathe in it, paying particular attention, of course, to the food they eat, and come home cured even in cases so bad that funeral arrangements had already been made in the home which they had left.'

"Whose treatment is that? Is it man's? No, that's the gift of the Great and Wise Creator. He makes those treatments way down deep in the bowels of the earth in a laboratory far greater than man could devise and forces them to the surface in the form of mineral water and gave them to us. The air we breathe and the water we drink. If that's the case —and you know it is—why don't we get those treatments that will do the work? I'll tell you why. Because the rich man has found out their value. He bought these places up, fenced them in, built immense hotels over them. He says any rich man can come, pay the price, and go home cured. But you folks standing here tonight that have to work for your money, you can stay away simply because you don't happen to have enough money to go to those mineral-water springs for treatment.

"My friends, these arguments are facts. This injustice has been realized for a number of years, and an analysis has been made of the mineral waters. We find that the natural mineral-water springs possess the greatest curative powers known to mankind. We also find that these curative powers of these waters are not the water, as is popularly supposed. Water is found the world over. It is the ingredients in the water that the water brings up out of the earth that do that great work for us. So we take the water and evaporate it; in the process of evaporation we get the ingredients. We duplicate those ingredients and we then have left what is known as the Natural Mineral Water Salt, which we place in packages of this size and character weighing about a fourth of a pound each. This package is for drinking and bathing purposes, making about twenty gallons of the original mineral water, stamped, numbered, and guaranteed by the U.S. Government as having been through the government's hands.

"Now it is not a medicine, so you do not have to cook it or prepare it nor fool with it in any way. Just take an ordinary drinking glass, this size glass; the ordinary drinking glass that you all have in the home is the right size. Now you will find the directions plainly printed upon the package. Now open it up; there you will notice a white powder or crystals. Now pour enough to cover the bottom of the glass, or what women call a level teaspoonful. Then fill up your glass full of ordinary drinking water, add a pinch of salt or enough to suit your own taste, stir it until dissolved. That makes a mineral water of it. Then drink it. The entire glassful twice a day for the first two weeks; after that once a day is all that is necessary in ordinary cases to keep your system in perfect working order and keep that uric acid out of the system when once you get it out. But in long-standing or chronic cases, such as rheumatism, liver, kidney, or bladder troubles, three times a day is necessary. It should be kept up until you see the natural improvement in yourself, then gradually reduce.

"Now you folks that have listened carefully are saying, 'I wonder what the action of that mineral-water salt is? What will it do? How does it operate on the human system?' Now, friends, this part of my work will interest every one of you, and I am not only going to show you, but I am going to prove to you what this simple mineral-water treatment does for you that your medicine has never done. I will be through now in one minute, after which we are going right on with the entertainment. And in that one minute's time, if you will all take the trouble to step in the circle a little closer, I am going to show you more right here and now about the action of your body than you ever knew before in your life. In other words, I am going to try and teach you in about one minute what it has taken thirty years to learn and a thousand dollars in money and hundreds of hours of hard work and study. Imagine, to teach every one of you how to save a lot of time, money, trouble, and expense in the future. For what you learn later in life by bitter experience and spend your good hard-earned money for the privilege and then have nothing to show for it. It is one thing for a man to tell you a thing and another thing for him to prove it. You can believe him or disbelieve him, as you see fit. Thank God that is your American privilege. But if a man makes a statement and then proves his statement you at least have to believe what your eyes see.

"Now the first thing that this Mineral Water Salt does in any case, man, woman, or child—I care not what you suffer from—is to correct the acidity of your stomach and start it to action. For the stomach is the beginning of the foundation or starting point of all your troubles. It must be the foundation or starting point of all cures. It then heals the ulcers that exist, places your stomach from a sickly condition to a healthy one, and never quits those organs until that work is done. That covers any stomach trouble, no matter what name you know it under, and we guarantee results inside forty-eight hours. From the ordinary stomach troubles such as indigestion, sour stomach, dyspepsia, dizziness, headache, loss of appetite, heartburn, constipation, et cetera. Say! if it never did anything else but that for you it would be well worth one hundred times the advertising price here and now.

"After your stomach is in proper working order it then works directly on your liver that reaches that pain across your back, also your rheumatism, malaria chills, and fever. Listen now, hardening of the arteries, better known to some of you younger men that were examined for the Army and Navy as high blood pressure, a disease which helps kill ninety-nine out of every one hundred workingmen and -women in America today due to the presence of that uric acid in the circulation of their blood. It then works directly on the kidneys, both sides alike. Understand that while operating on your kidneys it reaches your bladder, operating upon such cases as stone or gravel in the bladder, weakness or enlargement of the prostate gland, inability to hold the water or start the water in people of advanced age, and even your little children with weak bladders who wet the bed, and many other difficulties of a more private nature.

"My minute is up, gentlemen, and I hope and pray that these facts and the proof of them that I have shown will be of help to you in ridding your lives of pain and trouble. As I said before, I have no medicine of any kind or character to sell, and would not sell it if I had. But I am able to offer each and every one of you a package of this wonderful health-giving Mineral Water Salt which until now has been for the exclusive use and privilege of the rich. The price is only fifty cents a package, and those of you who wish to have lasting good health, that great gift of God and Nature, may now obtain it."

Salts always did well for the pitchmen and, so far as I know, never hurt any of the yokels who bought them.

Experience was the only thing that could teach a pitchman he had better stick to his pitch, whether it involved soap, salts, or herbs. It was a lesson I learned years later when I had given up Vital Sparks for herbs.

By way of varying my pitch—the men working for me were claiming my herbs would cure anything from hangnails to leprosy—I introduced a couple of noble-looking X-rays taken when I had had a series of operations. I fixed a rack with a light behind it so the yokels could get the full dramatic benefit of them.

I started the pitch by offering a thousand dollars to anyone who could prove the X-rays were not of my own body, and then flashed on the light. The crowd surged forward. I began with my gall bladder and moved on to my kidneys. The natives stood there with their mouths open so wide I could have thrown marbles down their throats. This was the stuff, I thought. I explained that if I had taken the herbs I probably would not have needed the operations; still, they had been a great help afterward. I hinted in a delicate way that I had even had bigger and better operations than the ones recorded.

When I sprang the sale they rushed the stand, but not to buy physic. They wanted to find out what my other operations were and if I had X-rays of them also. My pitch was wrecked, and I never pulled that one again.

Another time I was lecturing to an audience of about three hundred people when some yokel spoke up and said, "Is exercise good for a person when they are taking your herbs?" I usually lectured on an empty stomach, but that particular day I had just finished a rousing dinner with friends. When the yokel came up with his question I had a happy thought. I had always been able to touch my palms to the floor without bending my knees, so I said, "Yes, brother, I'll show you what a woman my age who takes these herbs regularly can do." I quickly bent over and touched the floor. It made me slightly dizzy, and everything began to go black. As I straightened up I produced a resounding belch. I was horrified, but my breath came back and I said quickly, "As you see, gentle exercise and the herbs will expel all the gas from your stomach." The pitch was saved, but the call was a close one, and thereafter I stayed with the original text.

My herb pitch was built up over a period of years, and of course it had to be presented with an introduction that would persuade my largely masculine audiences that a woman was worth listening to. It went like this:

"Now with your permission I will talk to you for ten or fifteen minutes. You will naturally say, 'Why should we waste our time listening to a woman even for ten or fifteen minutes? Now if it was a man talking we would listen for hours if necessary because when he got through talking we would know something. Why should we waste time listening to a woman?'

"You know, you menfolks have always had an idea you were smarter than a woman. Now I will tell you where you got that idea. When some men and women died they took out their brains and put them on a pair of scales and weighed them, and the man's brain weighed the most. Well, it ought to; he is the larger of the two. But remember this, when it comes to brains it is quality and not quantity that counts. You will say, 'Yes, but who ever heard of a woman that ever knew anything?'

"Do you know that the greatest discovery that ever was made in science or medicine was made by a woman? Madame Curie, a woman, discovered radium. She was also the first woman in the world to receive the Nobel Prize. It is not only a great honor to receive the Nobel Prize, but it carries a cash gift of forty thousand dollars. One of our greatest astronomers is a woman. Our greatest mathematician is a woman. Sarah Bernhardt is our greatest dramatic actor. The three greatest sovereigns the world ever knew were women, Elizabeth of England, Catherine of Russia, and Isabella of Spain. Also Maria Theresa of Austria. Why, if it was not for women you wouldn't have any religion. Mary Baker Eddy, a little frail woman, was the founder of the Christian Scientists. Katherine Tingley, Annie Besant, and Helena Blavatsky were the founders of the theosophists. If it were not for Mary, the mother of our Saviour, where would our religion be? You will say, 'Yes, we will admit there are smart women. But why are you boosting them up? Are you a woman suffragette or are you going to talk religion?'

"No, I'm not going to talk politics to you; they change so fast it would take all my time to keep up with them. Nor am I going to talk religion to you. To be perfectly frank, I am not interested in what happens to you after you die. The only time I am interested in people is when they are alive and can stand around and listen to me for a few minutes. You will say, 'Well, what are you going to talk about?' Principally myself, and you ought to have enough curiosity to hear what I am going to say to stand and listen for ten minutes anyway.

"Now I will tell you why I come out on the street corner to talk to you. How many of you people listening to me know what good health is? There are a lot of you who think you do. If I were to say to you, 'Are you healthy, and you and you?' you would say, 'Why, of course I am healthy. I was never under a doctor's care in my life. I have never been in bed a day; of course I am healthy.' Now I will tell you what good health is so you will never make a mistake about it again. Good health means that you do not know you have a body. Any time you are aware of the fact you have a body or any of the processes of the body, there is something wrong with it. For instance, can you hear or feel your heart beat? There is something wrong with your heart. Are you aware of the processes of digestion? There is something wrong with your stomach. Good health does not mean that every time you eat a meal you stand around all bloated up or belching gas for hours, or hobbling around with a lame back and lumbago. Good health does not mean you wake up in the morning with so much fuzz and fur on your tongue that you imagine you have swallowed the fur rug in the night and a corner of it is still sticking in your mouth. Good health means you don't know that you have a body.

"You say, 'Tell us more about this. We're a pretty healthy bunch here.' I'll tell you what I'll do. I will take this audience as a representative audience, men and women and children combined. I dare any ten of you to go to your own doctor and be examined, and I will prove that seven out of every ten of you have catarrh, six out of ten have something wrong with your stomachs. Even more than that have constipation, and how many of you have rheumatism, kidney trouble, and asthma God only knows, and I doubt sometimes if He does. You will say, 'Take catarrh, for instance. We all agree lots of us have catarrh, but what of it? Catarrh doesn't amount to anything; nearly everybody has catarrh.'

"Catarrh not amount to anything! Why, if catarrh never amounted to anything but the bad breath you had with it I would say it was a curse to humanity. Were you ever talking to anyone and as they were speaking you got a whiff of their breath and it almost knocked you down? I have seen husbands and wives turn their cheek to be kissed as the other party's breath was so bad they could not stand it. And did you ever notice that the worse a person's breath is the closer he will get to you? Why, if catarrh never got beyond its first symptoms, I would say it was the filthiest disease in the world. What is the first symptom? Now this is not a very refined thing for a lady to do on the street corner, but this is the only way I can impress it on your mind. This is the first symptom of catarrh. [Hack twice.] Isn't that right? Isn't that what they do? On the street, in the home; they do not even spare you at the dining-room table. You men that live in rooming houses, you can almost use that hacking and spitting as an alarm clock as the roomers wake up one by one and start hacking and spitting, cleaning out their head and throat. You think catarrh does not amount to much? Write to any consumptive sanatorium and ask them why and ask them what causes consumption and they will tell you nine hundred out of every thousand are there because of a neglected case of catarrh. I do not mean to say that all of you people standing around here who are troubled with catarrh are going to die of consumption. But I do say you are in a good position to get it. Catarrh causes ringing and buzzing in the ears, deafness, and even affects your eyesight.

"You will say, 'Yes, we will agree with you that catarrh is a dangerous disease, but what are we going to do about it? Catarrh can't be cured.' What makes you think catarrh can't be cured? 'Well, I ought to know; I have had it for fifteen years.' What did you do for it? 'Well, I used every salve I saw advertised or anyone told me about. I snuffed stuff up my nose, I used atomizers, and I gargled my throat, and it never did me any good.' No, and it never did anyone else any good. Salve simply softens the membrane of the nose, and gargles and atomizers simply wash them as you would your face, but they never cured a case of catarrh. Why? I claim catarrh is a germ that goes all through your body. You get catarrh of the stomach and bowels from the dropping mucus from your nose and throat. You must kill the catarrh germs all through your body. Now this package I am holding contains twenty-seven different herbs. If you will take one-fourth of a teaspoon of these powdered herbs, put them in a cup or glass one fourth to one half full of cold water, let stand two or three minutes to dissolve the herbs, stir, then drink at bedtime only, catarrh cannot live in your body.

"Is there anyone standing and listening to me suffering from sour acid stomach? Do you get all bloated up after eating and have to belch? Do you feel a lump in your stomach? Do you get so-called heartburn? Do you get palpitation of the heart or heart pains? Take one-fourth of a teaspoon of herbs every night at bedtime. Some people may be inclined to say, 'If I get sour stomach or gas I can take soda; it fixes me up.' Yes, temporarily, but later ruins you. You may say sour stomach and indigestion are not dangerous. Why worry about it? you think. Stomach trouble is not only painful and inconvenient but is also actually dangerous. How, do you say? Now you folks all know your heart lies this way [show], with the point hanging down. When you get sour stomach, a gas forms in your stomach and bowels. What happens? Your stomach swells up and presses toward the point of your heart. If it is only a light attack it simply causes you to feel stuffy and bloated and gives palpitation of the heart. If it is a bad attack you drop dead instantly of what? Acute indigestion. Your doctor may call it heart trouble or apoplexy, but if they hold an autopsy they will find your stomach is pressing against the apex or point of your heart.

"Stanford, the man who founded Stanford University, which has graduated thousands of your doctors, died suddenly on the train going to Palo Alto. The doctors said, 'Heart trouble,' 'Blood clot on the brain,' but when they held the autopsy they found his stomach, swollen like a toy balloon, pressing against his heart. He had died of acute indigestion. General Funston died of acute indigestion. You cannot pick up a newspaper after a holiday but you will read so-and-so died suddenly after eating a hearty meal. They will say, 'Heart trouble.'

"Nonsense! There is no such thing as heart trouble. So-called heart trouble is a result caused by some other part of your body being diseased—and most of it is caused by stomach trouble. If you have sour acid stomach, or fermented stomach, or gas in your stomach or bowels, take one-fourth of a teaspoon of herbs every night at bedtime.

"In the next three minutes I am going to tell you why people are unhealthy and how you can be healthy. There is a process going on in every human body every twenty-four hours called metabolism. You will say, 'What does that mean?' Well, for the sake of argument assume you eat two pounds of food every twenty-four hours. Now if you are not suffering from stomach trouble or constipation, one half of the food you eat is assimilated and taken up and made into blood and muscle; the other half is supposed to be eliminated and thrown out of the body through the body and the kidneys. Now any time that balance is destroyed and you have constipation and do not throw off that poison, your whole body is poisoned. You absorb that foul mass that lies in your stomach and bowels. How? You all know your stomach, intestines, and bowels are lined with tiny blood vessels. They take up this poisonous mass, absorb it, and distribute it all through the body. Then you suffer from toxemia and autointoxication. What does that mean? Poison of the blood. What are the results? The first result is pyorrhea. How many of you know what pyorrhea is? I will tell you.

"Someday you will be looking in the glass and you will notice your gums are turning purple and receding or going back from the teeth. The next thing you will notice your gums will feel irritated and bleed. Then someday you will find one of your teeth feels strange, as if it were loose. You will take hold of it and shake it and you will find your tooth is loose. I have seen people with their teeth so loose I could press every one of them out with my finger. I have seen people so bad with pyorrhea that if they bit into an apple or a crust of bread they would leave bloodstains on it. Now when you have pyorrhea what is the matter with you? How does it hurt you? The first thing, you have pus at the roots of your teeth. How does that hurt you? Well, you absorb some and you swallow some of the pus every day. You may say, 'I may absorb some because I can't help it, but I don't swallow any of the poison. Why, I brush my teeth and spit out every bit of it.' You can't help but swallow it; you all eat, don't you? Well, while you are chewing your food you are pressing those old loosened fangs into your gums and pressing the matter out of your gums and swallowing it with your food. Then what happens? Do you know that seven cases of rheumatism out of ten are caused by pyorrhea or infected tonsils? You remember when Colonel Roosevelt, our beloved Teddy, died. Do you remember the cause of his death? Here is what the papers said: 'Colonel Roosevelt did not die of jungle fever or wounds. He died as the result of an infected tooth.' He absorbed the poison from the roots of the teeth, it went to every joint, and he died of rheumatism of the heart. Viscount Grey, the ambassador from England, went blind from pyorrhea.

"So you see, it all comes back to keeping your system eliminating. Now some people will tell you pyorrhea is a disease of the mouth alone. Pull your teeth and you will be cured of your pyorrhea or your rheumatism. Nonsense! Pyorrhea is not a disease of the mouth alone; pyorrhea is a blood disease, a constitutional disease, and must be treated as such. Namely, get it out of your blood, out of your system. Pulling your teeth only removes the local infection in the mouth. Remember this, you must remove the cause before you get the results, and the cause is the poisons you are absorbing from your body. To show you pyorrhea is no recent disease caused by the present manner of living, that it must have some common cause like constipation or failure to throw the poisons from the system, here is a photo of a mummy thirty thousand years old who suffers from pyorrhea in an advanced stage. Here is a photo of his heart, showing he died of endocarditis, which was caused by pyorrhea. Now if any of you people are suffering from pyorrhea or if your gums are bleeding, take a fourth of a teaspoon of herbs every night at bedtime. Is there anyone standing here tonight who is troubled with constipation? Take one-fourth of a teaspoon of herbs at bedtime and it will cure you.

"Now when I mention constipation there are always a lot of so-called pure-minded people who will look at each other in horror and wonder what I am going to talk about next. The secretary of the Social Hygiene Society of Oregon, Mr. Waggoner, said to me, 'If more people had your bravery in speaking plainly, we would have a healthier race of people.' You will say, 'Yes, we admit you have a good medicine and it will do what you say. But I don't need it; I haven't got constipation; my bowels move once every day.' Do you think that is enough? Any natural healthy human being's bowels should move three times a day—morning, noon, and night. Just think, man is the only animal in the world who has only one movement of the bowels in twenty-four hours. If there are any stockmen in my audience they will know I am telling the truth. If you owned any animals and noticed they were in that condition, you would send for a vet.

"If you are suffering from constipation, take one-fourth of a teaspoon of herb mixture every night when you go to bed. You will have three natural normal movements of the bowels every twenty-four hours without gripes or pains. This is not a physic in the accepted sense of the word. That is, a physic like salts only works on the bowels each time you take it, while my herbs act on the glands in the stomach and bowels and cause them to secrete their fluids and cause the bowels to work naturally. No matter how long you have been troubled with constipation, take approximately one-fourth of a teaspoon of herbs at bedtime and you will have three natural movements of the bowels every twenty-four hours. If you have headaches or if you are bilious, take the herbs and the relief will be magical. If you have a lame back or your kidneys are weak, if you get up in the night and void the liquid from your body, take one-fourth of a teaspoon of herbs. Remember, most of the diseases of the kidneys are caused by constipation; your bowels are not throwing off the poison from your body, so your kidneys take up the extra burden and try to help them. That overworks the kidneys and they become weakened and diseased. If you have hay fever or asthma, take one-fourth of a teaspoon of herbs at bedtime. Some people think that unless you have a salve or an atomizer or some smoke to inhale, a medicine cannot help those troubles. No one was ever cured by any one of those temporary reliefs. Yes, hay fever and asthma are constitutional diseases, and they must be treated as such.

"Now I have told you what my medicine is and what it will do. I have come out here and told you the truth about your bodies. I do not come out to appeal to your sentiment; I come out to tell you the truth and appeal to your intelligence. Here is all I ask. If you have anything wrong with you, do not delay, do not wait until it is too late. Every disease in the world gets worse unless you take care of yourself. Do not wait until catarrh turns into consumption or your stomach trouble into cancer of the stomach or your pyorrhea into a deadly heart disease. Remember, no disease stands still. It either gets better or worse. Why take even the chance that it might get worse?

"Do you know that most people take better care of an old car than they do of their precious bodies? If the valves in a car get dirty or pitted you take it to a shop and get it repaired. If the valves in your heart go wrong you cannot get new ones. So any time you do not feel right, do not wait until the disease becomes incurable. Take care of yourself now, tonight. Here is all I ask of you. If you owned that old wooden building over there and the shingles were coming off the roof or the boards off the wall, you would get a carpenter or a hammer and nails and repair it. All I ask of you is to treat your body as well as you would an old wooden building. Remember, you can move out of a building into another any time you wish; the only place you can move your body is six feet underground. The price of this herb package is one package for one dollar. That is a three-month treatment and is generally enough for the most chronic cases. Now this is the way I am going to sell it to you. You people work for your money; you are entitled to get something for it. Now if this medicine will do what I say for catarrh, stomach trouble, constipation, or any of the diseases I mentioned it is worth twenty dollars. If it doesn't do anything I say it is not worth a cent. Now I am going to leave it to you. I will be in your town three days. Buy this package, take it home, take approximately one-fourth of a teaspoonful tonight and tomorrow night, and if you have not received some benefit from it bring the packages down here the third night and I will return your money to you without any questions asked or comments made.

"I am now going to conclude my talk with a little poetry. When God in His infinite mercy conceived the thought of man, he called upon His three high priests, Truth, Justice, and Mercy, and thus addressed them: 'Shall we make man?' Truth spoke up and said, 'Make him not, O God, for he will pollute Thy sanctuary.' Justice spoke up and said, 'Make him not, O God, for he will trespass on Thy laws.' But gentle Mercy, dropping on her knees and gazing up through tearstained eyes, said, 'Make him, O God, that I may watch o'er him and guide him through life.' So God made man and said, 'Go deal thou with thy fellow men.'

"Gentlemen, that is what I am doing tonight, dealing with my fellow men. You must be the judge as to whether I will deal fairly with you or not."

Madame Pasteur's Rejuvenation Pitch

"From time immemorial men have dreamed of rejuvenation, of the possibility of overcoming the devastating ravages of old age. It is a problem that has stolen like the shadow of a bat's wings into the consciousness of every man and woman who has ever walked these 'banks and shoals of time.'

"It is a grim specter, peering uncannily out of every mirror that reflects the graying hair, the deepening wrinkle, the dimming flash of the eye. It echoes the muffled drumbeat of the aching heart, tottering toward the sable curtain of the Night of Life.

"It is a goal toward which countless generations of physicians have bent desperate steps—eager to achieve success before the creeping paralysis of senescence covered them with its murky cloak. It is the prize for which the Dr. Faustuses of all the ages were ready to trade their immortal souls.

"The quest of Ponce de Leon for the Fountain of Youth was but a single expression of the great desire that has been pent up in the breasts of millions during the centuries. It was the cry of Catherine, who said, 'All my riches for another hour of life.' Caesars have offered their empires to have the fires of youth rekindled.

"Is it any wonder that scientists have labored through the ages to solve the greatest of all problems—the maintenance of virile power and the stamina of youth? So much of disappointment and discouragement has followed the quest that scientists had practically despaired of ever solving the secret of the ages and of holding in check the moving finger that writes their death sentences at an age when, according to the law of biological growth, they should be in their prime.

"Metchnikoff thought he had solved the problem, only to be swept away by the very toxins whose development he had hoped to prevent. And so with scores, if not hundreds, of devoted research workers in laboratories throughout the world—workers laboring week after week in search of that elusive substance or agent that would quicken the pulse of life and reanimate the sluggish cells, worn with the struggle against creeping age.

"Almost without hope—and then, like a ray of light in the darkness of doubt, comes a message—a message coldly scientific and carefully and scrupulously phrased.

"Interpreted into the language of the multitude, it means that Eugen Steinach, a comparatively unknown professor of biology in Vienna, has solved the problem of the centuries and has brought back, first to aging animals and then to aging men and women, the flower and bloom of vigorous youth.

"To this obscure Viennese professor belongs the honor of having been the first to succeed in producing the means of scientifically rejuvenating the human being without risking the perils of a dangerous or dubious operation. The world is ringing with the praises of this remarkable scientist! His great hospital in Vienna is the Mecca of thousands seeking new life and vigor, or the beauty of lovely womanhood.

"The new Steinach Rejuvenation Treatment is a process by which certain glands of the body, known as the endocrines, are energized by certain natural vegetable and animal substances which up to a very short time ago were obtainable only at Dr. Steinach's Vienna Clinic at great expense, entailing a foreign journey and a foreign residence for many weeks, if not months.

"Many sick and elderly people, as well as others in need of this treatment, are not prepared for such inconvenience and travel difficulties. A rejuvenation treatment has therefore been developed by our own company physicians which does here at home in the city of San Francisco what is done at the Viennese clinic for thousands of the foremost people of Europe.

"Dr. Louis Berman of Columbia University says, 'The problem is one of recharging all the glands of the internal secretion—the endocrines—at least the most important, the thyroid, pituitary, adrenals, and gonads. Long life is perhaps largely a matter of preventing or postponing their wane.'

"A. Bellou, one of America's foremost writers on scientific subjects, writes in a feature column for Cosmos News Syndicate an article entitled 'How Some of the World's Foremost Men Retain Their Mental Powers.' After describing the able and brilliant men of advanced years who run the world's affairs and telling how they do it, Bellou says, 'So we find that if the endocrine glands of men and women stand by them, they can grow to ripe old age in full possession of their mental and physical powers.'

"When the glands fail them, they fail, unless perchance they seek new life, youth, and health in the latest discoveries in the line of rejuvenation now offered by science. Clemenceau was able to carry on during the Great War because he had reached into the realm of science and grasped the new wonders that it offered in supplying continued glandular powers. Other foremost men have done likewise.

"Today the endocrine glands can be regulated and controlled by a natural herb and animal substance scientifically blended together to form a treatment superior to anything else known of by us. Our physician and laboratory men have perfected a treatment that will merit your investigation.

"My friends, would you believe it if you saw your best friend suddenly made twenty years younger? Do you believe an old lady could be made into a flapper, as illustrated in the well-known novel, *The Black Oxen*? As a fair illustration of this, we will take the well-known actress, Edna Wallace Hopper. This woman is well advanced in years, and yet she does not look a day over twenty. This great change was brought about by rejuvenation.

"You men and women who are nearly walking shadows of the persons you should be, and could be, you realize that there is something wrong, and down in your own hearts you have locked the truth, believing that you and no one else knows your secret. But your life is like an open book to the knowing eye.

"If you are tired of doctoring, patent medicines, poisonous drugs, drugstore prescriptions, and other trash, if you want the simple truth about these great subjects, avail yourself of the opportunity at this time, today, at this very hour, by securing one of our free consultation cards. These cards are being presented to you free of charge so you may have the opportunity of learning the great truth pertaining to yourself and to better acquaint you with our herb products. You may bring these cards for a free examination and consultation in our offices, which are right across the street. Turn around, all of you. Look over there. Those are the offices. Bring the cards with you, and absolutely no charge will be made for the consultation."

→ APPENDIX II ←
TALK
LIKE A
PITCHMAN

AL-A-GA-ZAM—Hailing sign of a pitchman, used to call attention from the crowd.

BALLYHOO—(n.) A flamboyant means of attracting attention to a product to be sold or show to be presented. (v.) To talk extravagantly or to provide introductory entertainment, leading to a product sales pitch or a main show. Also: Bally or Bally-Act.

BLOW-OFF—High-pressure selling used to liquidate stock before moving on to the next town.

BUCK-AND-WING DANCE—A solo tap dance with sharp foot accents, springing into the air, leg flings, and heel clicks. Commonly seen in minstrel, medicine, and vaudeville shows.

CHOPPED GRASS—Herb medicines.

CLOSED TOWN—A place where pitchmen are refused a license or can't buy a fix.

COCONUTS—Money.

CORN SLUM OR CORN PUNK—A cure that uses corn powder.

DOUBLE—To perform two or more roles in a medicine show.

ELECTUARY—A candied medicine or one mixed with honey or sugar syrup.

EMETIC—An agent that induces vomiting.

FIX—A payoff to operate without too much scrutiny from authorities, either as protection money or to prevent the police from interfering. Prior to the passage of the Harrison Acts, local authorities would give a license to "doctors" who sold patent medicines. A Fixer is the contact to whom payments are made; this could be an actual official or an intermediary.

FLEA POWDER—Powdered herb medicine.

FLUKUM—Either nickelplate ware OR liquid medicines.

GRAFT—Bribes; taking "fix" money. Mostly used to describe payments to elected and law enforcement officials.

GRAFTERS—Pitchmen.

GREASE—Salve medicines.

GRIFTER—A conman or scam artist. Has come to mean a specific type of conman who travels from place to place to enact their scheme.

GRINDER, GRIND—A continuous spiel or lecture. It was considered a less-skilled job than that of the lecturer or pitchman.

GUMMY—Any type of glue.

HACK—Taken from the word hackney, meaning a rented horse. It later came to mean a rented horse and buggy, then later a taxicab.

HIGH PITCH—A sales pitch (generally for medicine) delivered from a raised platform, often the back of a horse-drawn cab or wagon.

HOME GUARD—A pitchman who works only in their home city.

JAMB WORKER—One who sells worthless products or services; usually gone from a town before the customer discovers they've been cheated.

KEISTER—A portable display case for the pitchman's wares. A keister is set on top of a "tripe," a small, collapsible tripod table. Also refers to a wardrobe or prop trunk, or any luggage.

LECTURER—An individual who talks inside a medicine show tent explaining the various acts. Also: a conman who under the guise of educating is pitching a spurious product.

LIMEWATER—Water containing calcium carbonate or calcium sulfate. When combined with carbon dioxide, as when a person exhales into it, it becomes cloudy. It then becomes clear when an acid, like vinegar, is added. Used to 'diagnose' illness in support of pitching a medicine.

LOT LICE—Natives who hang around for the entire pitch or show without buying anything.

NOSTRUM—A medicine of secret formula; a questionable medicine.

PIKER—A gambler who plays for small sums of money.

PITCH—A high-pressure sales talk.

POKE—A carny's or mark's "stash" of money. In medieval times, a 'poke' was a pouch or bag.

POULTICE—A soft medicine, spread on cloth and applied to the skin.

PROPRIETARY MEDICINE—A patent medicine commonly called whether the name was registered at the U.S. Patent office or not.

ROAD STAKE—Money for traveling and living purposes while on the road.

RUBE—An unsophisticated person living in a rural area. See Yokel. The term is derived from the name Reuben. A scornful term for the outsider to show business; also "Elmer," "townie," "sucker," "native," "yokel," "chump."

SARSAPARILLA—A tonic beverage made from the Smilex vine.

SHILL OR SHILLABER—One who acts as a decoy for the pitchman, making purchases to encourage others to do the same.

SKID ROW / SKID ROAD—Formerly used in logging towns to denote where lumber was loaded. Came to mean any area of a city with cheap hotels, saloons, and prostitutes frequented by vagrants, alcoholics, and migrant workers.

SLUM—Cheap goods.

SNAKE OIL—Derived from Rattlesnake Oil, a cure-all liniment claimed to be made from snakes. Came to mean any spurious and obviously fake product.

SPIEL—Fluent and extravagant talk. See Pitch.

STICKS (THE)—Rural areas away from cities.

STRAIGHT MAN—An entertainer who feeds lines to the pitchman or a master of ceremonies for larger medicine shows.

TOW SACK—A large burlap sack; a gunny sack.

VELVET—Profit.

VERMIFUGE—A medicine concoction to expel worms from the body.

YOKEL—A naïve or gullible inhabitant of a rural area or small town. Often used to describe a conman's or pitchman's target(s).